CALIFORNIA TIMES AND TRAILS

****

by Joan and Gene Olson

"The world, you know, is composed generally of three classes — good, bad and indifferent. But California is an exception to this rule. I haven't made up my mind whether it always formed a component part of the earth, or whether it is an offshoot of some comet that dropped into this spot by the law of gravitation. California is either very good or very bad. The soil is very wet or very dry, the land is very high or very low, the people very good or very bad..."

— *A Pioneer*

WINDYRIDGE PRESS

Copyright © 1971 by Joan and Gene Olson

ALL RIGHTS RESERVED — No part of this book may be reproduced in any form without permission in writing from the publisher, except by a reviewer who wishes to quote brief passages in connection with a review in magazine or newspaper.

Library of Congress Catalog Card Number: 70-160291

PUBLISHED BY
WINDYRIDGE PRESS
780 OXYOKE ROAD
GRANTS PASS, OREGON

Printed in the United States of America

CHAVEZ RAVINE. Julian Chavez registered his brand April 23, 1853. He owned property now known as Chavez Ravine, the location of Dodger Stadium. Chavez served as a Los Angeles city councilman and a supervisor for the county of Los Angeles.

TABLE OF CONTENTS

CHAPTER			PAGE
One	*	**Early Exploration** GOLD AND VITAMIN C	1
Two	*	**Government** A GIMPY LITTLE MAN	13
Three	*	**The Indians** FIFTY AGAINST A THOUSAND	41
Four	*	**Westward Migration** BLOOD ON THE SNOW	79
Five	*	**The Gold Rush** THE LUCK OF JOHN SUTTER	115
Six	*	**Land Transportation** THE HARUM-SCARUM WHIRLIGIG	151
Seven	*	**The Women** "WHAT'S A LADY LIKE YOU DOING IN A PLACE LIKE THIS?"	185
Eight	*	**Agriculture** WATER, WATER EVERYWHERE	205
Nine	*	**Minorities** THE HYPHENATED CALIFORNIANS	233
Ten	*	**Commerce** ALL THE GOLD AIN'T IN THEM HILLS	267
Eleven	*	**Ecology** THE BLEEDING LAND	289

California Facts and Figures	306
Selected Bibliography	307
Index to Persons and Places	309

ACKNOWLEDGMENTS

Four important persons who contributed most over the years to the preparation and publication of this book were Martin Cole of Whittier, retired historian for the State Department of Parks and Recreation; Frank Arnich, librarian, Camarillo H.S.; Edna May Hill, reference librarian for Josephine County (Ore.) Public Library; and Howard Hansen, president, Southern Oregon State Bank, Grants Pass, Ore.

Among those who willingly manned oars when called upon were James de T. Abajian, San Francisco Public Library; Robert Angermeier, Stockton; Edwin B. Astone, City of Sacramento; Leonard D. Booth, Jr., Title Ins. & Trust Co., San Diego; Lee L. Burtis, California Historical Society; Art Chipman; Richard Clark, Sacramento H.S.; James H. Davis, Denver Public Library; Walter Dawson and Clarence Hagen, N.W. Textbook Depository Co.; Katherine DeJarnett, Placentia Public Schools; Mitchell DeJarnett; Frank N. Denison, U.F.W.O.C.; William D. Dillinger, State Dept. of Parks and Recreation; Ferol Egan; Sandra Elder, State Dept. of Parks and Recreation; Hans Engh, State Office of Tourism and Visitor Services; Gordon Finley, State Div. of Econ. Development; Norma Flanery, Redwood Empire Ass'n; Walter and Clarice Foelker; Helen Fontes, Higgins Library, UC Davis; Ruth French, State Dept. of Education; Melvin Gagnon, UC Davis; Charlotte Geary, Sacramento *Union;* Joan Gleichman; Elaine Highsmith, Sacramento *Bee;* Steve Hinderer, Dept. of Water & Power, Los Angeles; Robert M. Hooe; Gary Huckaby, Port of Sacramento; Marcy Huntsinger, Yorba Linda Public Schools; Kay Huntsinger; Alice Huntsinger; Jessie Kincheloe, Title Ins. & Trust Co., Los Angeles; Margaret Knispel, National Ed. Ass'n; George Kraus, Southern Pacific Trans. Co.; Greg Lipscomb, special assistant to Wilson Riles; Arthur Mann; William Matheson, Oakland Museum; Lawrence S. Nahm, Yosemite Nat. Park; Dolorez Nariman, Title Ins. & Trust Co., Los Angeles; Irene Simpson Neasham, Wells Fargo Bank History Room; Frank A. Norick, Lowie Museum of Anthropology, UC Berkeley; John Olguin, Cabrillo Beach Marine Museum; Obena Olson; Anna Parker, San Francisco *Chronicle;* Marjorie Priger; Lee Ryland; Lorena Sample; Security Pacific National Bank, Los Angeles; Leona Thomas; John Barr Tompkins, The Bancroft Library; Richard Winn, State Dept. of Water Resources.

The authors thank the following publishers for permission to quote from their published titles:

AFRO-AMERICANS IN THE FAR WEST by Jack D. Forbes; Far West Laboratory for Educational Research and Development (available only from Superintendent of Documents, U.S. Government Printing Office).

PASSAGE TO THE GOLDEN GATE by Daniel and Samuel Chu; © Copyright 1967 by Doubleday & Co., Inc.

Material about John Joseph Montgomery from "The Last Flight of John Joseph Montgomery," by Martin Cole, in American Aviation Historical Society Journal.

From *American Album,* by Oliver Jensen, Joan Paterson Kerr, and Murray Belsky. © Copyright 1968 by American Heritage Publishing Co., Inc. Reprinted by permission.

Thank you all.

Joan and Gene Olson
Windyridge
Grants Pass, Ore.

"An old photograph is a kind of miracle. It is not just because these ancient and fragile daguerreotypes and glass plates are so surprisingly sharp and clear, but because these scenes long vanished and people long dead spring out at us as though it were yesterday; as though these rigidly posed ladies and gentlemen will rise in a moment to bow to each other and, perhaps, to us; as though the steamboat at the landing will presently whistle, pull in its gangplank, and steam majestically off."

—Oliver Jensen

PHOTO CREDITS

California State Library—front cover, 19, 49, 125, 212, 302, back cover
Los Angeles Co. Museum of Natural History—4 & 5, 20 & 21, 35
Redwood Empire Ass'n—7, 12, 266, 269, 294, 296
Author—25, 150
Bancroft Library, UC Berkeley—29, 110 & 111, 178, 196, 227, 287, 291, 293
Southern Pacific Trans. Co.—38, 121, 164 & 165, 168, 171, 174 & 175
Art Chipman—44
National Archives—57 (US War Dept.), 238, 300 (Navy Dept.)
Lowie Museum of Anthropology, UC Berkeley—61, 67, 71
California Dept. of Parks and Rec.—78, 127, 198
California Dept. of Parks and Rec., Interpretive Services—89, 95, 100, 103
Title Ins. & Trust Co., Los Angeles—113, 130 & 131, 231, 253, 273, 278 & 279, 285
National Park Service—134 & 135
Wells Fargo Bank History Room, San Francisco—138, 145, 153
Title Ins. & Trust Co., San Diego—181, 182 & 183, 188 & 189, 203, 275, 277
California Hist. Society, San Francisco—186, 192, 261, 288, 305
San Diego Hist. Society, Serra Museum & Library—204
Los Angeles Dept. of Water & Power—209, 215, 220 & 221
California Dept. of Water Resources—225
F. Hal Higgins Library of Agricultural Tech., UC Davis—229
Library of Congress—241
Sacramento *Bee*—249
Denver Public Library—258
California Dept. of Education—263
Oakland Museum—271
Port of Long Beach—282 & 283
California Office of Tourism & Visitor Serv.—298

* * * * *

Historic cattle brands displayed throughout the book were made available by Title Insurance and Trust Company, Los Angeles.

AUTHOR'S NOTE

Californians who care about history live in a Garden of Eden. Writers who try to tell the state's story completely soon founder in a swamp of rich and redolent material. A final manuscript usually looks like a freeway interchange, with provocative arrows pointing off in all directions.

At the end of each of our chapters, there is a designation: "Sites to See." Here we point to some of the pertinent and fascinating places of historical interest which wouldn't fit comfortably into our text. There are many more; in fact, *California Historical Landmarks,* published by the State Department of Parks and Recreation, lists 827!

Los Angeles County Museum and Oakland Museum deserve to be listed after each chapter. To save space, we did not do this but make very special note of them here. California Hall in Los Angeles County Museum is complete, and completely fascinating; the California history exhibit in Oakland Museum is relatively new and utterly absorbing. Its use of light and art and space and especially of the written word sets a new standard for history museums everywhere.

A historical Garden of Eden—remarkable places like Maritime Museum in San Francisco and Briggs Cunningham Automotive Museum in Costa Mesa and Aerospace Museum in San Diego and Travel Town in Los Angeles and Pioneer Village in Bakersfield . . . and that's only a beginning.

So have fun. We did.

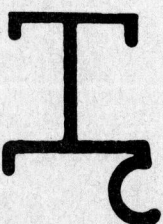

RANCHO LOS CERRITOS. The brand of Juan Temple was used at Rancho Los Cerritos and was registered May 15, 1852. Los Cerritos is now the location of Long Beach.

Chapter One ✽

Early Exploration
GOLD AND VITAMIN C

The Spanish of the 16th century were as greedy a band of freebooters as ever roamed the seven seas but it wasn't only a lust for riches that drove them to their dangerous explorations of the California coastline in tiny ships.

They were just as interested in Vitamin C.

It must be said at this point that those intrepid soldiers and sailors who represented the Spanish crown and the single-minded priests who carried the banner of the Catholic Church in the most far-reaching feats of exploration and colonization ever recorded on earth were much more than greedy; they were also brave, intelligent and fantastically hardy. Think of it—home base was thousands of miles away, transportation and communication were primitive, support from the Spanish crown was often lacking or slow in coming and frequently life had to be sustained in some of the world's most barren, hostile environments.

Yet much of what we now call Latin America was conquered, controlled and administered by the Spanish . . . and systematically plundered, as well.

One envisions men who could do such things as hardbitten, nononsense types, which these men certainly were. But there was a strong strain of dreamer in some of them, too, and when the truth is sifted out, most of their exploring objectives consisted of little more than romantic foolishness.

Consider, for instance, the first mention of "California" in the world's literature.

A Spanish author of far-out fiction named Garcia Rodriguez Ordonez de Montalvo wrote in a widely-read novel of 1510:

"Know ye that on the right hand of the Indies there is an island called California, very near the terrestrial paradise and inhabited by black women without a single man among them and living in the manner of Amazons ... Over this island of California rules a queen, Calafia ..."

Now what hardbitten, no-nonsense type would swallow that whole?

Well, apparently none other than Hernando Cortez, conqueror of Mexico and perhaps the mightiest Spaniard of them all. When Cortez discovered the southern tip of the peninsula now called Baja California, he thought it was an island—tall, dark Calafia's island—and named it "California."

(Californians must gulp and face the fact that their state has a secondhand name. But perhaps this is easier to accept than the earlier explanation of the name's origin, which was that it derived from the Latin *calida fornax,* or "hot furnace." How would that look in a chamber of commerce brochure?)

What about Vitamin C, you ask? Good question.

SOME PEARLS AND RUBIES

"Usually there came from Great China to Manila a large number of *somas* and junks, which are great ships laden with merchandise ... The goods which they usually bring, and sell to the Spaniards are raw silk in bundles of the thickness of only two strands, and other silk of inferior quality, soft, untwisted silk, white and of other colors in small skeins, much smooth velvet, and velvet embroidered in all sorts of colors and patterns; and other with the ground of gold and embroidered by hand with the same material; stuffs and brocades of gold and silver upon silk of various colors and designs, many other brocades ... tablecovers, cushions, carpets, caparisons of horse of the same stuff, and with bugles or seed pearls; some pearls and rubies, sapphires, stones of crystal ... large assortments of nails of all sorts, sheet iron, tin, lead, saltpetre and powder, wheat flour, preserves of oranges, peaches, viper-root, pears, nutmeg, ginger ... much fine thread of all kinds, needles, knick-knacks, little boxes, and writing boxes; beds, tables, chairs, gilt seats ... and a thousand other gewgaws and ornaments ... peppers and other spice; and curiosities, to recount all which would be never to come to an end ..."

Early Exploration

The mouth-watering shopping list composed by a Spaniard indicates plainly why his countrymen struggled so hard to develop the trans-Pacific trade during the 16th century. The westbound trip in the big, clumsy galleons was a breeze, literally; the lightly-loaded ships rode the trade winds to Manila in two or three months.

But the return trip was enough to make strong men weep...

It was necessary for sailing ships to strike out on a great northerly sweep into some of the worst seafaring weather in the world in order to beat their way eventually eastward. It was not unusual for a heavily-loaded galleon to slog for six or seven months through the stormy North Pacific before making a landfall.

The suffering of the crews was unbelievable. Sometimes only half a ship's crew survived the return voyage, with the survivors so weak that no one could stand upright. Captains' logs record instances of their being afraid to put in to land, even though the need for food and water was desperate, for fear that once the anchor was dropped, it could not be hoisted again by the dead and dying crew.

The villain was scurvy, dreaded curse of the ancient mariner. It caused ghastly blotches on the skin; often teeth fell out and gums swelled until suffering sailors couldn't close their mouths; eventually weakness beat victims to their knees.

Scurvy is a vitamin-deficiency disease—Vitamin C, in particular —but seamen of those days couldn't tell a vitamin from a viceroy.

But the Spanish seafarers knew enough to realize that it was a matter of desperate urgency that sheltered ports be discovered along the California coast where both galleons and the smaller exploring vessels could put in for rest and rehabilitation, then take on fresh water and vegetables (Vitamin C) before setting out on the easy leg of the voyage to their established bases on the west coast of Mexico.

History hangs on the blood and thunder of neurotic ambition; it also hangs on the need for proper nutrition.

* * *

A courageous Portuguese in the service of Spain, Juan Cabrillo, left Navidad on the west coast of Mexico in 1542 and beat his way

➡

This diorama from the Los Angeles County Museum depicts Cabrillo and crew anchored in San Diego Bay in 1542, about to "discover" the place. Indians dimly seen on the sandbar made up the reception committee, as usual.

north in two ships against the prevailing winds and currents, landing periodically to claim real estate for the Spanish crown. After three months, Cabrillo's motley crew in two tiny ships entered a sightly bay and again went ashore on a routine visit.

Only this time it wasn't routine; this time they stamped a big, bold mark in the annals of exploration.

That comfortable harbor entered by two tiny ships is now called San Diego Bay and Cabrillo and his crew were the first Europeans known to have set foot in Alta California.

Resuming his voyage, Cabrillo also put in at San Pedro, Catalina Island, Santa Monica and Ventura. Because Indian campfires were seen, he called Santa Monica "Bay of Smokes." Welcoming parties of Indians met his ships at Ventura, so it became "Town of Canoes."

Cabrillo never saw Navidad or his homeland again. After landing at San Miguel, he hurt his arm; blood poisoning developed and Juan Cabrillo died, but not before ordering his second-in-command, Bartolome Ferrelo, to sail on. Ferrelo obeyed, struggling north as far as the southern Oregon coast before turning around.

The explorers of the Cabrillo party passed up the best natural harbor on the Pacific Coast, San Francisco Bay. They had failed to discover the Northwest Passage or the golden kingdom of Calafia.

But they had staked out a vast new empire for imperial Spain and explored 800 miles of Pacific coastline; California could no longer sleep undisturbed in golden splendor under an eternal sun.

Now the English, along with the Russians, were coming.

THE PIRATE'S PLATE

When one walks into Bancroft Library at University of California, Berkeley, one must look sharp to keep from bumping into an unpretentious glass case bearing a small brass plate.

Drake's plate bears the inscription: "BEE IT KNOWNE VNTO ALL MEN BY THESE PRESENTS IVNE 17 1579 BY THE GRACE OF GOD AND IN THE NAME OF HERR MAIESTY QUEEN ELIZABETH OF ENGLAND AND HERR SUCCESSORS FOREVER I TAKE POSSESSION OF THIS KINGDOME WHOSE KING AND PEOPLE FREELY RESIGNE THEIR RIGHT AND TITLE IN THE WHOLE LAND VNTO HERR MAIESTIES KEEPEING NOW NAMED BY ME AND TO BEE KNOWNE VNTO ALL MEN AS NOVA ALBION FRANCIS DRAKE"

The plate surely is one of the most remarkable artifacts ever unearthed in California. Inscribed on it is a straight-forward message from an Englishman named Francis Drake, who coolly announces in brass that he is taking over all of the surrounding unsubdivided real estate in the name of Queen Elizabeth of England and from that day forward (June 17, 1579), the place was to be known as "Nova Albion"—New England. Drake seemed to feel that by giving the Indians a few trinkets, he had gained exclusive rights to the territory.

The plate was found in 1937, three and one-half centuries after Drake left it near the bay north of the Golden Gate where the English swashbuckler was known to have spent at least a month. (Now called "Drake's Bay," of course.)

"A fake!" cried cynics when the find was announced.

But metallurgists studied the plate and attested to its old, old age. In most quarters, this bit of brass is now accepted as authentic.

Apparently Queen Elizabeth of England, Drake's employer, was not impressed. Informed of Drake's bold conquest, she supposedly said: What was the good of owning a place if you had no one there to hold it?

A good point, as things turned out; Queen Bess was nobody's fool.

In the Spanish view, Drake was nothing but a pest. He had a bad habit of capturing galleons bound for Spanish ports and picking them clean of their pearls and rubies; the Spanish, naturally, considered this very bad form.

But Drake didn't plan to run for office in Spain. Instead he returned to England hauling the biggest load of booty ever carted up the Thames. His delighted queen knighted him in 1581 and it seemed like little enough to do. After all, this daring Englishman had not only fattened the royal treasury with a lot of Spanish loot but had also managed to circumnavigate the globe.

But in spite of Drake, it was the Spanish sun which was rising in the new world. The two Sebastians were waiting in the wings — Cermeno, a Portuguese, and Vizcaino, a Basque.

SMALL SHIPS, BIG STORMS

Cermeno, commander of a Manila galleon, had been ordered to moonlight; he was to explore the California coast while plying the regular Oriental trade route in 1595. His clumsy ship came a cropper when a storm slammed into it and drove it ashore in Drake's Bay,

Early Exploration

wrecking the vessel and destroying all cargo, including the vital provisions which were to sustain the party until its return to port on the west coast of Mexico.

The 70 survivors were put to work building a small boat. With only acorns and a pet dog for food, Cermeno ordered the little craft to sea. Despite near starvation, a remarkably accurate job of coastal mapping was accomplished.

Cermeno's ordeal ended the attempts to explore the treacherous coast with galleons. When the next attempt was made in 1602, three small vessels were especially constructed for the task and put under the command of Sebastian Vizcaino, who, oddly enough, was primarily a businessman, although his maritime experience was extensive, too.

One wonders if it wasn't this commercial background which caused the returned Vizcaino to sound like the president of the Monterey Chamber of Commerce, about three centuries before there *was* a Monterey Chamber of Commerce.

You see, Sebastian developed this thing about Monterey Bay . . .

A NOBLE HARBOR

As Vizcaino's little ships beat their way north along the California coast, the leader of the expedition apparently amused himself by naming everything in sight, blithely ignoring the names that had been recorded by explorers who had gone before. Vizcaino's names stuck, among them Santa Catalina, San Pedro, Santa Barbara, Carmel and Monterey.

For Vizcaino, there must have been little other amusement. By the time the ships put into Monterey Bay, scurvy was rampant, with only two sailors on Vizcaino's vessel able to climb the mainmast. One vessel loaded with sick was sent back to Mexico; the remaining two, after a three-week stay in the bay, bravely pushed on northward. Cold weather now was added to already enormous difficulties but Vizcaino refused to come about and head for home until they had reached a point close to the present California-Oregon border.

Vizcaino was not the only Monterey booster. The chronicler of the trip, a certain Father Ascension, described Monterey Bay as a "noble harbor . . . the best port that could be desired, for besides being sheltered from all the winds, it has many pines for masts and yards, and live oaks and white oaks, and water in great quantity, all near the shore."

Without doubt, Monterey Bay is immensely picturesque and has long proved to be a snug berth for a flotilla of fishing boats but a "noble harbor?"

There is some suspicion that the natural descendants of Father Ascension and Sebastian Vizcaino are still in California writing real estate advertising copy.

* * *

After his return to Mexico City, Vizcaino pushed hard for development of Monterey Bay as a major Spanish base but a change in viceroys thwarted him. The Manila galleons had to do without California's fresh water and Vitamin C; the long-sought safe harbor was there, all right, lurking behind fog-shrouded Golden Gate, but Vizcaino, mesmerized by Monterey, twice sailed right by.

Distracted by troubles in the old world and sapped by its other efforts in the new, Spain proceeded to let California simmer on the back burner for a full century and a half.

But when the Spanish finally did come back, they meant business. The leaders this time were men who would not be discouraged; their names now echo loudly through the musty corridors of California archives:

Father Junipero Serra . . . Captain Gaspar de Portola . . . Juan Bautista de Anza . . .

They performed incredible labors for God and crown but their mighty work, instead of giving Spain a new province, laid the foundation for what was to become two centuries later the most populous of the United States of America.

* * *

History is only the dead record of the past but remembered and nourished, it becomes heritage. Heritage is the foundation for the future.

Each generation must build on the foundation left by previous generations; it has no choice in the matter. We are, partly, what our ancestors were; no choice here, either.

Like it or not, we need to know those ancestors.

"Life must be lived forward," said Soren Kierkegaard, Danish philosopher, "but can only be understood backward."

Early Exploration

SITES TO SEE

CABRILLO NATIONAL MONUMENT, Point Loma, San Diego. (Worth the trip for the view alone. Don't miss the fine old lighthouse.)

DRAKE'S BAY, Marin County. (Sir Francis landed here to make his play for California.)

RANCHO SAN PEDRO. The brand of the Rancho San Pedro was also known at one time as "El Limon" (The Lemon). Brand was registered by Juan Jose Dominguez, who was granted the rancho, which consisted of 43,119 acres, in 1822. This is now the site of Los Angeles harbor area and the city of San Pedro.

Chapter Two *

Government
A GIMPY LITTLE MAN

A wise person once said that most of the world's work is done by persons who aren't feeling quite up to par.

Visit a mission on the Monterey Peninsula and you can believe it.

The hallowed place has an old look, as well it might. The drab room at Mission San Carlos Borromeo de Carmelo is small. Its furniture consists of a tiny straight chair and table, two trunks and a plank bed with a single blanket.

The man who lived in this room (and who died in it) obviously loved not luxury.

Death came in this stark little cell on August 28, 1784, to a frail, hobbling Franciscan priest whose statue now represents California in Statuary Hall, Washington, D.C. This same padre may become the first Californian ever lifted to sainthood by the Roman Catholic Church.

The little man was born on the Spanish island of Majorca. Spain issued a commemorative stamp in 1963 to observe the 250th anniversary of his birth. In the same year, the United States issued a National Medal honoring his name; he is the first priest to be so honored.

The remembered name is Serra.

Father Junipero Serra.

* * *

Physically, Padre Serra didn't amount to much. The record speaks of an "ulcerated" leg, which plagued him more or less constantly as

Charming little Mission Dolores in the heart of San Francisco looks like a chalet made out of sugar, about to be swallowed by the massive, modern church next door.

he plodded over thousands of miles of Mexican and California desert. He was no more than five feet, three inches tall. (Measurements were taken when his grave was opened in 1943). Even in his youth, he was not considered robust.

But somehow this gimpy little weakling managed to trudge across untracked country for weeks on end and live for decades in circumstances of great physical hardship while organizing and administering a chain of churches stretching from San Diego to San Francisco in an era when 30 miles was considered a good day's travel on the back of a horse.

Most of the time, he walked.

Obviously a fire burned within the man.

The fervor which drove Serra to his incredible effort is almost beyond comprehension today. The Spanish Catholic of Serra's day was a fanatic by modern standards. To Serra and his fellow priests, tens of thousands of unconverted Indians in California constituted a challenge that could not be ignored.

These quiet, friendly aborigines were "heathen," and the fact that they had perfectly serviceable, nature-based religions of their own seemed not at all important to the servants of the One True Cross.

The Franciscan priests first led by Padre Serra eventually established 21 missions in California; Serra is given personal credit for nine.

It worked ... for a time. And after a fashion.

Serra's early missions, of course, were nothing like the handsome structures which attract tourists today. Serra's Indians built mostly of brush and sticks.

Some of the missions today are still church property and serve religious purposes; others are state historic monuments, carefully maintained because they count with those who care about California's past; others are the treasured property of the communities surrounding them.

All of them are tourist meccas beyond compare.

El Camino Real — The Royal Road — is a tourist trail offering a historic richness that is the envy of most other states.

Today one can drive from Mission San Diego de Alcala in San Diego, the southernmost link in the chain, to Mission San Francisco de Solano in Sonoma, the northernmost, in a normal day's travel.

Part of the distance can be covered at 70 miles an hour over a freeway named after Padre Serra, who once limped over the same

"SEND AN EXPEDITION..."

The place: Mexico City. The time: 1766.

Jose de Galvez, *visitador-general,* felt his pulse race as he read his orders from the King of Spain:

"Send an expedition by sea to rediscover and people the bays of San Diego and Monterey."

Simple, direct, explicit.

One wonders if a king living in a royal ghetto an ocean away from the scene of the action had any conception of the difficulties involved.

But Galvez was an obedient man and a thorough man. He was just as interested as his king in the mysterious land to the north.

King Carlos III had called for a sea expedition; a sea expedition he would get. But had King Carlos ever been flattened on the unyielding deck of a galleon by a Pacific storm? Had he ever been laid low by the sapping scourge of scurvy?

Galvez decided to send a land expedition, too, just in case.

The little priest who had been appointed president of the California missions (an empty title at the moment, since there weren't any) agreed that it was an excellent idea.

Padre Serra also was a thorough man.

Still not comfortable, Galvez split the expedition into two columns which would be sent over different routes. Capt. Fernando de Rivera would command one column; the other would be led by Capt. Gaspar de Portola, who had just been appointed governor of Baja California.

Serra elected to travel with the column of Portola.

The fork thrust out by the suddenly vigorous Spanish had three tines called mission, pueblo and presidio.

One tine was sharp, two were dull. Pueblos were towns. Missions were churches. Presidios were military posts. In theory they supported each other; in practice they often stepped on each other's sore toes.

For instance, Father Serra first spotted the Monterey mission close to the presidio. *Uncomfortably* close, as it turned out. He saw fit to move it five miles away to a sightly spot along the Carmel River, where it stands today.

Better soil and more water was the *official* reason. A likely story...

Just two pueblos, Los Angeles and San Jose, thrived and survived. (Another one was planned near present-day Santa Cruz, but it didn't make it. It was to be called "Branciforte." Seems a shame that such a resounding name didn't survive.)

Only the missions were really successful. They worked because they were carefully planted in the middle of the best farm land and because there were lots of hard-working Indians around to coerce the soil into productivity. The missions, as a result, set the best table and provided entertainment with clock-around, year-around ceremonies and fiestas. They attracted population; they became community centers.

The missions, without doubt, were the only really sharp tine in the Spanish fork.

But only for a time. History has a way of passing by.

MULES MEDIUM RARE

The Spanish ships set sail into the prevailing winds. The columns of officers and soldiers and priests and Indians squinted into a dusty sun.

To the north along a threatening coastline and inland across a barren, light-scarred landscape lay exhaustion, scurvy, famine, lonely death and high adventure in a land called California.

Two ships, *San Carlos* and *San Antonio*, reached San Diego Bay in April but not without paying toll. Scurvy had cut a wide swath through the crews of both vessels; the men on the *San Carlos* were so weak they couldn't lower a boat to go ashore. Boats from *San Antonio* had to take the sick off *San Carlos*.

But what of the overland parties?

They had no scurvy problem but their way was anything but easy; death marched with both columns. Captain Rivera's group reached San Diego on May 15, 1769. The Portola-Serra segment, having taken a more difficult route, didn't arrive until July 1. These were the strongest and luckiest; about half of the expedition's men died or disappeared along the terrible trail.

It seems incredible but only two weeks later Portola, Fathers Crespi and Lopez and 62 others struck out northward through country Portola described as "rocks, brushwood and rugged mountains." Their goal: the fabled Monterey Bay.

The sight of the flowing column must have been a fascinating one for the natives who watched from hiding—leatherclad soldiers, Spanish officers in brilliant uniforms, priests in gray-brown cowls. Most of these usually rode horses or mules and were followed by Indians on foot, often leading pack animals.

Six months later, "smelling frightfully of mules," they returned to San Diego. Monterey Bay had been reached, all right, but the party didn't recognize it, with only Vizcaino's lyrical description to go by.

For good measure, they also stumbled onto San Francisco Bay but had no idea of the importance of their discovery. Father Crespi, who kept the trip diary, called it ". . . some immense arms of the sea which penetrate into the mainland in an extraordinary fashion . . ."

They'd have starved if they hadn't eaten their pack mules, 12 of them in 12 days . . . without barbecue sauce.

Small wonder they smelled like mules.

* * *

Only two days after Portola's party had left in search of mysterious Monterey, Father Serra had consecrated Mission San Diego de Alcala, the first link in what was to become a long chain.

But when Portola returned to San Diego, the situation was anything but good. Sickness and hunger stalked through the enfeebled settlement; no supply ships had arrived.

It seems highly peculiar but the Spanish in their world travels apparently had learned little about living off the land; in the New World, they might well have watched the natives and picked up a few pointers. There were fish in the streams and in the ocean; wild game, nuts and berries abounded in the woods.

Why didn't it occur to *somebody* in that hard-pressed community that the natives didn't depend on supply ships for food?

But Portola, apparently, was utterly dependent. Mournfully eyeing the decaying settlement around him, he decided grimly that if a ship didn't arrive from Galvez by March 20, he would abandon the effort and hightail it for Baja California.

History hangs on happenstance.

At dusk on March 19, a sail was sighted on the horizon!

THERE REALLY IS A MONTEREY

With renewed vigor, Portola led a party north toward the will-o'-the-wisp: Monterey. Father Serra, his leg troubling him terribly after the long march up from Baja, decided not to walk this time and boarded the *San Antonio*.

The year was 1770. As spring watered and warmed the glowing countryside, the mystery of Monterey was solved. Serra sailed in from the sea; Portola arrived overland. On June 3, a mission and presidio were consecrated.

Serra, the fervid priest of the Catholic Church, saw a land full of heathen Indians who had to be called to Christ.

Portola, the loyal soldier of Spain's King Carlos III, saw a rich new royal colony.

It was the same country, gold-green California, but seen through different eyes.

The missions founded by the Franciscans from San Diego to Sonoma not only survived, but thrived; they were the seeds which germinated and grew into modern California.

On the other hand, Portola's presidios—mostly staffed with underpaid, underfed culls and criminals—proved to be largely useless.

In 1812, Russian fur traders brazenly landed on the so-called Spanish coast of California and built a stockade; the military successors of Portola weren't strong enough to scare them off. Whenever an invader challenged the presidio at Monterey, the presidio crumpled; it never won a battle.

Put simply, the eyes of Spain were bigger than its stomach. After sending its staunch explorers into the tantalizing reaches of the New World, it couldn't sustain them. And so it happened that by reaching too far into the cookie jar, Spain lost Mexico. When it lost Mexico, it lost California. When it lost California, it lost the New World and retreated into the quiet, sun-splashed, tourist-trapped corner of the Old World that Spain occupies today.

THE DESERT *RATA*

In October, 1775, a remarkable man named Juan Bautista de Anza led a wildly-assorted group of 240 individuals trudging out of Sonora, Mexico, into a fearful waste of empty desert.

The assignment of this desert-wise officer, who had wandered this

In 1882, tombs of Fathers Serra, Lasuen, Crespi and Lopez were opened at Carmel Mission to halt rumors that the remains had been removed while the mission lay in ruins. Two years later, rebuilding of the mission began.

way before on a previous exploratory trek, was to found a mission and presidio on the shores of San Francisco Bay.

There were priests in the group and there were soldiers. The skills of both were needed, because there was a mob of hot and hungry civilians to manage, including more than 100 children!

This was primarily colonization, remember, not exploration.

(The de Anza trek has been mentioned historically along with the Lewis and Clark expedition. Not comparable, really. Did Lewis and Clark have 100 bored, tired and whimpering kids to manage? They did not. Or 140 pack mules, 450 saddle horses and 350 cattle? Certainly not; Lewis and Clark had only a self-reliant Newfoundland dog named Scannon.)

Yet de Anza, despite his squabbling, bawling menagerie, arrived at San Francisco Bay, after a harrowing journey, with more people than he started with. A woman had died along the way but three babies had been born.

A shepherd just can't do much better than that.

The de Anza expedition gave a tremendous boost to Spanish development of California. Chronically short of ships and sailors, weary of the hard sea journey along the Mexican coast, the Spaniards much preferred walking across a searing desert to floating over a surly sea as a means of supplying and populating the infant California settlements.

It was a good idea until 1787, when the Yuma Indians wiped out the Spanish garrison at a crucial crossing of the Colorado River, thus cutting the overland lifeline of the missions, presidios and pueblos. As a result, Spanish colonies in Alta California soon suffered from a lack of nourishment and protection. Forbidden foreign ships, including those of the snoopy *Yanqui*, entered the harbors. The Spanish presidio commanders could do nothing but smile politely and gulp because too often their troops were drunk or absent without leave.

THE FRUIT IS RIPE

At the turn of the 19th century, Alta California was a ripening plum just about ready to fall.

◀

On September 4, 1781, 11 families from Mexico, accompanied by four soldiers from San Gabriel Mission, founded Los Angeles. This diorama is in the Los Angeles County Museum.

Government

Spain knew it; Russia knew it; England knew it; the United States of America knew it.

All of these countries reached out a grasping, quivering paw . . . but oh, so tentatively, like four hounds carefully circling a porcupine while keeping a wary eye cocked at each other.

Spain, as has been pointed out, was overextended. The Spanish were hearing rumblings of revolt in Mexico and South America, even as their power and prestige in Europe were flaking away.

England was really more interested in the Pacific Northwest, where its Hudson's Bay Company was well established. But there was business to be transacted in California, too, and where there was business in the New World, there was Hudson's Bay. Somehow, in the old days of the American West, there was always Hudson's Bay. (One oldtimer cynically remarked that "H.B.C." stood not for "Hudson's Bay Company" but for "Here Before Christ.")

So what happened? Russia and England backed off from the porcupine when they decided it wasn't worth needles in the nose. Spain wanted California until it lost Mexico. The brash, young country called Mexico was so harried by its internal problems that it couldn't cope with a faraway colony.

Russia put in a tentative claim at Fort Ross but not with any grand notions of snatching California; it merely wanted to trade for furs and hides and buy supplies for its bases along the rim of the North Pacific. When the sea otter herds had been exterminated and it became plain that the button-bursting U.S. was in a mood for westward expansion, the Russians packed up their samovars and decamped.

England, as it turned out, had enough problems in the Northwest; it didn't need California troubles, too.

Before the game ended with the land called California clutched firmly to the bosom of the United States of America, the flags of seven countries had flapped over it!

There were hectic times when a new flag seemed to fly with each change of wind. There were years when Californians, if they didn't like the government in their neighborhood, could sample the one down the road.

Or just stay where they were and wait for the next political convulsion.

* * *

A bare outline of the squirming and thrashing seems least likely to compound the confusion.

First, there was the Spanish effort which consisted of fits and starts extending over several centuries. The Spaniards worked out of bases in Mexico, which was fine as long as they controlled that lovely land, but in 1810, a Mexican priest named Hidalgo triggered a revolt that led to Mexican independence. (It also led to Hidalgo's death before a firing squad, but that's another story.)

One might say that Mexico got Alta California in 1822 as a fringe benefit of revolution. Trouble was, the infant government of Mexico had problems at home which screamed for attention. Like Spain before it, Mexico had to let California drift through years of chronic shortage; there were never enough soldiers to protect it nor settlers to develop it.

Not that it was a bad life for the Californios, the Mexican families who owned and roamed the ranchos, and the "foreigners" (like John Sutter, the squire of Sacramento) who shared the lush life and the lusher profits. The hospitality of the rancheros was legendary—food piled high and gallons of wine and fiesta for all, with fat cattle roaming the golden hills and at the casas, slim senoritas dancing to guitars in the moonlight.

It was too good to last...

LAND OF THE LOTUS EATERS

California's lovely landscapes and comfortable climates have always lulled its natives of the moment into a state of heedless euphoria.

Before the advent of smog, traffic and taxes, it was easy to imagine that "Paradise" was the true name of the place and so why not have a bite or two of lotus, right? The newly-independent Mexicans succumbed, even allowed themselves the luxury of intramural bickering.

As usual, this was disastrous.

California might be a state of Mexico today if the fledgling Mexican government had been able, during the middle years of the 19th century, to give strong support to its lively emigrants in the north. It could not, though, and the Californios, typified by the remarkable Mariano Vallejo, quite naturally wondered if they wouldn't be just

The chapel at Fort Ross, only Russian outpost in California, as seen from a blockhouse.

as happy as Americans as they had been as citizens of Spain and Mexico.

Or even happier?

They were in love with the land, the climate, the way of life, and maybe it didn't matter too much what flag waved over this good ground. They were loyal to the earth which supported their life, not to a political system. Their experience led them to believe that politics was a rubbery product of people, twisting and squirming and reversing direction from year to year; the earth, on the other hand, was solid and dependable, subject only to the soft and distant commands of a majestic nature.

The Californios heeded the ancient call; they may have been really ecologists, at heart, with a strong dash of hippie.

But *who* was a Californian? In other words, who owned California?

A good question.

* * *

Jedediah Smith, the mountain man, was the first Yankee to lead an overland party into California from the east; this occurred in 1826. The Spanish told him to go back where he came from, but nobody ordered Jed Smith around; he went north instead and brazenly returned to California the next year.

Showing a face of utter innocence, Capt. John C. Fremont, topographical engineer of the U.S. Army, appeared in California in 1844.

He was a scientist, he said, and science was his game. Geography, to be specific. A mapmaker, pure and simple.

In 1845, Fremont again appeared . . . and in 1846, there was Fremont again, still protesting his innocence with military poise.

When Fremont and his small party displayed an American flag on a peak in San Benito County, Lt. Col. Jose Castro curled his lip and made a few angry gestures. Fremont withdrew.

If there had been guitar accompaniment, the action could have passed for an international dance entitled "Feint and Fall Back."

In its simplest form, the problem was this:

There were powerful politicians in the U.S., led by President Polk, who wanted in the worst way to grab California while the grabbing was good. But just sending soldiers in to snatch it was frowned on in international circles. (That is, unless the land involved was occupied only by Indians and the like; in that case, it was called "building an empire.")

At that time, the border between the U.S. and Mexico was in a state of flux. This is a polite way of saying that neither country was sure how much of that sun-browned sand in the Southwest was worth fighting over; this is the land that now is called Texas, New Mexico, Arizona and California. Americans were worried that if the U.S. didn't move into the developing vacuum, the English might. That, of course, would never do.

Some day somebody will write a history which blames most of the world's troubles on slow communications. A message from Washington, D.C., to Captain Fremont on the frontier couldn't be delivered for three or four months. A rumor seemed to make the same trip in a matter of weeks.

Under the circumstances, somebody was bound to get trigger-happy. Several somebodies did.

FIASCO BY SEA

On October 19, 1842, two American vessels sailed into Monterey Bay, looked their menacing worst and ordered the surrender of the port to the United States.

This ridiculous fleet was in charge of Cdr. Thomas ap Catesby Jones. (Jones was of Welsh derivation; the odd word "ap," means "son of" in Welsh.)

It seems that Commander Jones, stationed with his two sturdy vessels at a Peruvian port, heard a rumor that the U.S. and Mexico were at war. Hoping to implant his name in the history books, he promptly sailed north and invaded Monterey Bay.

On October 20, one day after his invasion, Cdr. Thomas ap Catesby Jones sailed out of Monterey Bay, trailing a wake of abject apology.

The U.S. and Mexico were not at war, it seemed, and all Jones could do was put to sea crying "Oops!"

But his name was in the history books, all right.

FIASCO BY LAND

At dawn of June 14, 1846, a small band of Americans (perhaps encouraged by a drop or two of unripe frontier whisky) descended upon Sonoma and surrounded the house of the respected commander of the presidio, Gen. Mariano Vallejo, who invited them in for a drink.

The Americans, led by William B. Ide, promptly seized the Californio leader and his officers, hauled down the Mexican flag and replaced it with a homespun creation of red flannel and brown paint, which was decorated with a star, a grizzly bear and the words "California Republic." (A monument marks the site of this Sonoma happening. California's present state flag is a slicked-up version of that early bit of laundry. Inevitably there were a few carpers who complained that the original bear looked more like a pig. One thing for sure: the modern version looks more like a bear.)

Whereupon Captain Fremont marched in with 72 riflemen to crash the party. Official war had erupted between the U.S. and Mexico a month earlier but neither Fremont nor the Bear Flaggers knew of it; they thought they were conducting their own private revolt.

Now the fat was surely in the fire.

* * *

Off Monterey Bay, Como. John Drake Sloat of the U.S. Navy read a stirring battle order to his nervous sailors:

"We are now about to land on the territory of Mexico with whom the U.S. is at war. To strike their flag and hoist our own in place of it is our duty. It is not only our duty to take California, but to preserve it ever afterwards as part of the United States."

On July 7, Commodore Sloat sailed into the bay, sent the American flag rippling up the pole at the customs house and claimed California, finishing off the 23-day Bear Flag Republic.

* * *

At long last, the last Mexican governor of California, Pio Pico of Los Angeles, and Gen. Jose Castro of Monterey were able to put aside their personal squabble long enough to gallop off in defense of their province.

Thus began a war of sorts, a stuttering series of disorderly engagements, often more noisy than bloody, with ragtag bands of "soldiers" on both sides romping over the countryside and flailing away at random with weapons that ran the gamut from lances to cannon.

On January 13, 1847, Gen. Andres Pico and Captain Fremont

A major figure of old California, Mariano Vallejo, relaxes before his Sonoma home about 1880.

signed the articles of Mexican capitulation at a ranch house in Cahuenga Pass.

More than a year later, with the signing of the Treaty of Guadalupe Hidalgo, Mexico officially gave up its rights and ambitions in California to the United States, in return for 15 million dollars and U.S. assumption of claims of three and one-quarter million.

Could anyone have guessed then that little more than a century later, there would be more Americans in California than in any other state?

Not the eminent Sen. Daniel Webster of Massachusetts, certainly. Bellowed Webster, in his best tub-thumping style:

"What do we want of this vast, worthless area, this region of savages and wild beasts, of shifting sands and whirlwinds of dust, of cactus and prairie dogs? To what use could we ever hope to put these great deserts or these great mountain ranges, impenetrable and covered to their base with eternal snow? What can we ever hope to do with the west coast, a coast of three thousand miles, rockbound, cheerless and uninviting, and not a harbor on it? What use have we of such a country? Mr. President, I will never vote one cent from the public treasury to place the Pacific Coast one inch nearer Boston than it is now."

At the time of Webster's tirade, the U.S. Congress was dominated by Easterners who intended to protect Eastern interests and had no intention of letting much public money be siphoned off to the upstart West.

There might have been a drawn-out argument in the Congress about admitting California to the Union except for one glowing fact:

There was gold in those sun-seared hills.

CALIFORNIA GOES LEGITIMATE

Stately Colton Hall in Monterey (which stands in restored grandeur today) was the scene on September 1, 1849 of the convention which adopted California's first constitution. Brash even then, Californians weren't interested in serving the usual probation period as a territory before being admitted to statehood.

On December 20, 1849, California did something even more brash—it came out flatfooted and declared itself a state of the United States of America, which simply wasn't done without the prior approval of the U.S. Congress.

That is, it wasn't done until California did it.

On September 9, 1850, California was admitted to the Union. The United States seemed just as anxious to admit California as California was to be admitted.

And why not? This baby knocking at the door carried buckets slopping over with gold and everyone agreed that it was a *most* appealing little tyke.

THE WILD RIDE OF JUAN FLACO

Everybody knows about Paul Revere and that clattering midnight ride over the cobblestones, but who's ever heard of Juan Flaco?

Juan *who?*

Compared to the California ride of Juan Flaco in September, 1846, Paul Revere's historic effort was a Sunday morning canter through Central Park.

The scene: Los Angeles. The situation: desperate. Young Capt. Archibald H. Gillespie had been left in charge of the conquered pueblo when Como. Robert F. Stockton advanced to the north.

Feeling his militaristic oats, Gillespie had clamped down hard on the proud Californios and before you could say "Paul Revere," he found himself and his 50 shaky soldiers surrounded by 600 angry Mexicans. Revolt was rampant all over southern California and the nearest assistance was 400 miles away in Monterey, where Stockton was supposed to be.

"I'll give $500," announced the tense Gillespie, "to anyone who will carry a message to Monterey."

Juan Flaco stepped forward and submitted to the indignity of having cigarette paper hidden in his long hair. Written on the paper was the exhortation: "Believe the bearer."

As darkness settled over the warm land on September 25, Flaco sneaked through the Mexican lines but was seen and pursued. He jumped his horse over a 13-foot ravine but the animal was struck by a bullet and had to be abandoned.

Carrying his lariat and spurs, Flaco jogged through the night to the home of a rancher, received food and another horse, then rode on . . . and on . . .

Four days later, Flaco reached Monterey, only to be told that Stockton was at Yerba Buena (now San Francisco).

Did Juan Flaco quit? He most certainly did not. Doggedly he

rode onward and finally delivered his desperate message after travelling about 500 miles in five days, an incredible effort for the time and place.

Perhaps Juan Flaco didn't make a deep mark in history because in a sense, he failed. Gillespie had to surrender before help could arrive. But Flaco's message triggered the formation of a relief expedition under Kearny, Fremont and Stockton which marched south and reoccupied Los Angeles on January 10, 1847.

If Juan Flaco had been able to stick to one name, he might have been better remembered. His name wasn't really Flaco; it was John Brown.

Or was it?

Apparently Flaco—or whatever his name was—started out as Johan Braune in Sweden, then joined the Swedish Navy, fought under Bolivar in Latin America, debarked in California and finally became an ardent American.

History can be peculiar, especially in California. It sends a name like Paul Revere flashing down the years, then ignores Juan Flaco, who earned many more saddle sores in just as great a cause.

But then, Paul Revere didn't have to leap the credibility gap.

Who could believe in a Swede named John Brown?

Even in California?

THE OLD WOMAN'S CANNON

Americans in California had their super-Paul Revere but Mexicans in California had their Barbara Frietchie (remember Whittier's "Shoot if you must this old gray head . . . ?"), a little old lady named Senora Reyes.

The story goes like this:

When the Californios objected to some of Archie Gillespie's more outrageous decrees, the captain is supposed to have snapped:

"You're a . . . cowardly foe not deserving of better treatment."

He might as well have waved a red bandanna in front of a fighting Spanish bull. The Californios began to plot against the popinjay, assembled a brigade of mounted lancers and soon lacked only one item for complete readiness: cannon. The Stockton-Fremont forces had captured most of the Californio field pieces and had even dug out four that had been buried for safekeeping.

The time was ripe for the strike; Gillespie's forces would never be weaker. But without cannon, what chance was there for victory?

Then, in the dark of night well after the hated Gillespie curfew had struck, an old lady left her house, was joined by shadowy figures and pointed the way to an adjoining vineyard.

The men dug at the spot Senora Reyes had shown them and soon their spades clanked on metal. Working furiously, they unearthed a cannon!

In the morning, mounted on wagon wheels, the cannon and the mounted brigade of lancers skirmished against the overbearing gringo at the Los Angeles plaza and forced his surrender.

The stubby four-pounder uncovered near the home of Senora Reyes on that dark, portentous night now rests in the museum of the United States Naval Academy at Annapolis. A former historian for the California Department of Parks and Recreation, Martin Cole of Whittier, tracked it down.

* * *

California's capital bobbed around like a yo-yo for a five-year period, from San Jose to Vallejo, then back to San Jose, back to Vallejo, to Sacramento, back to Vallejo, then to Benicia (named after Mariano Vallejo's wife) and finally, in 1854, back to Sacramento, where it stuck for a time and where it rests today. There hasn't been a serious move to dislodge it in more than a century, although every once in a while somebody half-seriously suggests that California be split into separate states, northern and southern. As recently as 1970, Assemblyman Willie Brown Jr. of San Francisco called for the creation of a commission to study division. Separation has seemed especially attractive to northern Californians since 1965, when legislative reapportionment by population gave southern California a majority in both houses of the state legislature.

There is more to it than that, of course. In the old days, San Francisco held sway as the state center of culture and commerce and as far back as 1880, many southern Californians felt like second-class citizens and began to think about separation from the overbearing North.

A separatist wrote in a magazine of the day:

"We are different in pursuits, in tastes, manner of thought and manner of life . . . our hopes and aspirations for the future are different. The restless, uneasy population of the north, ever drifting without local attachments, has no counterpart in Southern California;

neither has the wild spirit of mining speculation ever flourished here. With this peaceable life, possibly in part as a result of it, there has grown up in the people an intense love of their land. And it is for their own section of the State that this love exists. We call ourselves, not Californians but Southern Californians..."

Southern California, swarming with population now, developed slowly. In 1860, one-third of all Californians lived around San Francisco Bay and another third in the mountainous gold country. Less than five per cent lived along the southern coast. One hundred years later, the Bay area had only 20 per cent of the state's population, the mountain counties less than five per cent, and the southern coast, a whopping 50 per cent!

Nowadays a dedicated San Franciscan considers a resident of Los Angeles a purple-suited huckster or, if unclothed, a beach bum. The Angeleno, if pressed, will admit that there are just two kinds of people in San Francisco: hippies and effete snobs.

Both are right . . . and both are wrong. You can depend on it—a century from now the snippy dialogue will still be echoing through the smog both above and below California's Mason-Dixon line.

* * *

The Customs House in Monterey is said to be the oldest standing government building west of the Rocky Mountains. It is the centerpiece of the richest historical ground in California, the Monterey Peninsula. Here is the bay that Vizcaino advertised so excessively; here is where the U.S. first raised its flag in California; here is where Father Serra made his headquarters, where he died and where he is buried. Here also is a stunning collection of the oldest and most handsome adobe structures in the New World, some of them privately owned, some of them part of the Monterey State Historic Park, which surely is one of the most important historic treasures in the United States. Here is Colton Hall, where California's first constitution was carved out. Perhaps more so than any other California community, Monterey lives and breathes its heritage, respects it, cherishes it. Anyone who cares today about how it was in California in the old days must go to Monterey and go again, then leave reluctantly. In 1970, Monterey was capital of California, if only honorary capital, during the observance of California's bicentennial.

The Lugo family poses in its finery at the rancho in Bell; the year is 1888.

John Steinbeck wrote lovingly (and hilariously) of Monterey's Cannery Row in several novels. Cannery Row is inactive now but it still has the look of the Steinbeck era. Born at Salinas in 1902, Steinbeck reached the national spotlight with the publication of a novel, *Grapes of Wrath;* the powerful story centers on the migration of Oklahoma dust bowl refugees to California during the great depression of the 1930s.

Robert Louis Stevenson came to Monterey in 1879 and lived there for a time while pursuing Mrs. Fanny Osbourne, whom he married in 1880. The Monterey home in which Stevenson rented a room is now preserved as part of the Monterey State Historic Park; it contains many Stevenson mementos. The Monterey Peninsula so enchanted Stevenson that he used it as background in his classic *Treasure Island*.

Another famous author who used California settings in his work was Jack London, who lived on a ranch near Glen Ellen in Sonoma County. London, who fought a long battle with the bottle and lost, liked to clatter down the road from his ranch of an evening to partake of a happy glass or three with his cronies in Glen Ellen. (His favorite bar is now an unofficial historic landmark in the picturesque little village. As yet, the state hasn't taken it over.) London built a huge stone castle on the ranch and called it "Wolf House." Only a short time before he and his wife, Charmian, were to move in, the great structure burned. Crushed by the blow, London assumed the worst—arson. In 1919, the author's widow built another immense stone house, "The House of Happy Walls." The structure, along with the ruins of Wolf House and London's grave were presented to the state in 1960. At The House of Happy Walls, thousands of visitors every year look at a fine collection of London mementos, including a courageous display of some of the famed author's rejection slips!

* * *

Over the years, California attracted more than its share of authors who achieved immortality. Mark Twain did some of his earliest writing for San Francisco newspapers and stabbed away with such a sharp pen that his departure was mainly for the purpose of saving his hide. He rocked through some riotous months in the goldfields and poured his experiences into a classic book, *Roughing It,* and the short story which first exploded his name into national prominence, "The Notorious Jumping Frog of Calaveras County."

Upton Sinclair, who crashed upon the American literary scene with his muckraking novel, *The Jungle*, adopted southern California as his home.

California was called home for many years by two of the most prolific authors America has produced, Zane Grey and Erle Stanley Gardner. Grey, who lived at Altadena, established the classic pattern for that distinctively American product, the Western novel. Gardner, who lived on a ranch in Riverside County, wrote mystery novels by the dozen, often dictating his work to several secretaries simultaneously.

William Saroyan, born in Fresno, used the San Joaquin Valley as a setting for much of his writing. His book, *The Human Comedy*, has become a classroom classic throughout the United States.

In recent years, California has contributed several of its citizens to the national scene. Richard Milhous Nixon, 37th President of the United States, is a product of California's Orange County, born in Yorba Linda, raised in Whittier.

Earl Warren, chief justice of the U.S. Supreme Court from 1953 to 1969, was much in the news during his tenure because of the court's sweeping civil rights decisions during those years. Despite the controversy which swirled around him (or perhaps because of it), Chief Justice Warren is likely to be rated by historians as a landmark leader of the highest U.S. court. Warren was born in Los Angeles County, served first as attorney general of California, then as governor.

* * *

Like every other state, California sends only two elected individuals to the United States Senate, but is entitled to a small army of 43 in the U.S. House of Representatives, because representation in the lower house is based on population and California has more of that dubious asset than any other state.

California's constitution provides for election of a governor (four-year term), lieutenant governor, secretary of state, controller (chief fiscal officer), treasurer, superintendent of public instruction, attorney general and a board of equalization (four members who equalize taxable property valuations around the state and administer other taxes).

The state legislature consists of an upper house called Senate and a lower house called Assembly. There are 40 senators who serve four-year terms (half are elected every two years) and 80 assemblymen, who must present themselves to the voters every two years. Unlike

some smaller states, California's legislature meets every year, beginning a new term on the first Monday after January 1.

MISSIONS, BIRDS AND BEARS

It seems likely that every California history buff has his favorite mission. (So did grizzly bears; we'll get to that later.) Bird lovers, of course, vote for San Juan Capistrano in the south, where swallows return each year on St. Joseph's Day, March 19 (on or about). Carmel has its adherents, too, because it was Father Serra's headquarters, because the fantastic little man is buried there and because it's just plain handsome, a soothing sight for sore eyes.

Stately Santa Barbara, "Queen of the Missions," is the only one which stayed in operation without interruption from the date of its founding (1786) to the present. A process called "secularization," in which the missions were taken from church control for a time, caused many of them to slide into decay. Mission San Diego Alcala was the first to be established; Mission Solano in Sonoma the last. Mission San Luis Rey earned the title "King of the Missions" by becoming the largest and most populous in the chain. *No importa,* but San Luis Rey also boasts California's first pepper tree, planted in 1830.

The author's favorite is Mission Dolores in the heart of San Francisco. Dominated by the great church next door, Dolores just sits there in modest silence absorbing a flood of tourists and looking for all the world like an Alpine chalet transplanted to southern Italy. It has been said that Dolores is San Francisco's oldest building. Its cemetery contains the only monument to the California Indians, without whose labor Dolores, nor any other mission, could have existed. Many Indians —no one knows exactly how many—are buried in the churchyard.

The padres of Mission San Luis Obispo touted wayfarers on the mineral springs at nearby San Miguel. The padres insisted that bears came there at night to soak their lame legs. So let's give credit where credit is due, to Mission San Luis Obispo, the only mission recommended by bears.

Instead of a false front, California's capitol has a false top. In this photo taken in 1866 or 1867 by Alfred Hart of the Central Pacific, the first story is granite while the second story is revealed as ordinary brick, which was later coated with cement. Brick was used to hurry the building along in order to block transfer of the capital from Sacramento.

* * *

From Padre Serra to President Nixon, from brush huts at San Diego Bay to the eye-popping concrete marvel that is modern California—the change boggles the mind.

California made the fantastic leap in only two centuries.

Small wonder the state has suffered monumental growing pains.

SITES TO SEE

MISSION SAN DIEGO DE ALCALA, San Diego. (Father Serra's first.)

SERRA MUSEUM, near Old Town, San Diego. (Small, but high quality California collection; outstanding history bookstore.)

FORT ROSS, Sonoma County. (Restored Russian toehold in U.S.; exceptional museum.)

OLD SACRAMENTO, Sacramento. (Large, remarkable concentration of historic commercial buildings with great potential; much restoration work needed, though.)

STATE CAPITOL BUILDING, Sacramento. (Gleaming old-new structure has county exhibits on main floor, with surrounding grounds of great botanical interest and a sexy Senate chamber descended directly from the Barbary Coast.)

OLD GOVERNOR'S MANSION, Sacramento. (One governor called it a firetrap; this handsome, monstrous, Victorian relic is open to visitors; bring your own fire extinguishers.)

JUAN FLACO MARKER, Union and Weber streets, Stockton.

PUEBLA DE LOS ANGELES HISTORICAL MONUMENT, downtown Los Angeles. (Much has been done to restore some great old buildings around the site of the original plaza, but much remains to be done.)

RANCHO LOS FELIZ. The site of modern Hollywood, the rancho used the Verdugo brand issued to Maria Ygnacio Verdugo February 28, 1854.

Chapter Three ✻

The Indians
FIFTY AGAINST A THOUSAND

Even as one walks through the spiny, jagged area along government-tended paths a century after the trouble ended, one tends to crouch a bit and occasionally throw a furtive glance to the rear . . . especially if one's skin is white.

Even under a bright autumn sun which probes into the secret places, the caves and crevices reek of mystery and danger.

Especially if one goes alone in the off season when the tourist tide is at ebb . . .

This place is haunted, the grotesque lava shapes seem to mutter. *There are spirits here who want to speak of life and death, of peace and war, of cruelty and courage, of sunrise and sunset.*

The spirits, mostly, are Indian spirits. California Modoc Indian. For here, in this natural fortress of treacherous, upthrust lava, California's only major Indian war was fought and one of the most tragic episodes of American Indian history was allowed to drift to a bloody conclusion.

Now it is simply called "Lava Beds National Monument."

The federal government owns and controls and maintains the area in California's northeastern corner near the town of Tulelake. Tourist attractions include Indian petroglyphs, 50 square miles of lava flows, ice caves and extinct volcanoes. One expects this gray-black, sharp-edged, perforated stone to be as inhospitable as cold steel to plant and animal life but surprisingly, rabbit brush and sage abound, relieving the harshness with softening lines and delicate colors. The rocks are alive with lizards, snakes and marmots; this is mule deer country, too. Somehow life proceeds in this forbidding place. Only those kinds of life survive which know how to adjust and adapt and use this strange terrain.

During the winter of 1872-1873, a small band of Modoc Indians led by a young chief called Captain Jack used the terrain to perfection. They adjusted to it and adapted to it and for almost six months, this courageous band of about 50 Modoc warriors made American history and California history by holding off nearly 1000 U.S. bluecoats, volunteers and Warm Springs Indian scouts in one of the most dramatic clashes of white men and red men on the western frontier.

The American Indian way of life was dying in 1873.

It died hard, and nowhere harder than in Captain Jack's natural lava fortress—the Stronghold—which has since become a magnet for the history-minded who want to know how it was as the century ended and the fanatic remnants of the last great tribes fought to save the tatters of an ancient American way of life.

DEATH IN THE FOG

In the cold darkness of the lava beds at 4 a.m. on January 17, 1873, an army bugle sounded reveille. As the brisk notes destroyed the quiet of the night, shivering soldiers struggled out from under blankets, ate a hurried breakfast, then fell in before their commander, Lt. Col. Frank Wheaton of the 1st Cavalry.

Excited anticipation of the onrushing battle had made sleep difficult for many of the soldiers. In the restless camp not far from Tule Lake, they had talked of eating Modoc steak for supper on the following day.

There was only one order for this day: Kill Modocs, eradicate them, clean them out of the Stronghold forever.

The attacking force, including more than 100 volunteers, numbered over 300. There probably weren't more than 50 Modoc warriors in the Stronghold and they had women and children to care for, too.

Surely a great day had dawned for an army grown weary of abuse from settlers and politicians for not long since ridding the country of the Modoc menace.

On the evening before the battle, Lieutenant Colonel Wheaton had written in a letter: "A more enthusiastic, jolly set of regulars and volunteers I have never had the honor to command. If the Modocs will only try to make good their boast to whip 1000 soldiers, all will be satisfied."

But before many hours had passed, they were not so jolly, then not at all enthusiastic, and finally, some were screaming in pain as they died.

* * *

At dawn they marched to the edge of the bluff which overlooked the lava beds and the lake, then stared in astonishment.

The lake and the lava beds had disappeared!

Fog, thick and endless, completely concealed the terrain below. There was no sign of the Stronghold, no sign of the Modocs.

The soldiers had taken great comfort in their howitzers but suddenly there were no targets for the mighty guns; there was only gray, shapeless, fearsome fog.

According to plan, Captain Bernard was to attack the stronghold from the east; Wheaton's detachment would move from the west. But now there was no way to signal Bernard through the fog that plans should be changed, the attack delayed. An army does not change plans easily, even on a clear day.

Wheaton felt there was nothing to do but order the advance as planned, so down the narrow trail crept the soldiers, into the cruel lava, into the threatening fog.

They paused, waiting for their commander's order to proceed.

When it came, even the bugle repeating the command seemed strangled by the murky vapor.

An order was an order. Slowly they struggled into the ancient rocks, drifting along the dangerous way like ghosts, each soldier visible only to a few others. Lava tore at their boots. When they fell, lava gashed their knees and elbows. The first blood dripped onto the rocks.

They had started in line formation but soon the line broke in the face of huge lava boulders which loomed out of the fog and forced them into detours.

Despite the difficulties, morale remained high. Surely the fog would soon lift, the soldiers told themselves, and then they would link up with Bernard's strong unit and the two lines would swing around and touch in a classic maneuver, trapping Captain Jack's arrogant Modocs between the soldiers and the lake. Warfare by the book—the army manual. Everyone tried to forget that the officer who wrote the army manual had probably never seen the lava beds or a fog like this one.

But, the soldiers murmured, if it was foggy for them, wasn't it just as foggy for the Modocs?

* * *

In the Stronghold early that morning, the Modoc medicine man, Curly Headed Doctor, pranced through the mist exulting.

Hadn't Curly Headed Doctor promised that he, mightiest shaman of the tribe, would make mighty medicine to keep the soldiers out of the Stronghold? Hadn't he promised that not a Modoc would die?

And here, swirling its protective cloak around them, was the answer from the Great Spirit. As anyone could plainly see, the powerful ceremony of the night before had produced the fog.

In the rocks they knew so well, Modoc scouts prowled close to the soldiers and watched their every move without fear of discovery. In the Stronghold itself, Modoc warriors were at their posts in the rocks, staring over their leveled guns into the vapor, waiting for the first dim targets to slide out of the mist.

Then, suddenly, a distant, rolling rumble . . .

The advancing troops paused to listen, then cheered.

Gunfire! That would be Bernard's boys cutting loose; at last the agony of silent suspense had ended.

Cheers relaxed tense throats as the blue line plunged forward, moving as rapidly as the rocks would allow.

Then spots in the fog glowed ahead of them; a rifle's report knifed through the murk and a bullet streamed past with a banshee wail.

The first soldier fell and rolled, groaning, into the sharp rocks.

"Get me out of here!" he shrieked. "I'm shot! My leg's broke!"

Crouching, the soldiers searched the mist for the direction of the fire but now it seemed to come from all directions.

Another soldier fell and was unable to rise.

"Fire!" bellowed an officer.

The soldiers rose, lifted their guns and blindly triggered hot lead into the fog.

A desperate officer ordered: "Charge!"

The soldiers stumbled ahead for a hundred yards, loading and firing at the phantoms in the fog, loading, firing, falling, dying.

And still there were no real targets for the guns of the attacking army.

Where in the name of time were those infernal redskins?

Behind the guns killing white soldiers, that's where, and God help us now . . .

* * *

Soldiers and Modocs fought to the death in jagged lava during California's last Indian war.

By late morning, the soldiers had learned some painful lessons about lava. The holes and trenches and crevices could instantly cripple the man who fell into them but once in a trench, a soldier was safe from hot Modoc lead. In the open places, the footing was much better and the going easier. Easier, that is, until Indian sharpshooters, their gun barrels poked through holes in the rocks, knocked the soldiers screaming to their knees with well-placed bullets.

A CHANGE OF PLAN

At 3 p.m., thwarted at a bloody ridge, officers met and finally changed their original battle plan. They decided to send one unit around the left flank to attempt a linkup with Bernard's people on the lake side of the Stronghold.

The new plan worked no better than the old.

Modoc bullets found more victims.

The fog lifted for a moment just before 5 p.m. to reveal a red-orange sun sliding down behind Mt. Shasta. Soon it would be dark; with the blackness of night, the horrors of the day would be multiplied. Rather than waste their grim, day-long effort, the soldiers followed orders and pushed forward halfheartedly in a final attack.

It failed, beaten down by a fresh volley of deadly Modoc fire.

Then the dregs of courage dripped out of the attacking force and panic wrapped its clammy arms around them as they huddled in the rocks.

Now it was plain to Lieutenant Colonel Wheaton that the day's fight was finished. There would be no Modoc steaks for supper. There was nothing to do now but leave the lava bed and crawl up the trail to the safety of the bluff.

So the bugler sounded retreat . . . and immediately the cries of the wounded echoed among the rocks.

"Don't leave me here for them Modoc devils!" one cried. "Shoot me afore you go! My God, don't let 'em take me alive!"

An attempt was made to help some of the wounded soldiers but Modoc gunfire and Modoc war whoops stymied the effort. As night oozed over the ghostly battlefield, what remained of the attacking army stumbled and slogged back to the dismal camp they had left with high hopes only 10 hours before.

Cold, hungry, numb with fatigue, they looked back from the bluff. The fog had finally drifted away from the lava beds and now hung over the far shore of the lake.

In the Stronghold, a Modoc victory fire leaped up and splashed against the sky.

* * *

The end of day belonged to Curly Headed Doctor. Around the fire in the Stronghold, he bragged of his prowess as a medicine man and the Modocs listened. He spoke of the weakness of their chief, Captain Jack, who had argued, as always, for peace talk. And the Modocs listened . . .

Curly Headed Doctor's propaganda seemed to have a solid basis: In the day's hard fighting, not a single Modoc had been killed, while many soldiers had died.

There were only a few Modocs who were willing to listen to their chief as he rose at the end of the victory council.

"We have brought death to many white men today," said Captain Jack. "It is true. Modoc hearts are strong, Modoc bullets follow a true path. But hear me, my people! I am a Modoc and I tell you that white men, many white men, will come again. They are like fish in the lake and birds upon the shore! They will come again! We are strong but we are few. If we fight, in the end we must die.

"I am Modoc. When you say peace, I will make peace. But I know in my Modoc heart that we will never see Lost River again unless we stop this fighting!"

Captain Jack then slipped off to his cave. The Modocs continued their celebration. The fire finally died and the dancing stopped. The last exhausted warrior drifted toward his sleeping place in the Stronghold and the black chill of night gripped the rocks.

A part of a chapter of California history had been written, a few bloody pages of the last chapter of California's Indian chronicles.

The Modocs had won a battle in glorious style, but had begun to lose a war and an ancient way of life.

THE BEGINNING OF SCARFACED CHARLEY

How had it begun? How had a small, desperate band of American Indians been carried to this time and place on a surging tide of history?

Once the Modocs had been members of a Pacific Coast tribe called Lalacas; this tribe also included the Klamaths. But along about the year 1800, the Modocs and Klamaths quarreled and made war on each other. The Modocs won, then went to live by themselves in the Lost River-Tule Lake area.

But bitterness lingered. When white men came to California seeking gold, the Modocs and Klamaths were unwilling to stand together to protect their lands and privileges. Perhaps it didn't matter much; there were too many whites, too few Indians.

If whites had understood how Modocs and Klamaths felt about each other, Captain Jack might have died of old age, not at the end of a hangman's rope. But whites, streaming into a new, rich land which seemed to be theirs for the taking, surely weren't going to fret over fine points.

Indian-white troubles, at bottom, were simply a resounding clash between two utterly different ways of life.

The white way of life made the Indian way of life impossible. The horde of newcomers in wagons scared away the wild game on which Indian families fed. White woodcutters chopped down the trees which provided the Indians with pinenuts. Cattle herds owned by whites swallowed up the rice grass seed which Indians once had harvested each autumn. Herds of sheep ruined the tender desert plants upon which jackrabbits fed; soon Indian hunters found fewer rabbits to bring back to their villages. White miners spilled fish-killing poisons into the streams; Indian fishermen were forced to return to their lodges emptyhanded.

Some Indian tribes quietly accepted these depredations.

But not the Modocs...

* * *

In 1852, a party of Modocs which may have been led by the father of Captain Jack attacked at dawn to destroy a wagon train encamped on the shore of Tule Lake. Sixty-four emigrants died in the cruel ambush. The place became known as "Bloody Point" and the Modocs acquired their first black mark in white California history.

Before setting out to mentally hang these Modocs, though, we should ponder another episode which must have occurred not many years before. A Modoc warrior met a wagon train in a friendly way but was captured, tied to a horse and dragged to his death behind the animal. The Modoc's young son was forced to watch his father die. In time, this boy came to be called "Scarfaced Charley" by whites. The first shot of the Modoc War was fired by Scarfaced Charley. Captain Jack's strong right hand during the battle of the Stronghold

Here is Scarfaced Charley, mighty warrior of the Modocs.

was Scarfaced Charley. Charley's right cheek bore a ghastly scar but apparently there was another scar on his soul. White emigrants to California probably put it there.

The Klamath Basin Indians, including the Modocs, met at Yreka in 1864. Object: treaty. At the meeting were 710 Klamaths, 339 Modocs and 22 Snakes. The white spokesman was Esquire Elisha Steele, a Yreka lawyer who was acting Indian superintendent for northern California.

A treaty was signed. All of the Indians would occupy the Klamath Reservation. The whites would supply food, clothing and blankets for as long as the Indians needed them. In exchange, the Indians relinquished all claims to lands beyond the reservation.

Steele liked and trusted the Modoc, Kientepoos; apparently the feelings were mutual. During the conference, Steele gave Kientepoos the name of Captain Jack, after a miner he admired. The Modocs responded by setting down old Schonchin and electing Captain Jack their chief.

Emigrants in the area heard of the treaty and breathed huge sighs of relief. Finally the Modocs had been neutralized. Elisha Steele, without question, was a great man.

Unfortunately, the Klamaths and Modocs bore the throbbing scars of old enmity; they could not live together. The Modocs had cut trees to build cabins but in the night, Klamaths had taken what they considered their share of the logs. The Modocs complained to the Indian agent, a young, green army officer, but got no satisfaction. There were other irritations, other incidents.

Early in 1865, Captain Jack and some of the Modocs left the Klamath reservation and returned to Lost River, only to find that white emigrants had moved onto the land.

The Indians demanded "rent" from the whites. The whites complained to authorities.

Attempts were made to return the Modocs to the reservation. Finally a new Indian agent, Alfred B. Meacham, succeeded . . . temporarily. Captain Jack agreed to return if the agent would promise that the Modocs would no longer suffer the ridicule of the Klamaths on the reservation.

That promise and several others couldn't be kept. Three months later, Jack fled again, this time taking 371 Modocs along. Since Jack had brought only 43 of his tribesmen back to the reservation with him, this represented a net loss to the U.S. government of 328 Indians.

The Indians

Simple arithmetic indicated that the situation was sliding rapidly from bad to worse. Some of Jack's tribesmen voluntarily drifted back to the reservation but about 200 stayed out to create midnight fears for the settlers and nagging concern for the army.

LAND ON THE LOST RIVER

Superintendent Meacham, a good man, might have solved the problem without undue bloodshed if he had received the cooperation he needed. Since 1864, Captain Jack had pounded away at one point—a reservation on the Lost River.

"Give us back our land on the river," he pleaded. "Modocs can be happy there, no place else. Modocs must be by their river. Then we will fight no more among ourselves and peace will settle over the country."

In 1871 Meacham convinced Gen. E. R. S. Canby, army commander for the area, that a Lost River reservation should be given to the Modocs. But it was not to be; orders were issued to the 1st Cavalry to return the Modocs to the reservation "peaceably if you can, forcibly if you must."

Now, for sure, the fat was in the fire.

Soldiers streamed into the lava beds from as far away as Fort Vancouver and were joined by angry, determined volunteers from Oregon and California. Weeks passed in restless waiting as Lieutenant Colonel Wheaton refused to attack until the promised howitzers had arrived from Vancouver.

As the Modocs waited, Curly Headed Doctor wove a rope of red tules and strung it around the Stronghold.

Modocs within the circle, he promised, would be protected; none would die in the soldiers' assault.

And so the stage was set. On January 17, the soldiers moved fearfully into the fog toward the disaster of the first battle of the Stronghold.

It was the last time the United States Army would take lightly the fighting forces of Captain Jack, Modoc Indian.

* * *

Startled by the crushing defeat in the first Stronghold battle, officials in Washington, D.C., had second thoughts. Perhaps negotiation was the wisest course, after all. The army could not afford another fiasco in the lava beds.

And so a peace commission was appointed. Two of the men were excellent choices: A. B. Meacham and Gen. E. R. S. Canby. As winter wore on, the commission members acceptable to the Modocs met several times with Captain Jack in the Stronghold but could offer only a general amnesty and a reservation in Arizona or southern California.

But the Modocs still wanted Lost River . . .

Hooker Jim and Curly Headed Doctor argued that the amnesty offer was a fraud. Once the Modocs gave themselves up, they insisted, the Modocs would be hanged.

And so it was that the Modocs, safe for the moment in their rocky fortress, argued around the council fires and divided into opposing camps — doves and hawks.

Accept the offer, urged the doves. Fight to the death like Modocs, demanded the hawks.

It was supremely ironic that it should have been the leader of the doves, Captain Jack, who was soon to blacken his historic image forever by slaying the only army general ever killed during an Indian war in the United States.

A PLAN FOR MURDER

They called Captain Jack a cowardly woman, a squaw with white skin, and dressed him in women's clothes. It was too much for the proud Modoc; with a heavy heart, he agreed to the plan.

The plot was simple. They would ask for a meeting with the commission, take concealed guns with them and kill all the whites.

But the plan leaked; a woman talked.

A young Modoc woman named Toby had married a white interpreter named Frank Riddle. Toby Riddle (later called "Winema," the name she usually bears in history) passed along a warning from one of the Modoc doves in the Stronghold:

"Tell old man Meacham and all the men not to come to the council tent again — they get killed."

Two members of the commission, L. S. Dyar and Meacham, accepted the warning as truth. General Canby and the Rev. Eleazar Thomas could not believe that the Modocs would do such a terrible thing.

On the morning of the meeting, Meacham wrote:

"My dear wife:

"You may be a widow tonight, but you shall not be a coward's wife. I go to save my honor. John Fairchild will forward my valise and valuables. The chances are all against us. I have done my best to prevent this meeting. I am nowise to blame.

       Yours to the end,
       Alfred

"P.S. I am giving Fairchild six hundred and fifty dollars in currency for you."

Toby had spoken truth. Meacham's fears were well grounded.

*   *   *

The meeting began early on April 11, 1873, at a tent less than a mile from the army camp. Canby, Meacham, Thomas and Dyar attended as members of the peace commission. The Modocs were represented by Captain Jack, John Schonchin, Hooker Jim, Ellen's Man George, Shacknasty Jim, Black Jim, Boston Charley and Bogus Charley.

Fitful, fruitless discussion filled the nervous morning hours. Shortly after noon, Captain Jack suddenly leaped to his feet and yelled "*At-we* (all ready)!" Immediately two Modocs carrying rifles raced out of the rocks.

Captain Jack put a pistol to General Canby's head and pulled the trigger; the pistol misfired. He cocked and pulled the trigger again.

This time Canby fell with a bullet hole over his left eye. Boston Charley and Bogus Charley shot down Thomas; Schonchin went after Meacham; Hooker Jim chased the running Dyar and Black Jim moved toward Frank Riddle.

The attack was over in a few moments. Canby and Thomas were dead. Meacham had been shot three times, scalped and left for dead, but he survived, perhaps only because Toby had cried out, "The soldiers are coming!" causing the Modocs to run toward the Stronghold. Dyar and Riddle fled unharmed.

The brief encounter marked the end of the government's peace efforts. The chief of staff in Washington ordered the Modocs exterminated and a vengeful army eagerly prepared to launch a massive attack on the Stronghold.

*   *   *

The United States Army was not about to repeat its mistake of underestimating Modoc fighting ability in the Stronghold; the cruel defeat in the fog still rankled. Almost 700 soldiers were assembled for the new assault and again they were supported by Warm Springs Indian scouts.

The attack kicked off on April 15 and this time, fog did not protect the Modocs. Also, the soldiers remembered what they had learned about fighting in the lava. By nightfall of the first day, the troops had advanced two-thirds of the distance between Gillem's camp and the Stronghold.

Then, at nightfall, instead of pulling out as before, they dug in. Only three soldiers were killed and six were wounded during the first day's fighting.

On the second day, two army units joined along the shore of Tule Lake, cutting off the Modocs from their water supply. Other soldiers edged toward the Stronghold, crossing Curly Headed Doctor's red tule rope.

It was a bad day for the Modoc medicine man. The artillery had banged away all day, but caused no damage in the Stronghold; the medicine man gloated. Then a curious Modoc took his hatchet to an unexploded cannon ball and was torn to bits when it blew up. Perhaps Curly Headed Doctor should have warned his congregation that he could protect them against everything but their own stupidity.

So finally a Modoc had died. Curly Headed Doctor lost face and Modoc morale sank.

On April 17, the army advanced cautiously toward the Stronghold. The troops, expecting fierce opposition, encountered none. Only silence accompanied their careful progress.

"A trick," the lava bed veterans muttered as they hunkered down in the rocks.

But at noon the army discovered the startling truth: *The Stronghold had been abandoned!*

In the darkness before dawn, Captain Jack had led his people south out of the Stronghold.

Quickly the soldiers moved in and entrenched themselves against a Modoc return.

The main struggle had ended but not the suffering for either side. Colonel Gillem, commanding the troops, now had to prevent the Modocs from scattering. Patrols were sent out to locate the Indians and one of them, commanded by Capt. Evan Thomas and Lt. Thomas Wright, made a fatal mistake when it stopped, stacked its rifles and sat down to eat lunch. Some of the soldiers were so careless as to take off their shoes.

Even away from the Stronghold, the Modocs were at home in the lava. Shuffling quietly through the rocks, their scouts had tracked every step of the Thomas-Wright patrol.

The army had learned . . . but not enough. The soldiers were ordered by Wright to scout a nearby ridge; they died under the first Modoc bullets.

Half of the patrol didn't wait for instructions but simply ran, reaching Gillem's camp in less than two hours. Of those brave men who stuck fast, 25 died and 16 more were wounded.

Surely this was a satisfying day for Scarfaced Charley, who had watched his father being dragged to death behind a white man's horse.

Along about the middle of the afternoon, Charley yelled down at the cowering soldiers: "All you fellows that ain't dead yet better go home! We don't want to kill you all in one day!"

Then the Modocs slipped away. The relief unit from Gillem's camp didn't appear until morning, too late for the dead, much too late for the honor of the army.

So the Modocs had won another battle but they had won it in a way that virtually insured the loss of the war. The United States Army had been shocked by its humiliation in the first battle of the Stronghold, then thoroughly angered by the killing of Canby and Thomas. Driving Captain Jack's people out of the Stronghold had bolstered army morale but the Thomas-Wright disaster caused it to sag again.

Was there no way to beat down these madmen called Modocs? Were they devils incarnate, living in a devil's country, appearing, then disappearing, sliding away in the dark only to strike like poisonous snakes out of holes in these jagged, flesh-tearing rocks?

MODOC SUNDOWN

The Modocs were experts in psychological warfare.

But they were also naive and uninformed. They apparently believed that if they fought well enough and frightened enough soldiers, the United States government would capitulate and give the Modocs what they most wanted — their own land along the Lost River and a license to live their own life in their own way.

Captain Jack might have achieved this goal for his people but there was too little understanding, too little patience, too little time. And too often, the Modocs weren't content with just defeating the army against impossible odds; they had to spit in its eye as well.

Finally the army had to destroy the Modocs or let its own reputation on the frontier be destroyed.

Under pressure, the Modocs moved south, fighting as they went, and then had to leave the protecting lava beds entirely. The soldiers had driven away the wild game, and water, too, was in short supply. For the Modocs, life was hard and the end was near.

Soon Modoc was hunting Modoc. Hooker Jim's band was captured and then, like traitorous bloodhounds, four Modocs — Hooker Jim, Bogus Charley, Shacknasty Jim and Steamboat Frank — volunteered to lead the army to Captain Jack's refuge.

One by one, Captain Jack's band surrendered. Finally, on June 1, soldiers closed in on a canyon and the captain demanded surrender.

A Modoc stepped out on a shelf of rock and dropped his rifle. Filthy, ragged, exhausted, weak with hunger, the chief of the Modocs braved 20 rifles as he limped down to accept his fate at the hands of his tormenters.

He said only, "Jack's legs give out."

HANGED BY THE NECK

"The foregoing sentences (to be hanged by the neck until dead) in the cases of Captain Jack, Schonchin John, Black Jim, Boston Charley, Barncho and Slolux, Modoc Indian prisoners, are hereby approved; and it is ordered that the sentences in said cases be carried into execution by proper military authority, under the orders of the Secretary of War, on the third day of October, eighteen hundred and seventy-three.

U. S. Grant
President"

Then occurred an episode of almost unbelievable cruelty. The sentences of two of the six prisoners were commuted to life imprisonment on Alcatraz Island.

The prisoners weren't told. From their cells, they could see *six* graves being dug.

Barncho and Slolux weren't informed that their lives had been spared until the very last instant, just as they were about to climb the gallows ladder.

Hooker Jim and the other Modocs who had volunteered to help the army hunt down Captain Jack were not tried. Hooker Jim,

Wearing leg irons, three important Modocs hold still for a U.S. Army picture. From left, Boston Charley, Captain Jack and John Schonchin.

who had always argued against Captain Jack for a fight to the death with the whites, who perhaps had more white blood on his hands than any other Modoc, *was not tried* . . .

At Fort Klamath on October 3, 1873, the sentence was carried out and death came at the end of a rope to Captain Jack, Schonchin John, Black Jim and Boston Charley.

Now four Modocs, at least, had found the peace they had argued for.

Thus ended the Modoc War. When it was over, a bookkeeper concluded that this had been the most expensive war in U.S. history in terms of dollars per death. The war against Captain Jack had cost U.S. taxpayers at least a million dollars to wipe out 16 Modocs.

The Lost River reservation the Modocs wanted would have cost, at the outside, $20,000.

The war also cost the lives of 48 soldiers, a number roughly equal to the entire Modoc fighting force.

* * *

After the battles and the hanging, those who remained alive of the Modoc tribe were shipped in cattle cars to the Quapaw Indian Reservation in Oklahoma.

A few Modocs still live at Chiloquin, Oregon, and a few more still survive in Oklahoma. The Oregon Modocs insisted in 1968 that the Modoc story be told in the national monument, so a plaque was erected which at least started to tell the story. It said:

"Modoc Indian War 1872-1873. Within this lava fortress, under the leadership of Capt. Jack, a small band of Modoc Indians held off a much larger force of U.S. regular and volunteer troops for nearly six months."

THE GHOST OF OROVILLE

He materialized dimly out of the eerie light of dawn in the corral of a slaughterhouse, crouching against the fence, thin to the point of starvation, his hair burned off short, unclothed but for a tattered piece of canvas worn like a poncho.

The dogs saw him first and barked.

Awakened, the butchers who worked in the slaughterhouse approached the corral fence cautiously and stared hard into the half-light at the fearsome object.

Then one of them ran toward the house and feverishly cranked up the telephone.

"You better get right out here, sheriff," the man demanded, his voice tight. "We got us a wild man! You come get him!"

Oroville was only a few miles away. Sheriff J. B. Webber and several deputies soon were on the scene, edging toward the corral with guns trained on the cowering thing.

But there was no need for guns. The man let the sheriff handcuff him without struggle or protest. The reason was obvious to Webber: The creature was frightened almost to rigidity, and utterly exhausted.

Webber knew he had captured an Indian but that was all he knew. He could learn nothing more from the prisoner, who apparently couldn't speak English.

The sheriff took his captive to Oroville and put him in a jail cell reserved for the insane. Word of the capture had spread rapidly and already the townspeople and even a few outsiders were clamoring for a look. At the moment, jail seemed like the safest place for the pitiful man.

The date was August 9, 1911.

The last of the aborigines, the native Americans, had been forced to come to terms with the white man's civilization. The Yahi Indian who was to carry the name "Ishi" through one of the most curious and moving episodes of the white-red drama had come on stage expecting to die at the hands of his hated persecutors ... but had not died.

Not yet, not quite yet, and in the few years of life left to him, he was to bridge a wide gap of human history in California.

No Yahi were left to mourn him at his death; Ishi was the last. But mourned he was, long and well, by friends who represented a race he had feared for most of a desperate, harrowing lifetime. He died of a white man's disease but at the end, most of his friends were white. During half a century of savage slaughter, whites had killed his family, his friends and finally his tribe but at death, most of Ishi's friends and mourners were white.

The more hopeful humans might deduce from that simple fact that a man of one kind may yet learn to live with a man of another kind on a peaceful earth.

* * *

The following telegram was sent on August 31 by A. L. Kroeber, professor of anthropology at the University of California:

"SHERIFF BUTTE COUNTY. NEWSPAPER REPORT CAPTURE WILD INDIAN SPEAKING LANGUAGE OTHER TRIBES TOTALLY UNABLE UNDERSTAND. PLEASE CONFIRM OR DENY BY COLLECT TELEGRAM AND IF STORY CORRECT HOLD INDIAN TILL ARRIVAL PROFESSOR STATE UNIVERSITY WHO WILL TAKE CHARGE AND BE RESPONSIBLE FOR HIM. MATTER IMPORTANT ON ACCOUNT ABORIGINAL HISTORY."

Another anthropology professor, T. T. Waterman, took a train to Oroville that same day. Waterman thought the captive might be a Yana Indian, perhaps — and this possibility excited him immensely — from the southernmost branch of the Yana, the Yahi, believed to be extinct, a "lost tribe."

Waterman tried Northern and Central Yana words on the Oroville prisoner, saying each word as well as he could.

The prisoner listened courteously but did not react.

Waterman's list was running out. Finally, almost despairing, he uttered the word *siwini*, which means yellow pine, and tapped the wooden frame of the bed upon which they were sitting.

Suddenly the Indian's face glowed.

"*Siwini!*" Waterman repeated with hope leaping wildly.

The Indian repeated the word, correcting Waterman's pronunciation, and slammed his hand on the bed frame. For a few excited moments, they both whacked at the bed and prattled like parrots: "*Siwini! Siwini! Siwini!*"

They were communicating! It was hard to tell which of the two was happier about the breakthrough.

Waterman deduced that the Indian was indeed a Yahi and tried desperately to punch a larger hole in the wall between them.

Finally the Indian said softly, "*I ne ma Yahi?*"

Waterman understood; the Indian had asked, "Are you a Yahi?"

He was not, of course, but he nodded, and replied that he was. He knew what the Yahi meant by the question: *Was he a friend of the Yahi?*

Fear left the Indian's eyes. The last member of the lost tribe had started across the bridge from the old life to the new and he would make the journey with a white friend.

This is Ishi, photographed in Oroville soon after he turned himself in.

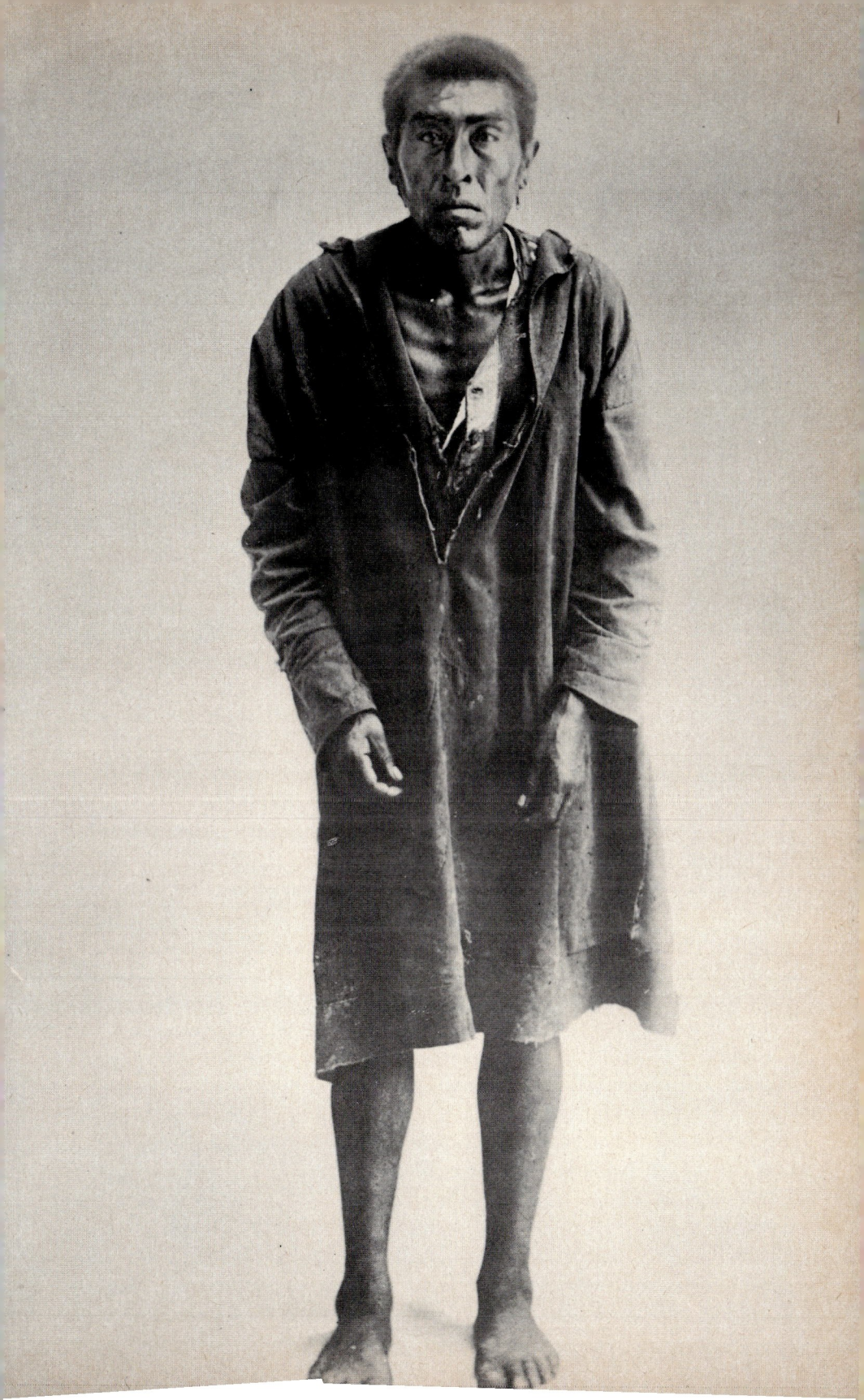

At about age 50, this native Californian who had outlived all his relatives and friends and who probably had never ventured beyond the tight boundaries of his tribal land, was about to plunge into the society and culture of the alien race which had brutally destroyed his own.

The Stone Age was about to confront the Twentieth Century.

GOLD POISONING

In 1850, about 10 years before Ishi was born, the Yana Indians, of which Ishi's Yahi people were the southernmost group, called approximately 2400 square miles of rugged, wooded country around Mount Lassen their land. There were several thousand Yana then.

Gold destroyed them.

The earlier Spanish-Mexican invasion of California had thoroughly shaken the underpinnings of the Indian way of life but numbers still favored the Indians. But when Anglo-Americans stormed west to root for gold, they came by the tens of thousands. In one year, 100,000 came. The population explosion of westbound whites destroyed the Indians. It was that simple. Indians only got in the way, so they were brushed out of the way.

The Yana tribes which numbered in the thousands in 1850 were reduced in a mere 22 years to no more than 30 individuals!

Many were murdered. Others starved. Some surrendered. Others were captured.

Life in the white man's jails and on his reservations took a quick and terrible toll. Diseases of the whites against which Indians had no immunity proved to be a worse enemy than guns.

In California during the second half of the 19th century, Indian hunting was both sport and profession. Two of the professionals in northern California were Hiram Good and R. A. Anderson. An admiring account of their prowess was written by Sim Moak, who came to California in 1863 at the age of 18:

"When I first met Hi. Good and R. A. Anderson, they were in the prime of life. Good was twenty-nine years old and as handsome a man as I ever saw. Anderson was twenty-five years old and as fine a specimen of manhood as one would wish to see . . . Anderson was elected sheriff of Butte County, two terms and if Good had lived he could have had any office in Tehama County he wanted. If it had not been for them, more white people living in Butte and Tehama counties would have been murdered by the barbarous Mill Creeks. Their business was never so urgent or time so precious they could not leave all to go forth to avenge the wrongs of the white settlers, committed by the red men. When a part of us settlers would start to clean up the Indians, we would elect a captain and it would always be Good or Anderson. The captain always was entitled to the scalps. At one time Good had forty hanging in the poplar tree by his house ... After Good had taken all the scalps, he took a buckskin string and sack needle and tied a knot in the end and salted the scalp and run the needle through it down to the knot, then tied another knot about two inches above the scalp and it was ready for the next one. The string was fastened to his belt and you can imagine a great tall man with a string of scalps from his belt to his ankle."

To avenge the wrongs committed by the red men ...

Several authorities who studied the record were able to authenticate no more than 20 murders of whites by Yana Indians and seven or eight of those took place beyond the normal range of Yanas.

But retribution against the Yanas killed thousands, in one way or another. The record shows plainly that whites in California added a wrinkle to the ancient slogan of revenge, "An eye for an eye ..."

In Yana country between 1850 and 1875, it was more like one hundred eyes for an eye.

Everyone believed that the Yahi had been wiped out completely, obliterated, removed from the face of the earth forever.

But it was not true; a few still lived in terrified concealment and a boy growing into manhood shared the soul-searing life and drank deeply, down to the last bitter dregs, of the tragedy of his people.

The boy would finally be called Ishi.

THE HIDDEN ONES

The remaining Yahi simply disappeared in 1872.

They lived off the land they knew so well, hunting and fishing and gathering. During those silent years, using all of their ancient cunning, the hidden ones allowed whites to see no more than flickering shadows in the brush, to hear no more than a shapeless sound in the night.

But by 1884, many of the Yahi hunters had died and the growing pressure of white settlement had made the old, natural life impossible. Yahis were forced to emerge from the shadows to steal a sheep or a calf, to pilfer from an isolated cabin.

White retribution was usually swift.

Near the end there were left only five Yahi, including Ishi, his aged mother and his sister.

Then three died or disappeared, leaving only Ishi and his mother. The record suggests that she may have died late in 1908. If so, Ishi was without human company from that date until his appearance at the Oroville slaughterhouse in August, 1911.

But the life story of Ishi, Yahi Indian, was not to end on that low note. In one of the most unlikely episodes of the white-red confrontation in America, Ishi was to live out the few years remaining to him in a San Francisco museum as an eating, breathing, talking exhibit in anthropology. But those years may well have been the happiest of his furtive, fear-ridden life and at death, he would be mourned not as an exhibit which had suddenly disappeared but as a loved human being who had ceased to breathe.

* * *

Shoes were simply too much for Ishi at first.

He put on underwear, shirt, pants and coat willingly enough but balked at footgear. With his new friend, Professor Waterman, he then bravely stepped aboard a train, even though his mother had warned him in his youth that trains were demons.

Quietly he rode the demon toward San Francisco Bay. The train went aboard a ferry boat to cross Carquinez Strait. They left the train and boarded another ferry for the journey across San Francisco Bay to the city, whereupon the last Yahi Indian, wide-eyed, got his first taste of trolley car travel.

At 11 p.m. on September 4, Ishi arrived at the museum of anthropology which was to be his home for the remainder of his life. He had been yanked abruptly out of the Stone Age; suddenly he was a resident of a great, noisy city, with a permanent home and even a mailing address.

Few human beings on earth had ever experienced a more rapid and complete change of culture and life style than did Ishi in 1911.

Could his tortured mind and emaciated body withstand the shock?

ANOTHER FRIEND

In the morning Ishi met Professor Kroeber, tried a few English words taught by Waterman and actually *blushed*.

The Indians

He needn't have. Kroeber was to become one of Ishi's foremost friends and guardians.

Kroeber had guarding to do almost immediately as newspapermen descended on the museum mouthing a thousand questions.

"What is his name?"

Then Kroeber had to spar. He knew that California Indians seldom spoke their real names and certainly would never offer them in reply to a direct question.

Krober said, "He shall be known as *Ishi*."

In the Yana tongue, it was the word for "man."

Ishi never did reveal his real Yana name. Ishi he became on that day and Ishi he remains in history.

* * *

When word of Ishi's arrival in San Francisco was trumpeted by the newspapers, flesh peddlers descended on the museum like an attacking army. Some wanted to sign up Ishi and Kroeber for a nationwide "educational tour;" others merely wanted to put Ishi in a cage for carnival crowds.

Quietly but firmly, Kroeber resisted.

Time passed; the promoting parasites gave up, but Kroeber worried about a new problem.

Whites had been Ishi's mortal enemies for most of his 50 years. Could the Yahi manage this new relationship suddenly thrust upon him? Ishi was unused to crowds; his life had been lived among a few trusted friends and relatives. Could he accept the throngs who now wanted to see him, talk to him, touch him?

As bad luck would have it, Ishi's arrival coincided with the scheduled opening of the new museum. The crowds, Kroeber knew, would be especially large as a result. Ishi was still physically weak; he could hardly be expected to stand in a receiving line while hundreds filed past.

Kroeber discussed the problem with Ishi. It was agreed that the Yahi would stay in a small exhibition room during the party. If he wanted to leave, he could.

It worked. Kroeber occasionally brought someone in to meet Ishi, who showed great interest in learning the names of those to whom he was introduced.

The affair was so successful that Kroeber announced to the newspapers that he and Ishi would be at the museum between 2 and 4:30 p.m. for several Sundays to come.

If the crowd was large, as it usually was, Kroeber would introduce Ishi to the audience, then translate the questions and answers. As a finale, Ishi displayed his Yahi skills—making fire or stringing a bow or chipping out an arrowhead.

Ishi's adjustment to his new environment progressed rapidly; his confidence in his new friends grew just as rapidly. He began to look forward to Sunday afternoons, when he would perform for the crowds.

Mentally and emotionally, Ishi had survived the transition from the Stone Age.

Put on the museum payroll as a janitor, Ishi had to learn to write his name in order to endorse checks.

Kroeber taught him. An actual reproduction of his signature looked like this:

Ishi

FOUR FRIENDS OF ISHI

First there was Waterman, the young anthropologist who escorted Ishi from the Oroville jail to San Francisco. Then there was Kroeber, another anthropologist who virtually adopted the Yahi.

There was also Juan Dolores, a Papago Indian from Arizona who occasionally lived and worked at the museum. In time Dolores learned to speak Ishi's Yana-English as well as Kroeber had.

And there was Dr. Saxton Pope—Ishi called him "Popey"—who was a surgeon in the university hospital next door to the museum.

These were the four close friends of the last individual of the lost tribe.

Slowly Ishi learned the white man's ways, adopting those he liked, ignoring those he didn't.

At first, when someone asked Ishi if he wouldn't like to put on shoes before going out, he might say, "I see the ground is stone here. Walking on that all the time, I would wear out shoes, but my feet will never wear out."

By midwinter of his first year at the museum, though, he had even accepted shoes.

Adjusted to his new life, Ishi demonstrates his skill in harpoon-making.

Trolley cars were his favorite amusement; he enjoyed them much more than automobiles. They ran on tracks, had lovely gongs and whooshed delightfully when their air brakes were applied. Airplanes impressed him less, perhaps because hawks flew so much better. Tall buildings didn't excite him, either; he had lived among mountains much taller.

He liked houses, though, and the furniture in them. He was fascinated by the roller shade. The first time Waterman let one snap up, Ishi exclaimed and tried to figure out its disappearance. He always retained his delighted interest in running a shade up or down.

He readily learned to use knives, hatchets, saws and hammers. A bench vise proved useful, too, substituting for his big toe in holding his work of the moment. But the two things in his new life which he considered most valuable of all were matches and glue. To Ishi, these were even greater inventions than gas and electricity. After a lifetime of laboriously creating fire by friction (which he still did frequently at the museum in demonstrations), he quickly took to matches. He considered glue almost as valuable and adopted it immediately for making bows and arrows.

His ready smile, his gentleness, his basic dignity gained him much affection. Sometimes as many as a thousand persons would gather around him during a single afternoon. Older persons, in particular, seemed to enjoy sitting quietly by him as he displayed mankind's oldest skills. It was almost as if Ishi were a sentimental bridge to the distant past along the far and ancient road of human history.

ISHI GOES NATIVE

In the spring of 1914, someone—certainly not Ishi—suggested a camping trip in Yahi country.

Ishi was horrified at the prospect of leaving his house and furniture but finally agreed to go. Kroeber and Waterman wanted Ishi to guide them through the land of his birth; there was much Ishi could teach anthropologists about the old Yana way of life.

The trip was a spectacular success. Even Ishi began to enjoy it, once he overcame his intense dislike for riding horses, and discovered that what his friends had in mind was to record the old way of life as completely as possible.

Here, perhaps, was a way for Ishi to help keep the Yahi people alive forever.

They swam daily in the cold, running water. They hunted and fished, using the old methods. Some members of the group went naked much of the time but Ishi insisted on wearing at least a loin cloth. Ishi taught a boy with the group to dance in the Yahi way. They hunkered around a campfire at night and told stories.

Ishi was the life of the party. These short days in the wilds with his white friends, as he proudly acted out the old Yahi life, glinted with pleasure and comradeship and overflowing satisfaction. White men had given these days to Ishi.

White men also gave him something else . . .

* * *

Ishi had suffered the first common cold of his life soon after reaching San Francisco in 1911. Soon thereafter, he developed pneumonia but beat down both illnesses. Had it been his lot to live on an Indian reservation, he might well have died then.

In December, 1914, he developed a cough and entered Popey's hospital for treatment. He seemed to rally but had to return to the hospital in early spring.

Then the diagnosis left no doubt: *tuberculosis.*

By late spring, his condition had improved considerably. Assured of Ishi's recovery, Dr. Kroeber left for Europe.

He would not see Ishi again.

Ishi's condition worsened. He returned to the hospital. He did not improve. His friends decided mournfully in autumn, 1915, that Ishi was dying and chose to send him home.

Home . . . to the museum. An exhibit room was cleared out and turned over to Ishi.

The storm winds of winter blew over San Francisco. Then spring spread sunlight over the bay.

On March 25, 1916, death came to Ishi at his home.

Having returned from Europe, Dr. Kroeber heard of Ishi's death in New York.

It was clear that the Yahi had become to those who knew him best a great deal more than an object of scientific curiosity; he had become an object of ageless human affection.

Said Waterman in a letter to Kroeber: "As you have heard from Gifford, the poor old Indian is dying . . . *He was the best friend I had in the world . . ."*

There is strong evidence that Kroeber, too, had lost his scientific objectivity. He wrote to Gifford from New York on the day before Ishi died: "Please stand by our contingently made outline of action, and insist on it as my personal wish . . . As to disposal of the body, I must ask you as my personal representative to yield nothing at all under any circumstances. If there is any talk about the interests of science, say for me that science can go to hell. We propose to stand by our friends . . ."

Ishi had told Popey that the proper way to dispose of the dead was cremation, so Ishi was cremated and his ashes placed in a jar bearing the inscription: "Ishi, the last Yana Indian, 1916;" the jar went into a niche in Mount Olivet Cemetery.

Mourning for Ishi was nationwide. A group of high school students in Kansas City, Missouri, held a memorial service. They had learned about Ishi from their teacher, who had visited the museum.

At Ishi's last home, gloom hung heavily for weeks after the Yahi's death. Those who padded through the silent halls knew that no more would anyone hear the soft sound of Ishi's favorite greeting:

"*Evelybody hoppy?*"

He had left his ancient world in desperation, forced to try his luck in a world totally new. To his enormous surprise, that new world not only didn't destroy him but finally, learned to love him.

Then finally betrayed him . . .

Ishi did not complain. From birth almost to death, he had been asked to cope with incredible terror and cruelty and hardship.

His body had been destroyed, at last, but dignity persisted; his spirit remained gentle, loving, unconquered to the end. The ancient Indian habit of calm acceptance had served him well.

Thus his way of saying goodbye in life became a suitable epitaph in death:

"You stay, I go."

Ishi, at left in front row, enjoys a performance at the Orpheum Theater in San Francisco. Next to Ishi is Sam Batwi, a Yana tribesman who was Ishi's frequent companion. The bearded man behind Ishi is A. L. Kroeber. Directly behind Batwi is T. T. Waterman.

LONE WOMAN OF SAN NICOLAS

The woman was tracked down by men from Santa Barbara who had been told of her presence by seal hunters working the channel between the mainland and San Nicolas Island. The year was 1853.

Brought to the mainland, the woman died within a few months, without telling her story to anyone.

She couldn't tell her story; no one understood her language. Apparently her tribe had died out, like Ishi's, and she was the only survivor.

But someone who heard the woman speak knew enough of the language to get four words down on paper. In time the words were identified as Shoshonean, similar to the tongue spoken by tribes in the Los Angeles region.

Then the story was pieced out.

The priests at Santa Barbara mission had decided in 1835 that the Indians on San Nicolas Island should be moved to the mainland. As the boat carrying the Indians fought through the surf after departure from the island, it was discovered that a small child had been left behind.

The leader of the group refused to turn back, to risk again the thundering surf, whereupon the child's anguished mother leaped into the water and quickly disappeared. When she could not be found during the days that followed, it was assumed that she had died in the surf.

Apparently she survived, though, and this was probably the woman the seal hunters saw in 1850. Her child had died, as had all of her tribesmen on the mainland.

The story of the lone woman of San Nicolas illustrates the desperate plight of California Indians, who had a unique problem: Enemies making up the God-gun-gold invasion came at them from every point of the compass. The Indians of California were caught in a four-way nutcracker.

Indians in most other parts of the United States were luckier; they were destroyed from only one direction, the east. In California, the western sea wall was breached first by Spanish explorers; then Spanish-Mexican missionaries, soldiers and settlers wended their dusty way overland from the south.

Then, once the tribes had been weakened by disease and dislocation of their natural life style, they had to cope with the eruption of gold-goaded Americans from all directions. Energetic, determined and generally contemptuous of Indian rights (in fact, mostly unaware that Indians had any), Americans quickly administered the *coup de grace* to California Indians.

"Diggers," sneered the Americans, seeing Indians poking around in the earth for acorns. "Indian" was a term of contempt; "digger" was a term for those beneath contempt.

In fact, there was no tribe of California Indians with a fair claim on the name. "Digger" was like "nigger," a term used by the unthinking.

Americans who came west were accustomed to Indians who wore spectacular feather headdresses and rode horses madly over the plains to skewer buffalo or other Indians, whichever happened to be in season.

California Indians, on the other hand, considered a horse something to eat, sometimes wore no clothes at all, and usually weren't mad at anybody.

Obviously shiftless, decided white Spanish and Americans. Mere animals...

Animals? It is a fact that at many Spanish missions, Indian workers —Christian Indian workers—were fed from open troughs in a courtyard. John Sutter did the same thing at Sutter's Fort.

When Father Serra founded his first California mission, the grim handwriting appeared dimly on the wall for California Indians. History makes it plain that the missions, with only meager help from Spain and the Spanish colonial government in Mexico, could not have existed for long without the slave labor of California Indians.

Ishi's friend, Dr. A. L. Kroeber, has written:

"It must have caused many of the Fathers a severe pang to realize, as they could not but do daily, that they were saving souls only at the inevitable cost of lives. And yet such was the overwhelming fact. The brute upshot of missionization ... was only one thing, death."

THE GIFT OF CHRISTIANITY

Was then Father Serra, this patron saint of California, little more than a slavemaster?

In this modern era, one has difficulty in understanding the strength and depth and quality of the religious fanaticism which motivated Serra and his Catholic countrymen.

Father Serra surely felt that in baptizing mission Indians into the Christian church, he had conferred on them a priceless gift—eternal life in the kingdom of heaven.

So what did it matter if a California Indian, to earn this priceless reward, had to eat out of a trough and work from before dawn until after dusk and die with a hoe in his hand?

The caste system brought to California by the Spanish was based on color. Those few persons of pure Spanish blood were at the top, securely; pure Indians were at the bottom. Mixed bloods occupied the middle.

There is a record of at least one Spanish mission in California where soldiers patrolled the church with long whips and prods after Indians had been assembled for mass. When a Christian Indian failed to stay long enough in a kneeling position, the whip or the prod reminded him of his religious responsibilities.

The indicated Spanish viewpoint seemed to be that Indians would acquire the rewards of heaven even if they had to be driven there by the sting of the lash or the poke of a sharp stick.

Spanish soldiers in California, condemning them as a group, were subhuman brutes.

You doubt? Read a report of that era written by Jose Maria Amador, second lieutenant in the weak, bored and weary Spanish army in California:

"We invited the Gentile and Christian Indians to come and eat pinole and dried meat. They all came over to our side of the river. Then when they were on our shore we surrounded them by the troops, citizens and Indian aides, and took them all prisoners ... We separated 100 Christians from the prisoners, and at each half mile or mile these were forced on their knees in prayer and were made to understand they were going to die ... each one of them received four arrows, two in front and two in each shoulder ... we baptized all the (remaining Gentile) Indians and then we shot them through the shoulder. Seventy of them fell at one shot. I doubled the charge for the 30 that remained and they all fell."

THE GIFT OF DEATH

Before the whites came, what is now called California was owned by approximately 150,000 Indians. No other area of what is now called the United States of America had a higher density of Indian population.

And why not? It was a warm, fertile land blessed with a remarkable variety of climate and topography, nearly all of it benign.

By 1890, only 17,000 Indians remained in California and many of these were of mixed blood. Most of the deaths were due to smallpox, measles and syphilis—white man's diseases.

Whites who saw California Indians living in thatched huts, eating acorns and strolling naked through a scenic wonderland weren't able to look beneath the surface. Having solved the problems of simple survival in this most comfortable of lands, the California Indian had branched out to develop a tremendously satisfying, sub-surface, psychological world.

He dreamed . . .

And he told his dreams around the night fires and built a life of mind and emotion as rich and rewarding as the physical, sensual world of the golden land he lived in. He had little reason to make war or wear flamboyant headdresses or paint his face, because frustration was not his problem; his ego was secure. He breathed pure air and drank clean water and enjoyed the pact of peace he had made with nature, a pact founded solidly on simplicity and respect, one for the other.

In 1954, a woman of the Hoopa tribe of California told a committee of the United States Senate:

"To most people, hunting and fishing is a sport. To the American Indian it is part of a religious custom. The American Indians are a very pious—I do not like the insinuations of 'pious'—but they are a very religious people. We did not believe in a church just one day; we believed in a church every day of the week and in every act that we did. And we have continued with that belief. Therefore, even the taking of food was a religious sacrament in a way, particularly in regard to the hunting of the deer. We had a set custom that we followed in the conserving of it and the way we used the meat and our sharing of it . . ."

Sometimes, especially during the wet winters, California Indians got together and "sang and danced for several days."

A simple life without smog, without water pollution, without traffic noise, a life based on a warm, cozy treaty signed and sealed with nature. *Nature* . . .

Ancient Californians had it . . . and lost it. Modern Californians want it and seek it with mounting desperation: nature and man, living together in a harmony of mutual respect. A dream? California Indians were the best of dreamers. Those who remain may still show the way.

* * *

The thing that immigrant whites, Spanish and American, failed utterly to understand was that they weren't moving into empty, ownerless land; they weren't bringing civilization to a place where there had been none.

Instead they were forcibly replacing one civilization with another. Colonization of the American West, often pictured in history as a romantic epic, may well have been little more than a bloody conquest. A reasonable person, then and now, might well see it in this light.

A fair amount of blind brutality suffered by Indians in the West was perpetrated by whites who had been considered decent, law-abiding citizens in their old communities east of the Rockies.

Brutality can seldom be justified, but it can be explained.

Many emigrants reached the West only after fantastic hardships which virtually wiped them out in mind, spirit and body. If they treated Indians brutally, they often treated each other just as brutally. The grim story of the Donner Party is an outstanding example. J. Goldsborough Bruff's graphic account of his struggle to survive in northern California after lagging behind his wagon train is another.

It must be remembered, too, that most whites started their western adventure filled with poppycock tales of Indian atrocities, many of which were merely campfire tales much mellowed and rounded off by re-telling. There is evidence that many of the troublesome Indian-white encounters along the trail resulted from a white frame of mind which bordered on panic. Too often when a white saw Indian sign, he shot first, then ran screaming for help.

Ignorance and exhaustion usually brew brutality; they did exactly this in California when white and red civilization met head-on.

THE QUIET BATTLE OF ALCATRAZ

During 1969, American Indians from all over the United States of America moved in force onto Alcatraz Island in San Francisco Bay to play out an ironic act of contemporary California history. A century was suddenly turned around...

The stark penitentiary had been abandoned in 1963 and the incorrigible convicts transferred; the federal government, left with a white elephant carved in rock, was negotiating with several individuals (including a Texas oil millionaire) for the island's sale.

Then the Indians paddled out, took over and announced through their Mohawk leader, Richard Oakes, age 27, that they would buy the island for "$24 in glass beads and silver, a precedent set by the white man's purchase of a similar island about 300 years ago."

In a parody of the kind of treaty the white man offered Indians a century ago, the Indian conquerors of Alcatraz expressed their concern for the few white caretakers living on the island by solemnly promising:

"We will give to the inhabitants of this island a portion of that land for their own, to be held in trust by the American Indian Government—for as long as the sun shall rise and the rivers go down to the sea—to be administered by the Bureau of Caucasian Affairs. We will further guide the inhabitants in the proper way of living. We will offer them our religion, our education, our life-ways, in order to help them achieve our level of civilization and thus raise them and all their white brothers up from their savage and unhappy state."

All the way from Alcatraz Island, California, to Washington, D.C., white faces turned red.

SITES TO SEE

STATE INDIAN MUSEUM, adjacent to Sutter's Fort, Sacramento.
SOUTHWEST MUSEUM, Los Angeles. (The West's largest collection of Southwest Indian artifacts. Don't miss the tunnel entrance.)
ISHI DISCOVERY SITE, Oroville-Quincy Highway, Oroville. (Stone marker in modern residential area indicates place of Ishi's surrender.)

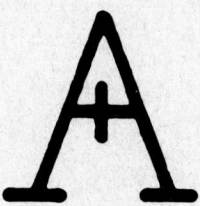

CITY OF ANAHEIM. For the purpose of branding livestock sold at poundkeepers' sales, the city of Anaheim adopted a legal brand on November 20, 1871.

Chapter Four *

Westward Migration
BLOOD ON THE SNOW

There it was in black and white on page 137 of *The Emigrant's Guide to Oregon and California* by Lansford W. Hastings:

"The most direct route, for the California emigrants, would be to leave the Oregon route, about two hundred miles east from Fort Hall; thence bearing west southwest, to the Salt Lake; and thence continuing down to the bay of St. Francisco."

Why, the man made it sound almost easy!

Yet those simple words published in a book were to lead directly to the bloodiest, most tragic act of the great pageant of westward migration in America. Before the curtain finally fell, men, women and children would be faced with the most grisly choice of all: They could turn cannibal and eat their own kind or they could die of starvation.

Not all of them died.

* * *

Bubbling with the spirit of high adventure, the Reed-Donner party had jumped off from Springfield, Missouri, in early summer, 1846. By mid-July, it had reached South Pass, crossed the Continental Divide and fetched up at the first important fork in the trail—the Little Sandy River in what is now Wyoming.

Three women of the Reed-Donner party were photographed in 1918 at a ceremony dedicating the monument at Donner State Park. Posed between the governors of Nevada and California are, from left, Patty Reed Lewis, Eliza Donner Houghton and Frances Donner Wilder. The pedestal under the statues rises to the height of the snow during the grim winter experienced at this place by the star-crossed pioneers.

Tracks led west from the Little Sandy toward Oregon and California via Fort Hall; Greenwood's Route, it was called. More tracks led southwest to fabled Fort Bridger and beyond along the new cutoff touted by Lansford Hastings south of Salt Lake.

The choice does not appear to have been difficult. After all, hadn't they read Hastings's book? Hadn't they also, as they worked their way through South Pass, received an open letter from Hastings in which this respected man of much frontier experience mentioned again his new and better trail south of Salt Lake?

More important, wasn't Lansford W. Hastings himself waiting even now at Fort Bridger to guide them safely past the perils?

Of course he was. They would follow the young explorer down the slope and across the desert to the Humboldt River in what is now Nevada, down the Humboldt to the Truckee and then make the great leap over the Sierras in September well ahead of the first snow. Beyond the high pass lay only a downhill drag to Sutter's Fort in the Sacramento Valley.

After all, wasn't it all right there in the book, printed in black and white?

On July 20, the 20 wagons of the Reed-Donner party turned left at the fork in the road, turned left toward a rendezvous with death.

THE PEOPLE

James Frazier Reed was 46 years old in the summer of 1846. Successful and respected in the Mississippi Valley, he joined his friend George Donner, 62, in the western adventure for a number of reasons. For one, his businesses had not been prospering as they had in the past. For another, his wife Margaret had been in ill health; perhaps California was what she needed.

It was the Reed family wagon which was conspicuous in the train; rolling majestically behind four yoke of oxen, it loomed over the others. Reed had built it for the comfort of his ailing wife and her mother, Mrs. Keyes. (Despite her son-in-law's consideration, however, Mrs. Keyes died soon after the trek began.) The wagon had spring seats, a stove and a second level for beds. Only Milt Elliott, a faithful employee of Reed's, was trusted to drive the overland yacht, which may have been one of the most palatial vehicles ever to stir dust along the trail. There was even room aboard the wagon for a hired girl, Eliza Williams, who cooked, washed and churned butter as the train wheeled westward.

Undoubtedly there were some in the party who envied the Reeds and resented that wagon; the wagon may have accounted for the party's choice at the Little Sandy of George Donner over James Reed as official leader of the party; later, the wagon may have been the real cause of the first serious crack in the party's morale.

They left Missouri as part of another wagon train, a roster of names. They entered California history through a veil of tragedy and emerged a grim puzzle ... and so they remain.

There were finally 87 persons — winners, losers, aristocrats, peasants, farmers, rich, poor, employers, employees, young and old; the brave and the cowardly, the strong and the weak.

Who were the heroes? Who the villains? Where is truth?

Even those who lived it and watched it and endured it couldn't agree.

Particularly about Lewis Keseberg, the learned man who may have survived in the Sierra snow by killing and eating his fellow man ...

WELCOME TO FORT BRIDGER

For four days, the Reed-Donner party rested at Fort Bridger. Lansford W. Hastings was not there but he had left a note. Since the season was rapidly slipping away, Hastings said, he had decided to move on with a party of 66 wagons after leaving instructions for those few who followed.

While they rested, the Reed-Donner emigrants warmed their hearts with the words of the famous old mountain man, Jim Bridger, and his business partner, Vasquez.

The new trail ahead cut off as much as 400 miles, Bridger and Vasquez said, with plenty of grass and wood available. There was water, too, except for one dry drive of 40 miles or so.

Reed was impressed; he wrote a letter to Springfield in which he spoke of the honesty and fair dealing of the mountain men and called them "two very excellent and accommodating gentlemen."

But Reed was unaware that as he wrote, there was a letter for him at Fort Bridger from a friend who had passed this way only two weeks before. The letter, given to Vasquez for delivery to Reed when he arrived — but never turned over to him — warned that under no circumstances should the Reed-Donner party attempt to take the cutoff recommended by Hastings!

The Reed-Donner party left Fort Bridger on the last day of July. If they had known what lay ahead, one wonders if any of them would have started down the trail.

MANY WAYS TO DIE

Trouble along the trail could take many forms — hunger, thirst, sunstroke, exhaustion, disease, Indian harassment, bickering, rage, thievery and always . . . death. Natural death. Accidental death. Violent death. Old bodies, finally worn beyond repair; young bodies, struck lifeless by gun or knife. Young and old, wiped out by the scourge of cholera.

During August, September and October as they hacked their way through the wooded canyons of what is now Wyoming and slogged hollow-eyed across the dazzling salt flats of Utah and the endless deserts of Nevada, the Reed-Donner party drank deep of trouble in all its forms, yet August and September were only a foretaste of the frightful ordeal which lay ahead in the Sierra snow.

On August 29, Luke Halloran died and was buried in a coffin made from wagon boards.

The longest stretch without water — the "dry drive" which Bridger and Hastings had called 40 miles or so — turned out to be 80 and when it was over, the emigrants were ready to consign Bridger and Hastings to the hotter regions of hell, from which the Reed-Donner party had apparently just emerged.

The passage across the desert had been nothing less than a disaster. Many wagons, cows and oxen had been lost. Indians had accounted for most of the livestock losses, shooting arrows into the beasts or driving them off.

The regular pattern of daily travel had been shattered. Horsemen rode away from the main party to hunt for livestock; wagons advanced if they could or stopped if they could not. Men left their families with others and scouted ahead for water and food. Tempers grew short; hoarding of food and water became the habit; soon friendships faded and only the survival of families mattered.

The stage was set for serious trouble. On the last day of September, the aching, weary, thirsty, hungry, sun-scalded party came upon a river flowing west. It had to be the Humboldt; now they had left the accursed Hastings Cutoff and had rejoined the major trail to

California.

Reaching the landmark should have lifted the spirits of the entire party. But the way had been too hard, the troubles too great. The reserves of human endurance had been drained. Tempers were on short fuses and fuses were burning. On October 5, James Reed killed John Snyder with a knife.

* * *

The first incident was trivial, but its result was disastrous.

John Snyder, driving a wagon up a long hill, found that he had to stop. Milt Elliott, directly behind with the Reed wagon, impatiently tried to pass on the narrow trail. His oxen tangled with Snyder's. Snyder and Elliott snapped at each other. Ordinarily a happy-go-lucky young man, Snyder now began to beat the oxen with the heavy end of his whip handle.

James Reed rushed forward to head off further trouble. Snyder threatened Reed, whereupon Reed drew his hunting knife.

Snyder swung at Reed with the butt of his whip and gashed his head. Reed struck back with his knife and drove it home near Snyder's collarbone.

Mrs. Reed rushed into the fray and was struck by Snyder, who then hit James Reed twice more.

Snyder started up the hill, then staggered as Patrick Breen rushed to his side.

"Uncle Patrick, I am dead," said Snyder.

Overwhelmed with remorse, Reed flung the knife into the river and tried to help the dying man. There were those who said that Snyder's last words were, "I am to blame."

The train encamped for the night, with the Reed family kept apart. James Reed was excluded from the feverish discussions which followed. Some had a notion that Reed should be brought to trial in California.

Keseberg, the thinker, had a better idea. As evening fell, he propped up his wagon tongue with an oxyoke in preparation for a hanging.

In a moment of high tension, with blood caked on three bad head wounds, Reed faced the scowls of the party which was on the verge of becoming a mob. Only two men, Milt Elliott and William Eddy, stepped to his side. Only three against many ... but the three were heavily armed.

The angry crowd backed down.

Then Eddy managed a compromise. Reed was to be allowed to leave the camp in peace and go on ahead. At first, the wounded man refused, thinking of his family, but when others said they would care for his wife and children, he sadly agreed to go.

* * *

Snyder was buried in the morning, not in a coffin like that built for Luke Halloran, but with just a board above to keep off the coyotes and one below for the sake of dignity. It was a sign; the party no longer had time for niceties. The veneer of civilization was flaking away.

Reed was sent away on his handsome horse, with no firearms. Except for the fact that the Donner section of the train was somewhere ahead on the trail, depriving Reed of guns would have been a death sentence.

As Reed faded from view, the train began to follow through a cloud of alkali dust. It was no longer a party; now one family was pitted against another. It was dog-eat-dog and so it was to remain.

Hardkoop, the old man from Belgium, was next. Getting sicker and weaker by the day, he had taken to riding in Keseberg's wagon. Then Hardkoop turned up missing. Keseberg said he knew nothing about him.

Eddy tried to borrow saddle horses from Breen and Graves to go back and look for the old man; Breen and Graves refused. Eddy, Elliott and Pike then wanted to go back on foot but the others said they wouldn't wait. Winter hung like a death sentence over the high mountains ahead; there was no longer time to fret about a sick old man.

Luke Halloran, the first to die, had been buried in a coffin. Then John Snyder was laid to rest between two boards. No one bothered to dig a grave for Hardkoop, except, perhaps, coyotes.

THE DESERT ENDS AT LAST

Near starvation, thirsty, bone-weary, sick in soul and body and mind, they crossed the last great desert. The only hope remaining was that Stanton and McCutcheon, who had been sent on ahead, would return in time. But would they come back at all?

They could understand why Stanton, a bachelor, once safe in the

Sacramento Valley, might not return but McCutcheon had a young wife and a baby with the wagon train. Would he let them starve? Surely not...

They knew that James Reed and his teamster, Walter Herron, had gone on ahead of the Donner wagons, too, intending to cross the mountains and return with help as quickly as possible. Where were Reed and Herron?

For three nearly foodless days, they struggled up a canyon. Then suddenly a shout arose from the head of the column.

"Hey, lookee! Stanton! It's Stanton!"

Moving slowly down toward the wagons were three horsemen and seven pack mules!

It was Stanton, all right, along with two Spanish-speaking Indian helpers he had picked up at Sutter's Fort. Soon bread was baking in Dutch ovens; they had brought flour as well as jerked beef.

When the worst hunger pangs had eased, they hammered at Stanton with questions.

McCutcheon had been taken sick at Sutter's Fort and hadn't been able to return, much as he wanted to. Captain Sutter had gladly sent the mules and the Indians and the food.

For Mrs. Reed and her children, there was even more welcome news—Stanton had seen James Reed and Walter Herron!

Only four days back, Stanton reported, he had entered Bear Valley, where he found part of Hastings's company encamped. On that same day, he had watched two men more dead than alive stumble down the mountainside leading a staggering mare too weak to carry even a saddle. The men were so used up and beaten down and burned out that at first, they could not be recognized. But it was Reed and Herron, all right; Stanton was sure of that.

The pass over the Sierras, Stanton reported, was still open, although there had been some early snow.

With Virginia Reed astride a mule behind him, Charles Stanton, of Chicago, Illinois, now an authentic frontier hero, led the tattered party west into the foothills of the Sierras.

* * *

On October 20, at Truckee Meadows, it was Stanton who argued for a rest stop. At this time of year, he pointed out, the snow in the mountains often melted between storms. Why not wait, rest up, then tackle the mountains with vigor? Only ox power could lift the wagons through the mountains and these oxen were only stumbling skeletons. Let them rest for a few days, Stanton urged; let them eat the long grass.

With some strong doubts, they took Stanton's advice and let the cattle feed. Prospects had taken a sharp upswing with Stanton's appearance but they suddenly dropped again when the specter of death reappeared.

A pistol exploded accidentally and killed William Pike.

They buried Pike without a coffin as his widow and two small children watched. *And now snow was falling...*

Staring through the snow toward the distant mountain mass, it must have been difficult for the emigrants to believe that fate could have anything worse in store than it had already settled upon them.

Stanton had said the pass was about 50 miles from Truckee Meadows. Before the pass, they would come upon a cabin built by emigrants two years earlier. Not far above the cabin was Truckee Lake; one could actually see the pass from there.

As they slogged upward under a gray sky, more snow fell. The air was bitter cold.

WEST INTO WINTER

It must be remembered that most of the members of the Reed-Donner party were flatlanders, no strangers to snow and cold, but greenhorns in the mountains. Until they rolled west from Missouri, most of them had never seen a real year-around snowcap. They did not understand that the American West has two winter climates: the generally balmy dampness of the lowlands and the thundering storms, paralyzing cold and fantastic snow depths of the highlands.

They had seen western mountains in summer and found them less fearsome than the life-sapping deserts. But these were not summer mountains; these were the towering Sierras surprised by an early winter, a winter that had already begun to lash the peaks and passes with blinding clouds of snow swept on gale force winds.

The rocky highlands around the pass are mostly barren of trees. It is harsh, bleak country whose cruelty is softened only by many little bright blue lakes with water clear and cold, even in summer.

Sutter's Fort (now Sacramento) lies 100 miles southwest of the lake called Truckee (now Donner) on a plain so low that its river water rises and falls with ocean tides. Due to lack of summer rain, the forests are thin in the foothills around Sutter's Fort. But between the foothills and below the high pass are some of the finest forests ever to grow on this earth. The mountain ridges run almost parallel, separated by deep canyons, both blanketed with magnificent stands of pine, fir and cedar. In the canyons flow hurrying streams which drain the mountain country into the Sacramento and spread the river helter-skelter over the great delta country on its surge toward San Francisco Bay.

In 1846, most of this country was wild; only the emigrant trail left man's marks upon it. Forty miles down from the heights was the first settlement, Johnson's Ranch, and wagons reached it only after twice being let down steep inclines by ropes. Beyond Johnson's, the country relented; a comparatively easy downhill pull for another 40 miles brought end of trail in sight—Sutter's Fort.

This was the lofty stage on which the drama of winter, 1846-1847, was to be played out. In late October, 1846, most of the cast had already moved into place.

NEW TROUBLE FOR REED

One can imagine James Reed's feelings when he was informed that the struggle between the Mexicans and Americans for control of California had burst out anew and that he could expect little help for the emigrants until the disturbance was over.

His reaction was typical of the man. Instead of bemoaning the cruel coincidence, he enlisted immediately to reinforce Fremont's force at Monterey, from where the colonel intended to march on Los Angeles. Reed was elected captain of the company being raised but he refused; instead he asked to be made lieutenant in charge of recruiting. He intended to do his first recruiting between Sutter's Fort and Truckee Lake.

Three days later, with 30 horses and mules grunting under loads of flour, beef and beans, Reed left Johnson's Ranch and headed into the wooded hills. He had the help of McCutcheon, now well enough to make the effort, and two Indians.

There had been no news of the emigrants' progress. It seemed likely, though, that they would encounter the party on the near side of the pass at Bear Valley, quite possibly nearing starvation and beginning to eat their precious oxen.

Rain began to fall on Reed and McCutcheon; then it grew colder.

The mountains above them turned ominously white. On the third day, they reached the lower end of Bear Valley, which lay under a foot and a half of new snow.

There were no wagons in sight.

The storm grew worse but still Reed and McCutcheon struggled on. They did not give up until McCutcheon was stopped by nearly neck-deep snow. They were still 12 miles from the summit.

With heavy hearts, these two fathers of families marooned on the white, lonely heights turned back toward Sutter's Fort.

Now, said Captain Sutter gloomily, there was no hope for relief until February, when the storms would ease off and the snow would harden. But the emigrants could butcher their cattle and freeze the meat in the snow, he assured Reed. They could live through; others had in years past.

Neither Reed nor Sutter could have known that the emigrants entered the mountains with far fewer cattle than were needed for survival.

The trap had closed on the Reed-Donner party.

WITHIN THE JAWS

Imprisoned by the storm near Truckee Lake, the emigrants did not seem overly depressed by this newest blow; they simply unpacked and dug in.

The Breens had arrived first and had moved into the existing cabin not far from the lake's outlet. The Kesebergs made themselves comfortable in a lean-to which they attached to the Breens' cabin. Another flat-roofed, windowless, pole structure had been built 150 yards away and still another half a mile below the lake. In this camp were 19 men, 12 women and 29 children, including six babies.

The howling blizzard had halted the Donners five miles back on the trail. Short of manpower, assaulted by banshee winds, they had been forced to move into hastily-built tents and lean-tos.

The short term prospect could be faced without great fear. They had shelter and clothing and firewood. The supplies Stanton had brought were just about gone but they could slaughter the animals for

The size of this retired freight wagon at Sutter's Fort proves that enough mules, properly driven, could pull almost anything to anywhere. Visitors willing to don earphones now can listen to the story of the old fort, as well as see it; the state has wired the whole place for sound.

meat, first the oxen, then the horses and mules, finally the dogs. Frozen in the snow, the meat would keep indefinitely. And they had guns; surely wild game and fish could be had.

But their first attempts at hunting were not encouraging. The lake was still clear of ice and they could see fish but failed to catch any.

Now confidence began to ebb. Some of the families, like the Breens and the bachelor, Patrick Dolan, had plenty of cattle for their own needs but others were desperately short. The available livestock wouldn't keep the group alive more than half the winter.

* * *

Inevitably the strongest began to think of escape.

On November 12, the first clear day after their halt eight days earlier, 13 of the healthiest men and two young women, encouraged by the melting of snow around the cabins, set out to assault the pass.

They were gone less than a day. Not far above the lake, deep snow was encountered and they had to return to the cabins in defeat.

On the next day Will Eddy killed an 800-pound bear, delivering the *coup de grace* with a club after running out of bullets. With the huge carcass in camp, stomachs swelled and spirits rose.

But on the next day, Eddy bagged only a squirrel and a duck. It was the last successful hunt recorded by the party.

Most families had to go on starvation rations. More and more now, they looked upward to the pass, hoping feverishly for the sight of figures working their way downward. Why didn't Reed and Herron come? Or McCutcheon?

Breen's diary stated: "Snowing fast wind W about 4 or 5 feet deep, no drifts looks as likely to continue as when it commenced no liveing thing without wings can get about."

Before their fearful, unbelieving eyes, it snowed for eight days!

And when it ended, the skies cleared to reveal a new disaster. During the storm, the remaining three or four oxen, the horses and Sutter's mules had wandered away and died. Now they lay buried in unmarked graves beneath the snow.

These were Easterners and plainsmen, strangers to these fearsome mountains, but if they believed part of what Lansford W. Hastings wrote in his book, they might well have heeded all of it. Hastings had glowing praise for California's winter weather but also pointed out:

"The remarks here made, in reference to the mildness, and uniformity of the climate, are applicable only to the valleys and plains, for *the mountains present but one eternal winter.*"

Westward Migration

* * *

Graves, from the snow country of Vermont, and Stanton, originally from northern New York, came up with an idea which should have occurred to someone sooner: Why not try snowshoes? They had the materials, rawhide and hickory from the oxyokes. Finished, they weren't beautiful but they worked, after a fashion. But before enough could be manufactured, another storm blew in.

The threat of starvation was no longer merely a threat; it was a winged specter fluttering in their shrinking stomachs. A German named Spitzer collapsed in the snow on December 8 and had to be dragged into a cabin. Bayliss Williams was near death as the storm raged on for five days, leaving a snow depth of eight feet on flat ground. With many of the emigrants now terribly weakened, it was becoming increasingly difficult to keep the cabins supplied with firewood. It became plain that those who were going to attempt the next breakout would have to succeed or die in the effort. There was no longer much that was worth returning to in the camps below Truckee Lake.

The women were coming into their own. Generally they remained physically stronger than the men, a phenomenon often noted when humans faced with slow extinction must reach down into the dregs of endurance.

There were finally 14 emigrants who felt strong enough to leave and for whom there were snowshoes; there were three others without snowshoes who wanted to follow.

They awoke on December 16, the appointed day of departure, and were cheered by clear skies. But they left in an aura of gloom and were waved on their way by the bony hand of death. During the night, Bayliss Williams had died.

FIRE IN THE SNOW

The snowshoers did poorly the first day, progressing only a few miles. When they camped, they could still see smoke from the cabins. But even so, two of the three without snowshoes had to turn back. Only one youngster, Lem Murphy, had stuck it out. In sympathy, the party cobbled up snowshoes for him out of some abandoned packsaddles.

Survival through the freezing night presented new problems. Thick green logs were cut and laid as a foundation on the snow. A fire was built on top. If the log platform was thick enough, the fire wouldn't burn through before morning and the flames wouldn't smother in the snow. Huddled under blankets around the fire, the party passed the night, resting, if not sleeping, in preparation for the struggles of tomorrow.

On the second day they crossed the pass, covered six miles and camped in 12 feet of snow. On the third day, they started downhill, if only slightly, but open ground and sunlight brought new trouble—snow blindness. Now counted among the weakest, little Stanton also was having great vision difficulty. He made camp late that night, and the next night as well.

At the end of the fifth day, they had food for only one more day. At the start of the sixth, the party was ready to leave camp when Mary Graves noticed that Stanton still sat by the fire smoking his pipe.

"Are you coming?" asked Mary quietly.

"Yes . . . I am coming soon."

But Stanton did not make camp that night. Brave little Stanton, who had known that morning that he was finished but wanted to make it easy for the others to continue. Brave little Stanton, who had once been safe in Sutter's Fort, but who had trailed back through the mountains with food, even though he had no family to feed.

Stanton was never heard from again.

Now they depended on the Indians to guide them but a mistake was made; they drifted away from Bear Valley instead of toward it. Early on the seventh day, their last food gone, they started out from camp but when it began to snow, they stopped, hoping that Stanton would appear to guide them. He did not appear.

On the ninth day, wandering aimlessly through a snowstorm, they began to think the unthinkable. They had not eaten anything for two days. They had not eaten nearly enough for many days before that. If any were to survive, they would soon have to start eating each other. It was Patrick Dolan who first dared to say, "I think we should draw lots."

Eddy agreed, but Foster objected. Eddy had another idea. Let two of them take guns, he said, and fight until one or both were dead. This way a man would have a fighting chance to live. Even if he died, he would not be butchered like a pig.

But again there was an objection.

Then Eddy said there was only one thing to do—struggle onward until someone died. Glancing at the gaunt faces and defeated eyes of those around him, he felt that the moment was not far away.

With most of the party more dead than alive, they stopped that night and managed to build a fire. Antonio, one of the drovers, was the first to die; Eddy knew he was gone when his hand fell into the fire and burned to a coal.

But the storm's fury increased before they could eat. For a time they could only pile wood on the fire to stave off death from freezing. Then, as someone staggered off to cut more wood, the head flew from their only hatchet and was lost in the snow.

As the fire died, Eddy roused them and helped them form a circle on the snow with blankets under them and over their heads. The snow soon covered the blankets, trapping their body heat. They cowered under the blankets that night, which happened to be Christmas Eve, through the next day and the next night and into the afternoon of the following day before the storm finally ceased. An old man "Uncle Billy" Graves, had died, then Patrick Dolan. Lem Murphy, 13, was delirious and near death when they came out from under the blankets and started to make a fire in a dead pine tree.

Now, finally, it was time. The barriers of civilization fell. They cut flesh from Dolan's legs and arms and roasted it. Only the Indians and Lem Murphy, who was too far gone to eat, refused. As the moon set that night, Lem Murphy died.

They remained in camp for the next two days. It was easier now; the wall had been breached. The Indians finally ate, too. They stripped the flesh from the bodies, roasted and ate what they could and dried the remainder to take along. Pathetically, they observed one rule only: No one ate flesh of a member of his own family.

FOOTPRINTS IN BLOOD

There were 10 who left that terrible camp—Eddy, Foster and Fosdick; the two Indians, Luis and Salvador; and five women. Foster and Fosdick were whipped, groggy, defeated. It was the magnificent Eddy and the women who drove the group along. Without a hatchet, they could build fires only by scraping snow away from the base of a dead tree and setting it aflame. Having lost their way entirely, they could only move toward the west on painful feet, leaving bloody footprints on the snow, laboriously climbing the canyon walls, crossing streams on snow bridges, living for more than a week on preserved human flesh.

Even after they left the deep snow and caught distant glimpses of the Sacramento Valley, their troubles continued. Luis and Salvador fled the party when it became plain that Foster and Fosdick intended to kill them. Then Fosdick died and was eaten.

Though barely able to lift his rifle, Eddy killed a deer. What remained of the party stumbled onward and finally straggled into a camp of Indians, who could offer only acorns to eat but pointed them toward the trail to safety. Now they were living on grass; plenty of deer were seen but no one had strength to lift a rifle.

On the morning of January 17, Foster and the five women, no longer able to walk on their bloody, frost-bitten feet, gave up and lay down beside the trail to die.

But there was still strength in the amazing Eddy. With Indian help, he pushed on.

* * *

Near sunset, Harriet Ritchie opened the door of her parents' cabin near Johnson's Ranch. Two Indians stood outside, holding between them the bedraggled shape of a man who asked weakly for bread.

It was Eddy.

The little community sprang into action. Soon four men bearing packs and guided by the two Indians were moving up the back trail. They found Foster and the five women in time. When morning came, men on horseback rode farther back up the trail and had no trouble following it; it was plainly marked by bloody footprints.

Fifteen persons had left the camp below Truckee Lake 33 days earlier—nine men, a boy and five women. Only seven survived, two men and all five women. It seems likely that these seven lived only because they were able at the final moment to cast aside the last taboo of civilized society and eat their own kind.

* * *

Bones, boiled long enough, produce a juice. The juice, mixed with water, tastes something like soup. The nourishment is slight. It is mainly food for the mind.

At Truckee Lake, with December wearing on, bone juice and

These are stumps of trees cut at snow level by the Reed-Donner party. The picture was taken about 1925.

animal hides were preserving life, after a fashion. Hides were carved into strips, then held close enough to a fire to singe off the hair. Then they were scraped and boiled in a kettle until pulpy. When the mess cooled and grew stiff, it was ready to eat.

Eating boiled hides was like eating not-quite-hard glue. Not everyone could stomach the sickening concoction, even with starvation glaring hollow-eyed from every dark corner of the cabins.

In the Murphy cabin, a hide was used as a rug near the fire. Children, lying near the fire, began to cut off little chunks and crisp them in the coals, then eat them. Before long, the rug was gone. The children had eaten it out from under themselves!

The cabins were less crowded now that the snowshoers had gone but conditions had grown much worse. Filth cast its stench everywhere. Vermin multiplied, despite the cold weather. Men, women and children with bodies unwashed for months lay down most of the time, too sick, too tired, too weak, too disheartened to move.

On December 20, Milt Elliott came back from the Donner camp with bad news. Four men, including "Uncle Jake" Donner, had died. They hadn't starved, exactly; they had merely sickened and drifted off. The Donners had only tents and brush shelters and as a result were wet most of the time. They were eating mice, when they were lucky enough to catch any. George Donner was in bad trouble. He had cut his hand and the wound wouldn't heal.

For Mrs. Reed on Christmas Day, a pot of smelly glue was not a suitable dinner for her family, which had once known the best. White beans, half a cup of rice, a few dried apples, tripe and a two-inch-square of bacon—these were the treasures she produced from hiding places and set before her children.

"Eat slowly, children," she said firmly. "There is plenty for all."

A German, "Dutch Charley" Burger died on December 30. Breen noted in his diary that Keseberg had taken over the dead man's valuables. Breen made similar notations from time to time. Keseberg was not trusted; it was as if Breen wanted a record, just in case . . .

The next breakout attempt, not surprisingly, was spearheaded by Mrs. Reed. On January 4, she and her oldest daughter, Virginia, Milt Elliott and Eliza Williams left camp and pushed along the lake toward the pass. The younger Reed children had been left behind, but not without tearful pleas that must have torn their mother apart; they were deathly afraid of being abandoned.

Eliza Williams withstood only one freezing night, then turned

Westward Migration

back. After the first night, Virginia had so little strength that she had to crawl up slopes on hands and knees; sometimes Milt carried her.

It was a tribute to their determination that they even managed to get through the pass, but they did . . . and then got lost. After four nights in the open, they staggered back into camp, defeated.

Another storm swept down on them from the pass. On January 13, Breen wrote in his diary:

"Snowing fast wind N W snow higher than the shanty must be 13 feet deep dont know how to get wood this morning it is dredful to look at."

SEVEN AGAINST STARVATION

Fourteen men mounted on horses and mules left Johnson's Ranch on February 4 and rode through rain and snow toward the mountains, their animals laboring with heads bowed, slipping and sliding through the greasy, sucking, adobe mud of the trail. On the night of Friday, February 5, it was raining so hard that they could not lie down to sleep; they stood all night around a fire. But a serious attempt at rescue had gotten underway at last.

The most remarkable member of the party was William Eddy, who was venturing back into the mountains after only two and one-half weeks of recuperation from his harrowing crossing with the snowshoe party. But Eddy knew better than anyone else in the rescue party how bad it was in the bitter camp by Truckee Lake; his wife and children were there. Because of them, he was going back long before he was ready. And even then, too late . . .

(Breen's diary reported for Friday, February 5, almost as an afterthought: ". . . Eddys child died last night." On the next day he wrote: "Mrs. Eddy very weak.")

At daylight on Sunday, the incredible storms ceased, the sun shone and the rescue party stopped to rest and dry its sopping supplies and equipment.

On Monday, February 8, the party resumed its trek. (Breen at the lake wrote in his diary: "Spitzer died last night about 3 oclock . . . we will bury him in the snow. Mrs. Eddy died on the night of the 7th.")

Now only little Jimmy lived of the family William Eddy was hurrying to save.

Tuesday the party reached Mule Springs and was dismayed to find deep snow. There was no food for the animals; only men with back packs could go on. It was a crushing blow. They had hoped to take the animals as far as Bear Valley.

It was too much for William Eddy. He and a man named Verrot were chosen to take the animals back to Johnson's. Two others were assigned to stay at Mule Springs and guard a supply cache, leaving 10 to go forward into the white mountains without snowshoes.

Now they were only 50 miles away from the cabins at the lake but they might as well have been 1000, so far as Milt Elliott was concerned. Breen recorded Elliott's death on February 9. Now Mrs. Reed's burden would be much heavier. Only two days before his death, the faithful employee of the Reeds had called on Mrs. Reed to make sure that she had hides to eat. The line between life and death at the lake was growing so thin and short that if the rescue party didn't break through within a matter of days, there would be nobody left to rescue.

On February 13, with the party at Bear Valley only 30 miles from the lake, three members flatly refused to go farther. The seven who went on were Aquilla Glover, the leader; Dan Tucker, Sept Moultry, Ned Coffeemeyer, Joe Sels and two brothers, John and Daniel Rhoads. (Said Sheriff McKinstry later at Sutter's Fort: "I will give you a list of their names, as I think they ought to be recorded in letters of gold.")

No one among them was a mountaineer of any great experience; in fact, Coffeemeyer and Sels were sailors. The other five had crossed as emigrants during the previous autumn.

At dusk on Thursday, they entered the trees where Eddy had said the cabins were. There was only snow to be seen. Were they too late?

Then a hollow shell of a woman emerged from a hole in the snow and tottered toward them.

"Are you men from California," she croaked, "or do you come from heaven?"

* * *

On Monday, a group of 23 had been chosen to accompany the relief party on the return trip. Of the 17 children among them, three were only three years old. Two of the children, Tommy and Patty Reed, were to be the cause of still another heartbreaking decision for their mother.

The snow was firmer now than when the first party of snowshoers had left but the least strong members of the party—Leanna Donner, two of the Reed children and the Englishman, John Denton—simply could not keep up with the main body.

Then Mrs. Reed faced her moment of truth.

She might save Jimmy and Virginia if she stayed with the party, but then Patty and Tommy would be left at the cabins with death their likely fate. But if she went back to the cabins with all the children, mightn't they all die?

Glover promised that once he led the party to safety, he would return immediately to rescue the Reed children.

The parting between the Reed youngsters and their mother was tearful. Young Tommy didn't seem to realize what was going on but eight-year-old Patty understood completely and accepted her fate like the heroine she was.

"Well, Mother," said Patty, bringing some of the strong men in the group to the point of crying, "if you never see me again, do the best you can."

On the way back to the cabins with Moultry and Glover, she told the men that she was willing to go back because of her little brother, who would need care, but she was sure she had seen the last of her mother.

John Denton was the first to die. He simply sat down by the trail and announced that he could go no farther. (In his last hours, it developed later, he had written poetry about his native England.) Little Ada Keseberg was next to go.

As the party advanced, they found to their horror that their food caches had been raided by animals. The group broke up, several men moving ahead as rapidly as possible to get food for the others. Again there was blood on the snow as the refugees were forced to walk on frost-bitten feet which swelled, then burst.

On Friday afternoon, down to a diet of rawhide again, they thought they were within a day's travel of Bear Valley.

On Saturday, they saw human figures winding through the trees ahead of them. It was a relief party!

"Bread! Bread!" cried the starving children as they stumbled forward.

The lead rescuer said, "Is Mrs. Reed with you? Tell her Mr. Reed is here."

As Virginia rushed forward to throw herself into her father's arms, Mrs. Reed, overwhelmed, slumped into the snow.

Reed, it turned out, had expected to meet the party on this great day. In camp the night before, he had baked bread and even a few

sweet cakes for the children. Reed, the resourceful . . .

Then Reed's party of rescuers resumed its march toward Truckee Lake; the rescued slogged on to Bear Valley, where the problem suddenly became not too little food but too much.

William Hook sickened from overeating and was given tobacco juice to induce vomiting. But he had not learned his lesson. During the night, he slipped over to the store of provisions and ate all he could. When he was found in the morning, it was too late for tobacco juice. And so, safe at last, another died . . .

On March 4, Mrs. Reed and the other refugees in her group reached Sutter's Fort. But Margaret Reed could not keep herself from looking back; her heart and mind were still in the mountains with her husband, with Tommy and Patty.

RESCUE!

The organized rescue effort, so slow in beginning, was now operating efficiently. Between Sutter's Fort and Truckee Lake, men and supplies were moving with frenzied haste. During the remainder of March and most of April, no effort was spared to save those who had been left in the grim camps by the lake.

By March 5, when Mrs. Reed's group arrived at the fort, 26 of the Reed-Donner party were safe. Twenty-eight others were dead. Thirty-one remained in the mountains.

James Reed arrived at the cabins by the lake on March 1. A little girl jumped off the corner of a cabin roof to meet him but fell and could not rise.

With fear gripping his throat, James Reed picked up his daughter Patty and asked about Tommy.

Patty pointed at the cabin; Tommy was in there sleeping, she said. Reed descended into the cabin and woke the skeleton which his son had become. Tommy did not recognize his father at first; it was necessary for Patty to assure him that yes, this truly was his father . . .

The condition of the emigrants was almost beyond belief. For several days, the rescuers worked in the stench of death and depravity to clean the rotting filth of months from the children first, then from the adults and finally from the cabins.

Working in the Murphy cabin, Reed had been forced to look at

Here is Patty Reed, young heroine of the tragedy in the Sierra snow.

what remained of the body of Milt Elliott, his trusted employee. His head was intact, but most of the rest of him had been torn away.

Those who survived at the cabins had managed only by eating the bodies of the dead.

The curtain had begun to fall on the grisly drama by the lake. On March 3, Reed was ready to lead another party to safety.

Then an old enemy struck another ghastly blow. On March 6, the eighth great blizzard of the winter trapped the Reed party en route and threw the entire rescue operation into chaos.

Reed and some of the refugees, including Tommy and Patty Reed, managed after terrible hardship to reach Bear Valley and safety. Along the way, Patty again impressed with her heroism. Although barely able to walk, she refused again and again to be carried. Only after she reached Bear Valley did the doughty eight-year-old reveal that she had brought with her a small doll, the last of her possessions. (That very doll is now on display at Sutter's Fort State Historic Monument in Sacramento.)

The next rescue party, led by William Eddy, reached the cabins on March 13 and found that an already terrible situation had worsened. James Eddy had died and Keseberg raved to the grieving father that he had eaten the body!

William Eddy almost killed Keseberg then but took pity on the crippled, emaciated man. Eddy vowed, though, that some day he would kill Keseberg.

The departure of the Eddy group forced Tamsen Donner to make a harsh decision. Her husband, George, was near death but she had no intention of leaving him so long as a spark of life remained. Yet her three young daughters deserved a chance to live. With incredible courage, she sent them with Eddy and turned away from the cabins by the lake to walk through the woods toward her dying husband.

The Eddy party reached safety with much less difficulty than had the others. Of those few persons left in the mountains, only one would survive — Lewis Keseberg.

THE LAST ACT

The final scenes added no luster to anyone's reputation. The men who left Johnson's Ranch on April 13 to go back into the snow were

This is Patty Reed's doll, less than four inches tall, in its case at Sutter's Fort.

led by a mountain man named Fallon. They were motivated mainly by greed; money and other valuables remained in the mountains.

They found only Keseberg alive, lying semi-conscious among human bones on the floor. A pot of blood was on the stove. The half-crazed man admitted that he had eaten Tamsen Donner, in fact bragged of her fine flavor, but denied murdering her.

By the end of April, the Fallon party had brought Keseberg through the mountains to safety. The epic had ended, its tragic chapters written in blood on the snow.

Eighty-seven emigrants had set out on the Hastings Cutoff. Five had died before reaching the Sierras, 34 in the mountains and one after reaching the lowlands. Two rescuers perished as well — Luis and Salvador, the Indians sent by Sutter. Only 47 survived.

It was the worst disaster of the entire westward migration; it left its bloody mark forever on the California Trail.

The entire James Reed family came through without loss; the Breens were the only other family which hadn't lost at least one person.

Some of the survivors became important persons in their adopted communities. James Reed bought a large parcel of land near San Jose and became one of the first subdividers in the developing region. The Breens settled around San Juan Bautista; the Donners joined the Reeds at San Jose, while the Murphys went to Marysville.

William Eddy, one of the truly heroic figures of the episode, lost everything but did manage to recoup in California. He remarried and fathered another family but died relatively young in 1859.

And what of Keseberg?

Apparently Captain Sutter put little stock in the ghastly talk about the man, for Keseberg was given command of a Sutter schooner. When the ship put into San Francisco and William Eddy heard who was aboard, he armed himself and set out to fulfill his vow. However, James Reed and Edwin Bryant talked him out of it.

In one of history's most ironic and gruesome twists, Keseberg later went into business in Sacramento — he opened a restaurant!

But Keseberg was not fated to escape unscathed. He had talked too often of his cannibalism in the free-and-easy atmosphere of early California. As time passed, civilization smoothed off the rough edges of California society and fingers began to be pointed at the German. On occasion, it was said, children even threw rocks at him. He lost his money and sank out of sight. When he resurfaced in 1879, it was discovered that his wife had died and he was living in poverty with two mentally defective daughters. At least, Keseberg did not live happily ever after.

The story of the Reed-Donner party has always attracted a certain amount of morbid interest because of the cannibalism connected with it. At first, several members of the party weren't at all bashful about admitting — even boasting — that they had eaten human flesh in the mountains. But as years passed, survivors wanted to forget the horror; some of them even went so far in scrubbing up history in their memoirs as to deny flatly that cannibalism had occurred.

They needn't have been so squeamish. The Reed-Donner story remains one of history's brightest testimonials to human courage and the will to live.

Consider this fact: Despite incredible privations which extended over many months and strained many minds to the breaking point, despite frustrations and disappointments enough to crush even a strong spirit, not a single member of the party is known to have committed suicide. In fact, there is no clear record of anyone even giving suicide serious consideration, which is as fantastic as anything else about the massive tragedy.

Californians are not likely to forget the name "Donner." Truckee Lake became Donner Lake; a freeway now crosses Donner Summit through Donner Pass.

"GOODBYE, MOSE!"

There was a cabin waiting, remember, when the vanguard of the Donner Party neared Truckee Lake and thereby hangs a tale.

In autumn of 1844, a party led by Elisha Stevens found the trail through the mountains now called Donner Pass. In the group was a spindly, awkward 18-year-old named Moses Schallenberger.

The party reached a point east of the pass in mid-November and decided to split up to improve its chances of getting through. Six strong young persons were chosen to strike out ahead on horseback. Three others were appointed to build a cabin below Truckee Lake and spend the winter there guarding six wagons. Moses Schallenberger was one of these.

The main body moved west into the mountains. Schallenberger and his companions, Foster and Montgomery, returned to the lake and built their cabin. Their livestock consisted of two skinny cows, which certainly wouldn't provide a winter's food. But the young men were good shots; they would live off the land. (Two years later, the Reed-Donner party still thought this was possible.)

However, soon three feet of snow covered the ground, with more threatening to fall. They made crude snowshoes, saw plenty of fox and coyote tracks but nothing to shoot at. The deer had gone to lower elevations and the bear had already hibernated.

Suddenly fearful that they would starve if they stayed, they killed the cows, dried some of the meat and set out toward the pass on snowshoes. They reached the summit by the first night but Moses Schallenberger, exhausted and shivering, knew he had gone as far as he could.

His only remaining chance was to return to the cabin and try to rough out the winter alone. At the moment, it must have seemed like no chance at all.

As Schallenberger told the story: "We did not say much at parting. Our hearts were too full for that. There was simply a warm clasp of the hand accompanied by the familiar word 'Good-by'."

Young Moses was so played out when he reached the cabin that he had to take hold of his foot and lift it over a sill nine inches high!

He knew that he couldn't exist for long on the beef remaining and he doubted if he would have any luck hunting but he remembered seeing some traps in one of the wagons . . .

Those traps saved his life.

Wrote Schallenberger: "As soon as daylight came I went out to inspect the traps . . . After some hesitation I commenced the examination, and to my great delight found in one of them a starved coyote. I soon had his hide off and his flesh roasted in a Dutch oven. I ate this meat, but it was horrible. I next tried boiling him, but it did not improve the flavor. I cooked him in every possible manner my imagination, spurred by hunger, could suggest but could not get him into a condition where he could be eaten without revolting my stomach. But for three days this was all I had to eat. On the third night I caught two foxes. I roasted one of them, and the meat, though entirely devoid of fat, was delicious. I was so hungry that I could easily have eaten a fox at two meals, but made one last me two days . . . Once I shot a crow that seemed to have got out of his latitude and stopped on a tree near the cabin. I stewed the crow but it was difficult for me to decide which I like best, crow or coyote . . . I caught, on an average, a fox in two days, and every now and then a coyote. These last-named animals I carefully hung up under the brush shed on the north side of the cabin, but I never got hungry enough to eat one of them again. There were eleven hanging there when I came away. I never really suffered for something to eat, but was in almost continual anxiety for fear the supply would give out. For instance, as soon as one meal was finished I began to be distressed for fear I could not get another one. My only hope was that the supply of foxes would not become exhausted . . . It is strange that I never craved anything to eat but good fat meat. For bread or vegetables I had no desire. Salt I had in plenty, but never used. I had just coffee enough for one cup, and that I saved for Christmas . . .

"Fortunately I had aplenty of books . . . I used often to read aloud, for I longed for some sound to break the oppressive stillness. For the same reason, I would talk aloud to myself. At night I built large fires and read by the light of the pine knots as late as possible, in order that I might sleep late the next morning, and thus cause the days to seem shorter. What I wanted most was enough to eat, and the next thing I tried hardest to do was to kill time. I thought the snow would never leave the ground, and the few months I had been living here seemed years.

"One evening, a little before sunset, about the last of February, as I was standing a short distance from my cabin, I thought I could distinguish the form of a man moving towards me. I first thought it was an Indian, but very soon I recognized the familiar face as Dennis Martin . . ."

The boy's heroic ordeal was over. Martin, who had been urged to make his dangerous journey by Schallenberger's sister, made new snowshoes for the boy. They set out the following morning and were able to reach safety in the valley before the next storm hit.

In ironic contrast to the Reed-Donner party, the Stevens party reached California with two more members than it had when it started out. No one died and two babies were born along the way. They were a courageous, well-organized group. One member had brought traps and another had brought books.

A boy named Moses would be everlastingly grateful.

WEST OF SOMEWHERE

The first wagon train to California arrived in California without any wagons.

The year was 1841. John Bartleson was the elected captain of the group but John Bidwell actually held the group together. (Bartleson apparently let the party know that unless he could be captain, he wouldn't go, and six or seven others wouldn't, either. Bartleson was elected captain.)

The group began its journey well supplied with ignorance and misinformation. Before the party arrived in California after abandoning the wagons in the Sierras, John Bidwell would be reduced to eating the windpipe of a coyote.

In truth, these pioneers weren't exactly sure where California *was*, except that it lay somewhere west ... or to the west of somewhere.

But the party had one big thing going for it—youth. Most of the members, fortunately, were young, strong men.

The expedition entered history as the Bidwell-Bartleson Party, first across the plains to California, despite the fact that it was a failure in every respect except the all-important one—it arrived in California.

Faced with the Sierra wall, Bidwell wrote in his journal on October 29, 1841: "If California lies beyond those mountains we shall never be able to reach it."

But they did reach it and members of the party took root and flourished into a lush crop of prominent first citizens of California. Bidwell went to work for John Sutter and waxed rich. The town of Chico now stands on what once was Bidwell's Arroyo Chico Ranch.

Josiah Belden of the group became San Jose's first mayor. Charles Weber founded the city of Stockton. Tehama County grew up around the huge Tehama Ranch owned by Robert Thomes, another Bidwell-Bartleson pioneer.

Bidwell was elected to the U.S. Congress and in 1892 ran for President as the candidate of the Prohibition Party. In his spare time, Bidwell gave California agriculture a healthy boost by bringing plants from all over the world to his ranch.

* * *

At first, travel along the California Trail just sputtered along. In 1848, it was estimated that only 450 persons made the overland journey. In 1849, 22,500 came and in 1850, 45,000!

The reason, of course, glittered in the gold discovered at Sutter's Mill in 1848.

The Oregon Trail had suddenly developed a busy branch. At the fork, it was said, there was a sign: "To Oregon."

There was no sign pointing the way to California—just a chunk of gold ore.

"All of those who could read," said smug Oregonians, "went to Oregon."

* * *

The big year along the trail to California was 1852, when 52,000 made the trip. As the gold petered out, so did tourist travel. In 1857, only 4000 travellers were counted along the trail. Without gold pouring out of the Mother Lode, California's infant economy couldn't support its resident population, much less an annual flood of immigrants.

Westbound wagon travel continued to trickle along, though, and didn't end until 1869 or thereabouts when, at Promontory Point, Utah, the driving of a spike made of California gold tied the country together with iron rails. The covered wagon was never built that could compete with a railroad, especially after the battling lines tangled in price wars. On one gladsome day during the period when the Southern Pacific and the Santa Fe were at each other's throats, a westbound emigrant could buy a ticket from New York to California for one dollar! (Presumably, this was coach fare, not Pullman.)

When the last yoke of oxen had been unhitched west of the Sierras, more than 165,000 persons had lived through the epic journey.

* * *

The California Trail was by no means a single set of well-worn ruts. It had branches, cutoffs, bypasses and detours. Then, as now, whenever a real estate promoter wanted to entice some tourists, he opened a new "trail." There is no record of any of them putting up a sign: "Travel at your own risk."

One of these operators was Peter Lassen, owner of a large ranch southwest of what is now called Mt. Lassen. (In Lassen County, incidentally.)

Lassen wanted to form a town around his ranch and become a feudal baron, rather like John Sutter of the Sacramento area. So, in 1848, Lassen coaxed a batch of emigrants off the trail near the Humboldt River in what is now Nevada, then steered them northwest

➡

This mighty panorama of San Francisco in 1863 was photographed from Telegraph Hill; Golden Gate is in the distance.

along the Applegate Trail which Oregon-bound trains had used in '46 and '47 and finally turned them southwest at Goose Lake, on the present Oregon-California line.

As a guide, Lassen turned out to be a splendid deep-sea diver. When the leader got lost for the third or fourth time, wiser heads took over and the train broke into fragments, most of which survived, but only after terrible hardship.

Lassen's northern California empire didn't materialize but he probably was happy to have escaped with his life; surely, before the party had finished its stumbling around in the northern mountains, with nobody quite as lost as Peter Lassen, more than one strong man in the misguided group wanted to grip the leader by the throat and shake hard.

* * *

It was bound to happen, with all those trails headed (supposedly) for the same place. A man named William H. Nobles developed a "short cut" from the big bend of the Humboldt into California. East of Mt. Lassen, for a distance of about 20 miles, Nobles found it handy to use Lassen's route . . . but in reverse. As a result, a wagon rolling south along Lassen's route toward California might meet a wagon rolling north along Nobles's short cut to California! It isn't difficult to imagine the bad jokes passing between the wagons.

* * *

There were often unusual sights to be seen along the trail. The 1850 migration included a woman, walking, carrying everything she owned upon her head. And several ladies in a train of 1852 dared to wear *bloomers*.

* * *

Nothing new under the sun; the trail even had billboards. The first one was placed in 1847 at Deer Creek, west of Fort Laramie, Wyoming. It advertised the Mormon ferry near the present town of Casper, Wyoming.

* * *

Water supply was often a problem along the trail. Then an emigrant discovered that water smelling sickeningly of sulphur could be made drinkable by brewing it into strong coffee. Another emigrant

They don't build schools like this any more, even in Russia. This ornate institution served pupils of Artesia along about 1898.

found that his horse wouldn't drink the water but would drink the coffee. (Without sugar and cream, it is hoped.)

When it was all over and California had become a respected and reasonably respectable state of the union, it was plain to see that immigrant Americans, after the landing of the Pilgrims, had managed to travel west only 1000 miles, just one-third of the way to the Pacific. They reached the edge of the forest and stopped. But then, to make the next great leap to Oregon or California, they had to cover—not in 200 years, not even in one full year, but in *a single summer season*— twice the distance their ancestors had managed in more than two centuries! And with the same equipment—wagons, horses, oxen and shoes.

Somehow, they did it.

SITES TO SEE

BIDWELL MANSION, Chico. (Charming old house was headquarters of John Bidwell's huge Rancho Chico.)

DONNER MEMORIAL STATE PARK, Nevada County. (Memorial, museum and cabin sites are of interest.)

PIONEER VILLAGE, Bakersfield. (This remarkable Kern County effort is a very special collection of old buildings moved to the site, restored and furnished; worth half a day of anybody's time. The adjoining Kern County Museum has a dog-powered butter churn!)

SUTTER'S FORT, Sacramento. (Beautifully restored showplace of state park system.)

RANCHO SAN RAFAEL. Now occupied by the city of Glendale, the prominent brand of the rancho was granted to Jose Maria Verdugo in 1785. The rancho consisted of 36,402 acres.

Chapter Five *

The Gold Rush
THE LUCK OF JOHN SUTTER

Soaked by a heavy rain, bone-weary after spending the night under an oak tree, James Marshall arrived at Sutter's Fort on January 24, 1848, immediately sought out his employer and tensely announced, "I must talk with you alone, Captain Sutter."

They went to the main building, where Sutter closed and locked behind them the door of a bedroom-sitting room.

Marshall asked for materials to make a small scale. Puzzled, Sutter rose and quickly brought a scale from the apothecary shop.

Marshall opened his handkerchief and nervously dumped several small yellow fragments onto the table.

Captain Sutter looked them over carefully, took down an encyclopedia from the shelf and read for a moment. Then he tested the material with nitric acid; there was no reaction.

With growing excitement, Sutter glanced at Marshall, then measured out a volume of silver equal to that of the yellow stuff and put both on the scales. Without question, the yellow material was heavier!

It was enough to satisfy Sutter.

"It's *gold*," he said, his eyes flashing.

* * *

Gold it most certainly was. Marshall, building a sawmill for Sutter on the south fork of the American River, had spotted a few golden specks in the tailrace. Although he was not aware of the extent of his discovery on that stirring morning in Sutter's Fort, the solitary, cantankerous carpenter had dipped into one of the greatest gold discoveries of all time, the Mother Lode, 2 miles wide and 120 miles long, California's fantastic golden backbone.

It must have seemed to Captain John Augustus Sutter then that Lady Luck had at long last decided to take up permanent residence under his roof. Bankrupt in his native Switzerland at age 31, he had left his family to go to New York, then to the Mississippi Valley. Still dissatisfied, he had shipped to the western frontier via Hawaii, charmed the Mexican government of California out of a huge land grant in the Sacramento Valley and then proceeded to turn it into an empire which by 1848 found 150,000 acres under his control, including some coastal land that he had purchased from the Russians at Fort Ross and Bodega Bay.

Wrote Sutter proudly in his reminiscences:

"Business increased to such a happy extent that I soon employed six hundred men in the harvest field; to feed them I had to kill four to five oxen daily. I could raise forty thousand bushels of wheat then without inconvenience, reap the crop with sickles, thresh it out with horses, and winnow it in the wind . . . I had twelve thousand head of cattle at the same time fifteen thousand sheep. I had all the Indians at my call whom I could employ."

Of course, he was up to his ears in debt but an entrepreneur often must borrow in order to expand and expansion was the name of Sutter's game. With 27,000 head of livestock and 40,000 bushels of wheat in a single season, why worry?

It had been necessary for Sutter to become a Mexican citizen to acquire the land. When America wrested California from Mexico, Sutter quite happily became an American. A businessman had to be flexible about politics because politicians, particularly in early California, tended to be in office today and nowhere tomorrow. Besides, he liked Americans, always had; they had big ideas and lots of energy and weren't afraid to stick their necks out. Yes, Sutter decided, he would make a splendid American.

Outgoing, affable, freehanded, the captain had lots of friends. Ever since the first immigrants led by John Bidwell had stumbled out of the Sierras—exhausted, sick and near starvation—Sutter's Fort had been a lifesaving oasis and to these grateful pioneers, the chubby Swiss assumed a position at the right hand of Santa Claus.

So everything finally was going Sutter's way . . . but there was a cloud on his horizon no bigger than a speck of gold glittering in a millrace.

The Gold Rush
HOW NOT TO KEEP A SECRET

Sutter and Marshall seemed to feel that it would be a good idea to keep their discovery secret but inevitably leaks developed. In fact, Sutter himself wrote to a friend, Mariano Vallejo of Sonoma: "I have made a discovery of a gold mine which, according to experiments we have made, is extraordinarily rich."

Sutter had an immediate problem—he didn't own the precious land where color had been discovered. He promptly arranged a three-year lease with the Coloma Indians, one of the few cases in Western history where white men bothered to recognize Indian land rights. (The Russians at Fort Ross put another case on the record.) Then Sutter sent an employee, Charles Bennett, to have the lease confirmed in the Monterey office of Col. R. B. Mason, governor of California.

Sutter could have chosen better. Bennett seems to have shown his gold sample to almost everybody who would stand still, especially in the streets of San Francisco.

But Sutter's secret remained safe for the moment; almost no one believed Bennett!

No one, that is, except a soft-spoken Georgian, a former gold miner, who quietly bought proper tools and set out for Coloma, 150 miles away. Isaac Humphrey was the first of the stampeding tens of thousands who would soon be frantically grubbing for gold just as, in the words of one cynical observer: ". . . 1000 hogs let loose in a forest would root up ground nuts."

Speaking of hogs, it should not be assumed that Sutter's attempts at secrecy meant that he wanted to keep all the treasure for himself. The Swiss was not so gold-giddy that he forgot about the saw mill and the flour mill he had a-building and he knew what would happen to men earning their keep plus a dollar a day when gold fever struck. Time enough to pass the word about the strike when the mills were operating.

The saw mill was finished two months later, whereupon the crew quit and went prospecting.

The men building the flour mill soon followed suit.

Leather tanners working at the fort walked away from two thousand hides and went to seek their fortunes.

Sutter's Indians stayed long enough to harvest the new wheat crop, then left it to rot on the ground.

In one of California history's most bitter twists, Sutter's empire, so secure a few months earlier that the middle-aged tycoon was thinking of retiring, was beginning to crumble about his ears.

John Sutter, man of far-reaching vision, had stumbled over a mountain of gold and was not to rise again.

GOLD FROM THE AMERICAN RIVER!

It was Sam Brannan, part-time Mormon and fulltime wheeler-dealer, who finally triggered the big rush by riding through the streets of San Francisco in May, waving his hat and bellowing:

"Gold, boys! Gold from the American River!"

Everybody knew Sam; one of his distinctions was that he was one of the few individuals ever excommunicated *twice* by the same church.

Sailors, both military and civilian, jumped ships as if they were sinking, some of them sacrificing four years' pay in the process. As more ships slipped through the Golden Gate, their crews smelled gold and evaporated. Soon there were literally hundreds of crewless vessels lying dead in the water of San Francisco Bay.

One formerly sober citizen, after his first glance into the filled pouch of a returned miner, described his feeling thusly:

"A frenzy seized my soul; houses were too small for me to stay in; I was soon in the street in search of necessary outfits; piles of gold rose up before me at every step; castles of marble, dazzling the eye with their rich appliances; thousands of slaves bowing to my beck and call; myriads of fair virgins contending with each other for my love . . . were among the fancies of my fevered imagination. The Rothschilds and Astors appeared to me but poor people; in short I had a very violent attack of the gold fever."

As real gold began to arrive in the settlements, most of the working men simply dropped everything and panted toward the Mother Lode.

The Californios on their rich ranchos seemed to have a natural immunity, however. Luis Peralta, elderly squire whose land included the present cities of Oakland, Berkeley and Alameda, was eloquent in his advice to his sons:

"My sons, God has given this gold to the Americans. Had He desired us to have it, He would have given it to us ere now. Therefore, go not after it, but let others go. Plant your lands, and reap; these be your best gold fields, for all must eat while they live."

The old man was right; the gold in those distant hills ruined more men than it enriched.

* * *

An interesting thing happened to John Augustus Sutter on his way to destruction.

Some men were ruined by too much gold acquired too quickly. Sutter got into trouble not because he had so much of the precious stuff but because his creditors thought he did and descended like hungry locusts to demand full settlement of long-standing debts, some of them so old that Sutter had forgotten about them.

Pestered until he was half out of his mind, Sutter turned over his holdings to his recently-arrived son, August, and fled to the mountains to lick his wounds.

Then Sam Brannan had an idea. Why not, he suggested to August Sutter, lay out a town between Sutter's Fort and the river, name it Sacramento City and sell lots? Why not indeed?

It worked. Lots sold fast and August was able to pay off the most insistent of his father's creditors and gain a little breathing room. As a by-product, he had spawned a capital city for California.

The respite for John Sutter was only brief, however; his luck had turned with a vengeance.

With his father still wandering the hills, August sold Sutter's Fort for $40,000. It might have been worth much more but now Sacramento City had taken the play away from it. Even so, the money should have been enough to bail out the toppled tycoon but August wasn't able to maintain contact with his footloose father and made the mistake of paying everyone who presented a claim, real or phony.

Enter Sam Brannan again. Slick Sam's little conspiracy cheated the Sutters out of the best lots remaining in Sacramento City. When the deed was done, Sutter had left only Hock Farm, the first patch of land he had cultivated in California.

At this place was reunited the family that Sutter had left in Switzerland 14 years earlier.

The bighearted Swiss was waiting at his isolated outpost when the early immigrants staggered out of the Sierras; he fed and clothed and housed their emaciated bodies, gave them employment, loaned them money, again and again sent rescue parties to bring stragglers down from the smothering snow.

California had given him everything but gold; then at last it gave him that, too, and gold did him in.

THE RIP-ROARING YEARS

Nobody wanted to take time out for a census but it is likely that there were as many as 10,000 miners in the Mother Lode when hectic 1848 clattered to a close. During the year they took out gold worth a cool ten million dollars, which is about two-thirds of the price paid by the U.S. to Mexico for California and a promising little place called Texas, plus several other sprawling parts of the West!

The year of the jackpot was 1852, when 80 million dollars worth of precious metal was torn out by 100,000 miners.

Eighty million dollars ... enough cold cash to stuff a steamboat.

First the gold attracted the people, then it financed the building of towns all over California. Greatest beneficiary of the treasure trove was San Francisco, which boomed, then boomed some more, and quickly became the commercial hub of the emerging state.

There are those who point to the Mother Lode as the reason for California's modern position as the richest and most populous state in the country. For certain, the infant got a running start when James Marshall picked up the golden flakes.

Also for certain, it has yet to stop running.

There are also those who say it couldn't have happened without the Comstock Lode, which wasn't even in California.

A frenzied new rush immediately erupted and Virginia City, Nevada, called by some the wildest mining camp ever to roar and screech into history, was the focus of the excitement.

A flood of silver cascaded from the Comstock during the peak years of production between 1860 and 1880. Although the strike was not in California, most of the cash flowed into the pockets of Californians. Millionaires were made in months and some of their names dominated California commerce for decades to follow — William Sharon, William Ralston, John W. Mackay, James Fair, James Flood, Adolph Sutro. Most of them sooner or later built eye-popping mansions on the hills of San Francisco.

The Comstock eventually petered out, too, but not California's luck. When the silver flow slowed, oil was discovered, just in time to keep the economy energized.

This single building is all that remained of Sutter's Fort before restoration began in 1925.

LIARS AND HISTORIANS

Mark Twain, who got his writing start as a free-swinging journalist in Virginia City, once snorted:

"A mine is just a hole in the ground owned by a liar."

During this fantastic period in this incredible place called the Mother Lode, lies and truths were hard to separate; one might be as hard to believe as the other.

Like this:

During the peak of gold fever, getting dirty clothes washed in San Francisco was either impossible or prohibitively expensive; new clothes cost a fortune. But early San Franciscans thought big, even about laundry. Ship traffic was heavy, so sometimes dirty clothes were shipped to Honolulu, washed and returned to San Francisco. A few even sent their grimy garments as far as Canton, China! So the story goes, anyway.

* * *

Carrying mail during the winter across the snow-choked Sierras was a vexing problem until a Norwegian immigrant named Thompson went to work. He fashioned skiis out of oak, shouldered an eighty-pound mail sack and crossed the mountains in four days between Placerville and Genoa, Nevada. Eating only dried beef and hard biscuits, "Snowshoe" Thompson soon cut his elapsed time to three days headed east, only two days westward, where the long slope of the mountains gave him a boost. For years Snowshoe was the only means of communication through the winter-locked heights. Even so, he asked no pay for schussing over his dangerous ski run. Then, when he asked the federal government for some belated pay to help him through old age, bureaucracy blocked him; he got nothing. Buried at Genoa, an amazing man called Snowshoe Thompson earned only crossed skiis carved into his tombstone.

* * *

The first flake of gold found at Sutter's Mill is in the Smithsonian Institution in Washington, D.C.; the museum at Sutter's Fort has a picture. An actual flake of similar size found in the same millrace in 1947 is on display at the fort.

* * *

John Sutter's hospitality wasn't reserved only for immigrants just off the trail; he also housed miners in transit to and from the goldfields. Apparently there was always room for one more in the attic. A sign on the wall of the main building at Sutter's Fort quotes a guest during the winter of 1849-50, when as many as 250 men might be bedded down in the attic at one time: "The men were packed in like sardines. They were dead tired, cross and cranky, they swore at each other and all swore at the latecomer for disturbing them. Being sworn at wasn't so bad. It was the atmosphere that tried the stoutest stomach —the combined smell of boot leather, tobacco smoke, sweaty clothes, sweating bodies, garlic breaths . . . if you raised up on your elbow and looked around, it was just like looking over a rolling ocean of men—twisting, squirming, turning over, talking in their sleep, some mumbling prayers, others sobbing, others cussing, some all of these. And good lord, how they snored!"

The federal census for California in 1860, considered to be the first accurate one, demonstrated plainly that the pull of the Mother Lode had been felt around the world. Nearly 40 per cent of the 379,000 persons had been born outside the U.S. China sent the most, 34,935, followed by Ireland, 33,147; Germany, 21,646; Great Britain, 15,897; Latin America, 9150; France, 8462; Canada, 5438; Italy, 2805. American Negroes were well represented, too, with 4086 individuals. Most were free Negros, not slaves. A large percentage of the Latin Americans were Mexicans from the border state of Sonora; most of the Latins not from Mexico came from Peru and Chile.

* * *

Benjamin Butler Harris came to the Mariposa County mines from Texas in 1849. He wrote: "My first crowbar, pick, shovel and battered second hand property of a disgusted miner were purchased for sixteen dollars. My diggins were about eighteen inches of bedrock. I managed to crevice and dig out about a dozen pans full per day from which about an ounce was daily realized. Out of this it required about $10 per day to supply my food which was usually beef or pickled pork, hard bread and coffee. By extra economy I sometimes managed to subsist on $8 per day. About this time my fancy was caught by a widely circulated caricature of the return of two ragged, famished prospectors having washpans heaped with shining gold—voraciously regarding a lot of Irish potatoes at a trading booth and balancing in the scales their weight in gold. One of them is saying 'this yer gold dust looks mighty yeller, but them thar 'taters looks yeller-er'."

* * *

The same Benjamin Harris went to Sonora in Tuolumne County and described the miner's day of rest. "A Sunday in Sonora, then having several thousand population, had its main street about its entire length blocked . . . from many Monte tables at intervals piled with gold dust and thronged with bettors. Late in the afternoon, after most of the day's sights had been taken in, I asked D. G. L. . . . how much gold dust he had seen that day in Sonora. He replied that he thought he had seen about 'ten barrels of it.' "

* * *

More from Harris: "Rough two dollar cowhide boots were sold for six ounces. ($96; gold then was worth $16 an ounce.) Lumber shipped from Maine hauled to the mines or lumber whip sawed in the vicinity readily brought $1 per foot. About this time I read of a New Englander who wore buck skin clothes in the mines returning home with his 'pile' and throwing away the old suit from which his thrifty wife gleaned from pockets and seams $13 in gold dust. The profits from the mines so possessed men's imaginations that United States private soldiers and sailors on this coast deserted on every opportunity, often with much risk. They were encountered everywhere in the Sierras. No one seemed to blame their yielding to the irresistible temptation. Luck seemed to smile on them more than on the others and with these were verified the proverbs that 'sailors make money like horses — but spend it like asses.' "

And still more Harris: "In the early days of mining, it was difficult for public speakers to obtain audience room under shelter. Store tents or shanties had the largest space and these were invariably accompanied with a bar and tables rent to gamblers. Often have I witnessed merchandising, whiskey selling and drinking, preaching and gaming all going on in the same tent on a Sunday and other days. It looked queer at first to see quiet men listening to the 'divining of the word' rise orderly from their goods box seat, softly approach the bar, take a drink, and as orderly resume listening to the sermon. On one of these occasions while two or three monte tables were running and Preacher

Blacks and whites worked side-by-side in the California gold fields. This Long Tom was operating at Spanish Flat in 1852.

P....... who had an unpleasant, raucous, rasping voice was holding forth; Yank Humphreys was annoyed thereby in the matter of ruining his game. He approached the preacher saying, 'Money is what you are preaching for—you are interrupting my game. Here's $2 I'll give you, if you'll dry up and quit preaching.'

"The preacher meekly pocketing the lucre remarked, 'The Lord sent it but the Devil brought it,' continued preaching as before. Such a guffaw went up as was rare in those 'diggins.' Discomfited, Yank also continued his game — preaching to the contrary — notwithstanding $2 loser in the operation . . ."

* * *

After most Americans left the placers, Chinese moved in and sifted through the leavings along the stream beds. When they were done, money and machinery were needed to gouge out remaining gold deep in the earth. One of the largest mining companies was Idaho-Maryland of Grass Valley, which finally sank shafts more than 5000 feet and took out many millions of dollars worth of gold, giving up only when forced to by rising costs and a government-fixed price of $35 an ounce.

Another popular mining method was called "hydraulicking." Great gouts of water were forced from huge hoses against gold-bearing banks or hillsides. The biggest nozzle could fire a nine-inch stream for 400 feet, washing the gold-laden mud called "slickens" down to immense sluice boxes where the gold was extracted, then dumping the leftovers into the streams in a monumental effort of pollution.

When you stop to think that about 425 hydraulic operations were at work in the late 1870s, using 72 million gallons of water per day and pouring 46 million cubic yards of slickens into streams flowing into the Sacramento River, it's not difficult to imagine the result — thoroughly gummed-up water courses.

Silt had raised the Yuba River bed *thirty* feet by 1878, putting Marysville below water level; only levees prevented flooding. There was violence, usually with downstream farmers pitted against miners, before legislation and court rulings ended the abomination. The ghastly effects of hydraulic mining can still be seen in scars on the

Wicked Bodie, ghost town left over from gold rush days, is carefully neglected by the state to preserve its charming decrepitude.

land, particularly in Butte and Nevada Counties.

The last phase of gold mining in California saw dredges employed; these were nothing more than shallow-draft factory boats. Near Oroville, the tailings dumped by dredges provided most of the material making up the tallest earthfill dam in the world. (This is rather like a meat packer using every part of the pig *including* the squeal.)

* * *

During the great depression of the early 1930s, unemployed persons from all over the U.S. trekked to the California gold fields again. (This was not a stampede, though; it was more like a funeral march.) Life in California was healthier than selling apples on a city street corner and there was always the honeyed thought: Had the '49ers, by any chance, missed a rich pocket or two? The average depression miner's take was about 50 cents per day, not much even in those low-priced times, but it beat standing in a bread line in Philadelphia. After all, nobody ever found a nugget in a slice of whole wheat.

* * *

Tourists now swarm through the Mother Lode from end to end, most of them sticking to State Highway 49, which winds slowly and beautifully across the historic ground, revealing one relic after another. The gold discovery site at Coloma is a state park; a monument to James Marshall is nearby. Columbia, in Tuolumne County, has been restored by the state and offers visitors a redolent glimpse into the past. Many other towns in southern and northern mining regions — Mariposa, Nevada City, Grass Valley, Downieville, to name just a few — offer rich rewards to the history buff; many of the old buildings still stand proudly, if not too securely.

Not all the worthwhile spots are reached via Highway 49. One of the most fascinating is a desolate place called Bodie, east of the Sierras and off Highway 395 south of Bridgeport. Bodie was just plain *tough*, no question about it. The story goes that when a Nevada family decided to move to Bodie, a young girl in the family murmured fearfully: "Goodbye, God. We're going to Bodie." Bodie residents violently objected to the story, calling it nothing but a libel, insisted that the girl really said: "Good! By God, we're going to Bodie!" With about 100 of its old structures still standing surprisingly erect, Bodie is now a state historical park, like Columbia, but unlike Columbia,

Bodie has not been reconstructed; the state has allowed Bodie to be its ghostly self. Another off-trail gold town worth visiting is Weaverville on Highway 299 between Redding and Arcata. Weaverville has a special attraction for those who are interested in the somber path of the Chinese through the gold fields; a restored joss house is a highlight.

* * *

Law enforcement sometimes suffered in early California because proper facilities weren't available. The struggling town of Bishop, for instance, lacked a jail, although it had a great need for one. Officers solved the problem — or so they thought — by shackling prisoners to the wheels of freight wagons. Running out of wagons, they handcuffed a prisoner after wrapping his arms around a small tree. Next morning, he was gone. As near as the lawmen could tell, the prisoner had clambered up the tree until it bent over, then dropped to the ground. Not only did Bishop lose the prisoner, but the handcuffs, too.

* * *

In many gold mines, mules were used to pull ore cars. Since it was a nuisance to transport the animals up and down the shafts, some mules spent their entire lives underground! This practice continued until modern times. As late as 1940, a mule named Mae West (she had a lazy way of moving and a plump posterior) was brought to the surface and retired with honors in Alleghany after spending much of her life in the depths. Mae West became a town character, wandering the streets, calling regularly at stores and homes for carrots and apples, probably convinced that she had ascended to heaven.

* * *

The Mother Lode today is anything but the rip-roaring place it was when gold was king and nothing was cheap but life, but on a summer evening in a storied place like Sonora, it's not hard to hear echoes of the drunken shouts of roistering '49ers and the wild strumming of guitars in fandango halls, as the old ones again wander down the halls of history.

This exceptional view of a hardrock mine at Ludlow in the Mojave Desert shows clearly that gold mining could be hard, dangerous work. Note men working at upper right.

THE HIGHWAYMEN COME GALLOPING

Inevitably, given human nature, there were sly, soft-handed souls in the gold fields who recoiled from the notion of staking a claim and bending their backs. To these unmuscular types, it seemed wiser to let others grub for gold, then take it from them, by one sneaky means or another.

It might be said that the sly ones mined the miners.

But once the metal had been mined or filched, it had to be transported to a place where it could be banked or invested; San Francisco was the usual destination and a stagecoach was the usual vehicle.

As soon as Wells Fargo began to ship gold in volume, a new opportunity for gainful employment opened up along the dark and lonely roads travelled by the rugged Concord coaches.

A few unprincipled and reckless individuals were bound to see and snatch the golden opportunity; they would mine those sly ones who had already mined the miners.

* * *

If Robin Hood hadn't existed, man would have had to invent him.

Hero hunger was evident in early California, too, and from it grew a legend of a robber of the mountains, abused and embittered in his youth, who finally rose in wrath, mounted a sleek black horse, flashed angry lightning from his eyes, then rode forth to plunder the rich and avenge the poor.

But in California, they didn't call him Robin Hood; they called him "Joaquin."

A Mexican name, Joaquin. In time, there were at least five of them: Joaquin Carrillo, Joaquin Valenzuela, Joaquin Ocomorenia, Joaquin Botelleras, Joaquin Murieta.

Mexican names, all of them, borne by a mostly mythical hero who carried the romantic banner of resistance against the swarming Anglo invaders.

Proud Mexicans who had lived in California when it was a province of Spain, then of independent Mexico, weren't eager to step aside when the land was swallowed up by the United States of America. Mexicans in California, unlike the Chinese, refused to accept the status of foreigner. They did not care to take the low posture and burrow through the tailings as the Chinese did so peacefully and profitably.

The Gold Rush

And so it happened that Mexicans became the primary targets of Anglos in the gold fields. So it was that Joaquin, the Mexican Robin Hood, became the scourge of the gold roads. Americans had taken over the mines; it seemed only fair that Mexicans should exact a toll on the roads leading down from the mines.

THE HEAD IN THE JAR

May, 1853 — Spurred by the $1000 reward offered by Governor Bigler for any Joaquin captured or killed, a Texas transplant named Harry Love rode out with a company of 20 armed men that he liked to call "rangers." They rode and they rode and they rode, through the mountains and through the valleys and through the foothills.

They found no suitable Joaquin.

On July 25, as their enlistment was about to run out, they encountered some Mexicans sitting on the ground around a fire; their horses were some distance away. An argument sparked and itchy fingers triggered guns. Two Mexicans died at the scene, including Three-Fingered Jack Garcia, a long-sought robber and murderer; another was hanged by a mob after having been delivered to Mariposa by the rangers.

A pistol ball had messed up Garcia's head so badly that there was not much point in turning it in for the reward; however, his three-fingered hand was cut off and preserved.

The other dead man had claimed to be the band's leader, although he had not announced his name. *Joaquin?* It was good enough for Harry Love, who ordered the man's head cut off and preserved in a jar of alcohol. The posse then rode toward Sacramento to present the head and hand and collect the governor's reward.

Apparently there was no argument about the identity of the original owner of the pickled head. The reward was paid and Love's rangers also collected 90 days' wages.

The head then went on display as that of the one, the only, the

➤

This dramatic scene might very well be the only picture ever taken during an actual stage holdup in California. The camera was held by Agnes Wilkinson of Philadelphia, a passenger on this Yosemite stage in 1907. Miss Wilkinson said the highwayman had "great blue eyes and a lovely voice" and posed only after carefully arranging his mask and linen duster.

original Joaquin Murieta. Almost immediately newspapers began to scoff and ugly rumors flew. Said the San Francisco *Alta:*

"It affords amusement to our citizens to read the various accounts of the capture and decapitation of the 'notorious Joaquin Murieta.' The humbug is so transparent that it is surprising any sensible person can be imposed upon by the statements of the affair which have appeared in the prints ... It is too well known that Joaquin Murieta was not the person killed by Captain Harry Love's party at the Panoche Pass. The head recently exhibited in Stockton bears no resemblance to that individual, and this is positively asserted by those who have seen the real Murieta and the spurious head."

A long-playing controversy had begun to spin.

* * *

The grisly object called the head of Joaquin Murieta was displayed for years thereafter in museums, along with Garcia's hand. The clouded question of identity became positively murky when one of the first posters advertising the exhibition spelled the name "Muriatta."

It remained for a part-Cherokee newspaperman who wrote under the name of "Yellow Bird" to turn Joaquin Murieta into California folklore. In 1854, John Rollin Ridge (Yellow Bird) wrote and published a book in San Francisco called *The Life and Adventures of Joaquin Murieta, Celebrated California Bandit.*

An eager reading public took it as fact, but Ridge unquestionably had stirred a large dollop of fiction into his romantic brew. He knew that the public wanted a Robin Hood, so he created one, a handsome young man of impeccable reputation who took the outlaw road only after American miners had raped his beautiful wife, Rosita, as Joaquin watched; hanged his brother on a false charge, then whipped Joaquin himself after first roping him to a tree.

This explained to everyone's satisfaction how Joaquin could remain pure in heart and still swear "an oath of the most awful solemnity, that his soul should nevermore know peace *until his hands were dyed deep in the blood of his enemies!"*

The book was reprinted in several languages, turned into poetry and plays and finally written as "biography" by Walter Noble Burns in 1932; he called his book *The Robin Hood of Eldorado.*

With a title like that, how could it miss?

Joaquin Murieta had become — and still remains — a blazing

figure of folklore in the annals of California. The known facts of his life are few but no matter; Californians for over a century have taken Joaquin to their hero-worshipping hearts and no doubt will continue to do so. After all, Robin Hoods don't burst upon the scene every day.

Joaquin!

Leaping gracefully aboard his coal-black stallion, his dark eyes flashing, storming through the night to rob the rich in order to give to the poor, striking with his lightning knife at injustice wherever he chanced upon it, dashing through the canyons of California with his loyal followers thundering after on an errand of heavenly vengeance...

So it isn't history, if history is only dry fact. Californians desperately wanted to believe that Joaquin rode the lonely night trails through the shadowed canyons, so Joaquin rode.

It's quite possible that he always will.

GOLD FROM THE GRINGOS

The hard treatment suffered by Mexicans in California during the so-called rancho period may well have accounted for the high incidence of Spanish names among the outlaws of the day.

Forced by Americans to settle for the leavings, brutalized, cheated, not allowed the protection of gringo law, a fair number of Mexicans of an angry nature turned to violence and lawlessness.

Juan Soto, Tiburcio Vasquez, Jesus Tejada, Procopio, Narrato Ponce (a native of Chile, actually, not a Mexican), Eduardo Gallego, Pancho Ruiz, Bartolo Sepulveda — all cut wide swaths through the poorly-policed parts of early California. A notable villain of southern California was a certain Salomon Pico, who had a quaint habit of cutting the ears off his gringo victims, then stringing them so they could be hung from his saddle and referring to them as "my pearls."

When miners working their claims found they were losing more to roaming thieves than they could bear, they reacted as one might expect from such simple, rough-hewn men — they formed lynch parties and carefully chose their guests of honor.

Knowing a bad thing when they saw it, the thieves rode out of gold country into the San Joaquin Valley and the worndown mountains of the Coast Range; it was in the low coastal mountains that

Black Bart was a dapper gent with only two bad habits.

the terrible Vasquez made his last stand.

THE MAN IN THE WHITE HAT

Harry N. Morse was a '49er at age 15. He failed to get rich as a miner, saw the light and went down to Oakland, where he worked as a butcher boy, then as an expressman. At age 28, he was elected sheriff of Alameda County and served for the following 14 years.

California outlaws who wanted to continue in their chosen line of work would have been wise to stuff the ballot boxes, or more appropriately, steal them, because young Harry Morse, indefatigably riding the lonely canyons, was to be their nemesis.

It was Morse who finally caught Soto and Black Bart; it was Morse who laid the groundwork for the capture of Vasquez. In shootout after shootout, Morse miraculously survived and outlaws surrendered . . . or died.

It was Morse, working tirelessly as sheriff of Alameda County and as a special operative of J. B. Hume, Wells Fargo's ace detective, who sent the California highwaymen to prison or to the gallows; it was Harry Morse, as much as any other person, who convinced Californians that their dusty roads were safe at last.

BLACK BART, CRIMINAL POET

Trailed by twin ribbons of July dust, the Wells Fargo stagecoach left Quincy for Oroville and rolled through Sierra foothills warmed by a strong morning sun. The driver was relaxed, happy in his work. And why not?

The treasure box held only $378, plus a diamond ring said to be worth a mere $200 and a silver watch. Nothing there to attract trouble, surely.

Besides, almost a year had passed since Black Bart had stopped a stage. There had been several robberies in late 1877 and early 1878, but none had looked like a Black Bart job; the bandits hadn't worn the flour sack with cutout eyeholes, nor the linen duster; nor had they left original poetry at the scene of the crime; nor had they ordered in deep, distinctive tones:

"Throw down the box!"

But on this special morning, as the stage approached a slow and difficult turn in a spectacular canyon of the Feather River, Black

Bart struck again.

"*Throw down the box!*" ordered the deep voice from the flour sack worn on the head of the man at the side of the road.

Backing up the order was a double-barreled shotgun aimed at the suddenly nervous stomach of the driver.

Wells Fargo expected loyalty and bravery from its employees, but did not ask that either be carried to the point of suicide; salaries weren't that high. The box was thrown down.

Then, as the shotgun waggled, the driver whipped his horses away from the tense place.

What else could a sane man do, plainly confronted by none other than Black Bart, scourge of the Sierras?

A few hours later, a posse member at the scene of the crime picked up a piece of paper upon which was scrawled this snatch of doggerel:

> "Here I lay me down to sleep
> To wait the coming morrow,
> Perhaps success, perhaps defeat,
> And everlasting sorrow.
> Let come what will I'll try it on,
> My condition can't be worse;
> And if there's money in that box
> 'Tis munny in my purse!
>   Black Bart, The PO8"

A California newspaperman, who perhaps could take his poetry or leave it, soon wrote that Black Bart, by leaving his verse on the road, had only added insult to injury.

It is likely that no more inoffensive man than Black Bart ever robbed a stage.

There are those relentless souls who insist that he worked off his meanness by writing poetry, then signing it "PO8." True, only a vicious punster would commit such an act; a person who would take such a step into outer darkness could rob Wells Fargo a thousand times and not lose an hour's sleep.

Otherwise, though, an inoffensive man. There is no record of Bart's ever firing his ominous shotgun at a human being; maybe the double-barreled weapon wasn't even loaded. He may have considered his pen mightier than his blunderbuss.

It was Bart's habit to walk to the scene of his next robbery, then camp nearby until the stage loomed out of the dust. He apparently

The Gold Rush

whiled away the hours by perpetrating poetry, often inscribing each line in a different syle of handwriting. He may have been hedging his bets; a critic who couldn't give him his due as a poet might be willing to admire his penmanship.

It is ironic that California's most expert stage robber, the disappearing dervish who drew blood from Wells Fargo no less than 28 times between 1875 and 1883, was finally snared by a bit of written evidence.

A mere laundry mark on a handkerchief...

BART COMES A CROPPER

Sheriff Ben Thorn of Calaveras County was a careful, calculating man.

Some greedy citizen had robbed the stage to Copperopolis on the cold, clear day of November 3, 1883, and it was Thorn's job to catch the culprit.

At the scene of the skullduggery, he picked up a fair amount of litter: a belt, a magnifying glass, field glasses, a handkerchief full of buckshot, three linen cuffs and a couple of flour sacks.

Apparently it had been a bad day for Bart. Among other inconveniences, he had been shot at four times, at a minimum; often enough, at any rate, to cause even an intrepid highwayman to scatter a fair amount of incriminating debris over the landscape as he fled.

Sheriff Thorn methodically examined the handkerchief and made note of small letters on it: "F.X.O.7."

The identifying mark of a laundry? Worth looking into, maybe.

*   *   *

Said Harry Morse, special operative for J. B. Hume of Wells Fargo:

"After diligent search I was rewarded by finding the identical mark on the books of a laundry agency, Mr. Ware, 316 Bush Street (San Francisco). The handkerchief had been left there three times... I found on inquiry that the washing belonged to one C. E. Bolton."

Soon Mr. Ware was describing C. E. Bolton in detail. He lived, said Ware, in a small hotel, Webb House, at 37 Second Street, Room 40.

Black Bart, the man of letters, had been undone by another man of letters who held in his innocent hand a laundry stamp.

Said Morse to the newspapers:

"He was elegantly dressed, carrying a little cane. He wore a natty little derby hat, a diamond pin, a large diamond ring on his little finger, and a heavy gold watch and chain. He was about five feet, eight inches, in height, straight as an arrow, broad-shouldered, with deep-sunken bright blue eyes, high cheekbones and a large handsome gray moustache and imperial; the rest shaven clean. One would have taken him for a gentleman who had made a fortune and was enjoying it. He looked anything but a robber."

His debt to society paid, Black Bart left San Quentin prison on January 21, 1888. He talked to newspaper reporters and vowed to go straight. (Presumably he was talking about stage robbing, not PO-8-try.)

Then Charles E. Boles, alias C. E. Bolton, alias Black Bart, faded from the scene.

In the months immediately following Bart's release, a few stages were robbed in California. Inevitably Black Bart was mentioned. These rumors had to be balanced against reports from South America that Black Bart was there, all of a sudden, and had pulled off a peccadillo or two.

No one could prove any of this, though, and no one again laid a legal finger on Black Bart. Whereupon PO8 disappeared from California history.

California's gain was literature's loss.

THE HUMPTY-DUMPTY ROAD AGENT

There was still another sort of highwayman in California — the loser. One of them, in fact, has to be considered a world's all-time champion loser, a determined but misguided soul who tried mightily to gallop into criminal history aboard a snorting charger but who concluded his career as a rump-sprung pedestrian in Folsom prison.

This was the road agent ridiculous: Dick Fellows.

Dick had *most* of the qualifications of a successful highwayman; he was smart and greedy and sneaky. He could talk the bark off a tree and the birds off the limbs. What's more, he wanted to be a successful brigand so badly he could taste it.

It wasn't just gold that Dick Fellows wanted, though; like Black Bart, he yearned for an image as well. (History is littered with the broken carcasses of men who have stumbled over the same obstacle.)

Unfortunately for Dick, the image established by Joaquin, Vasquez and their ilk involved a four-footed beast called "horse" and right there is where Dirty Dick Fellows came a cropper. When Dick was born, surely horses around the world nickered and neighed and marked him for a patsy, a load to be unloaded.

And this is how the story goes . . .

* * *

A young man named Dick Fellows first entered San Quentin prison as a non-paying guest on January 31, 1870. During late '69, he had committed several social blunders, first holding up a lone traveller near Los Angeles, then trying without success to rob a stage at the outskirts of Santa Barbara. The prison register marked him as a Kentucky native, 24 years old, with no prior record of criminal activity.

Rumor had it that he had been graduated from Harvard. True or not, he soon had a job in the prison library and almost as soon, he had organized a Bible class among the inmates. In time Dick Fellows was recognized as the leader of the religious element in the prison. This is true . . .

Then, with less than half of his sentence served, saintly Dick was pardoned and released.

How could anyone argue against the complete conversion to rectitude of a man who before leaving San Quentin held a prayer service for those few cynical convicts who doubted his sincerity?

CASH AT CALIENTE

The wild little railhead town of Caliente just north of the Tehachapi Mountains drew Dick Fellows in early December, 1875. Did Dick know about the $240,000 gold coin shipment which Wells Fargo intended to transfer from train to stage at Caliente for the trans-mountain trip to Los Angeles on December 4? Was Dick in Caliente for a prayer meeting? Or was Dick, for once in his life, just plain lucky? The record is unclear.

At any rate, Dick watched wide-eyed as three express boxes were carefully transferred from train to stage. Even more interesting was Dick's observation that the shotgun messenger was none other than J. B. Hume, ace Wells Fargo detective.

Three heavy express boxes? And J. B. Hume?

It was a situation designed to make a larcenous heart beat faster. Dick held a hurried conference with an ugly friend and made a plan: He would rent a horse at the livery stable, ride out to meet his friend about a mile from town, then together they would gallop over hill and dale to intercept the stage at a private place in the mountains. It was a simple, straightforward plan which might have worked except for one thing — Dick forgot to let the horse in on it.

At the appointed moment, Dick mounted the horse and rode sedately out of town toward the meeting with his companion in crime.

Half an hour later, the riderless horse trotted back into Caliente. Dick lay unconscious in the road, where he had landed on his head.

* * *

Holding his aching skull, Dick straggled back toward town. Now he faced only unpleasant prospects and had to sort them out with a buzzing brain. His partner wouldn't rob the stage alone; when Dick failed to show at the rendezvous, the ugly one would assume that the law had gotten wind of the scheme and had snatched Dick. Either that . . . or Dick had lost his nerve.

Dick had his pride to think of. Dick Fellows a coward? It would never do to have that get around. He would have to tell the truth; a dumb animal had bested him.

During the afternoon in town, Dick brooded. Then an idea flickered through his tortured mind and he fastened onto it with delight. Of course! There was only one way to prove his nerve and his horsemanship in one fell swoop. After all, that morning southbound stage wasn't the only stage in the world.

There was a northbound stage due in Caliente from Los Angeles between eight and nine o'clock that very evening.

What he would do, Dick Fellows feverishly vowed, was *rob that stage from the back of a horse.*

SUCCESS OF SORTS

Perhaps hoping to change his luck, Dick didn't rent a horse this time; he stole one, brazenly untied it from the rail in front of Sisson & Wallace's store and rode off.

What's more, he stayed *on* the horse until he met the stage half a

Dick Fellows, dismounted, showed plenty of poise.

mile from town, drew his pistol, stopped the stage, got the treasure box on demand and watched in triumph as the plundered vehicle rolled dustily toward Caliente.

Now that was the way to rob a stage, murmured Dick. If only his ugly friend could have seen it!

But as was usually the case with Dick, his moment of triumph was short-lived. He had left Caliente in such a hurry that he had forgotten that one didn't open a Wells Fargo treasure box with a fingernail; an ax was the normal tool.

Now time was of the essence. The stage would be in town soon and the alarm would sound. There was nothing for Dick to do but hoist the heavy box aboard the horse and ride off with it. Which he did...

Moments later, Dick was sprawled in the road again with the box in his lap and his erstwhile mount headed for home on a dead run.

So there was Dick, afoot again, with the worst kind of incriminating evidence in his possession and the law rapidly closing in. Showing true grit, Dick shouldered the box and lunged off through the darkness toward the half-built tunnels which would carry the railroad across the Tehachapis to Los Angeles.

Whereupon he stumbled over an eight-foot dropoff, breaking his left leg above the ankle and smashing the instep of his left foot when the box landed on it.

The end? Not for Dick Fellows, a man among men, possessed of all the manly virtues except an understanding of horses.

ONE GOOD HORSE DESERVES ANOTHER

Dragging his shattered leg behind him, pushing the Wells Fargo box ahead of him, Dick made his way for several painful hours to a camp of Chinese railroad workers, where he commandeered an ax and finally broke open that infernal box.

Eighteen hundred dollars went into Dick's pockets then and he must have wondered if it would be enough to pay his medical bills.

After hiding out during the following day, Dick Fellows did an incredible thing: He went to a farm owned by a man named Fountain and stole a *horse*.

A horse just made for Dick, one which happened to wear a mule shoe, making tracking easy. A few days later, J. B. Hume of Wells Fargo arrested Dick Fellows in Bakersfield. A simple-minded nag had done Dick in again.

Six months in the county hospital put Dick back on his feet, although he needed the assistance of the crutches the county had kindly supplied him. He left the hospital for the jail, where he was to await transportation to San Quentin. Bakersfield, only recently picked as the seat of Kern County, hadn't had time to build a proper bastille; Dick was placed in a temporary jail made from planks.

Crutches and all, Dick soon burrowed out through the floor, spent 48 hours hiding in the Kern River swamps, then sought out a ranch and—believe it or not—*stole a horse.*

The Gold Rush

The animal wasn't saddled, so Dick led it to a nearby farm, tied it to a corral post and went rummaging in the barn for a saddle. He found one, staggered out of the barn under his load of saddle and crutches and frightened the horse out of a year's growth. The horse reared up, broke his tie and raced for home, leaving Dick afoot again and fair game for the posses which soon captured him and sent him to San Quentin for the second time.

Chances are excellent that he didn't travel to prison by horse. This is evident from the fact that on June 16, he *arrived* and the big doors closed behind him.

IS THERE NO END TO THE HORSES?

Five years later, Dick Fellows went free, stayed honest (by his standards) for a couple of months, then apparently slipped back into his charitable habit of lightening the loads of stages. San Luis Obispo, Soledad, Santa Cruz, the Santa Clara Valley—he ranged far and wide.

Professional lawmen and posses sniffed hard along his trail. Finally a certain Constable Burke of Santa Clara, diligent but not overly bright, made the capture in a barn near Mayfield.

With Dick in handcuffs, the smug constable and his quarry got off the train in San Jose, where Burke planned to turn over his famous prisoner to Capt. Charles Aull of Wells Fargo.

As a parting gesture, Dick offered to buy the constable a drink. Benumbed by Dick's flattery, Burke accepted the offer. As so often happens, one drink followed another, making it possible for Dick, when they emerged from the saloon, to hammer down with his handcuffs on Burke's neck.

Then Dick was gone again, swallowed by the dark . . .

Six days later, a certain Doctor Gunckel who lived a few miles out of San Jose had occasion to go to his barn and move a bale of hay.

Behind the bale was a bearded stranger who had just finished a meal made up of canned fruit from the doctor's cellar and a half bottle of the doctor's very expensive imported London stout.

It was Dick Fellows, naturally. Within minutes, Dick had talked himself out of still another trap. Gone again . . .

But now the bloodhounds of the law and Wells Fargo were in full cry. Early on the following evening, up a quiet canyon in the Coast Range, two officers named Haskell and Edson investigated a lighted cabin window. Dick Fellows sat at the table, waiting for his host to serve supper.

And so, back to San Jose to jail, with three shifts of wide awake guards watching their slippery prisoner, along with 700 citizens of the town who would have been satisfied with just a glimpse of the vaunted stage robber.

It seemed that they were holding Dick for the sheriff of Santa Barbara, who wanted to return the bandit to face—what else?—a robbery charge. Dick was duly taken to Santa Barbara and was sentenced to Folsom prison for as long as he cared to live. End of story? Not quite...

* * *

Dick had talked his way out of many a sticky situation and purely charmed his way out of others; he frequently showed inventiveness and fortitude, to say nothing of physical stamina that made normal men look puny. J. B. Hume knew this; Constable Burke knew this; Dr. Gunckel knew this.

Apparently Santa Barbara officials didn't know this. Dick, after all, had made his reputation in the northern counties.

So, on April 2, 1882, just as they were about to take Dick from Santa Barbara to Folsom, the road agent leaped off a shelf in his cell, landed on his jailer's back and before you could say "will-o'-the-wisp," was gone again...

LOCO HORSE, LOCO RIDER

It so happened—it was *inevitable,* really—that a horse had been staked in a pasture two blocks from the Santa Barbara jail at this special point in time.

It was also inevitable that this particular horse had chomped on loco weed a week before and was still nervous about its psychedelic experience.

It was inevitable, too, that an escaped prisoner named Dick Fellows should leap on that horse and immediately insist that the confused beast race to freedom with a horse-loving human frantically clutching at his neck.

It didn't work, of course; it was against nature.

In the public square of Santa Barbara on that balmy April morning, Dick Fellows landed hard in the dust at a point marked "X", the precise place at which a loco horse had finally sounded a closing

THUMP to his career of crime.

Captured, escorted to Folsom under heavy guard, Dick wrote one final letter, to the editor of the *Santa Barbara Press,* and it is a measure of the man that he did not blame horses in general or any particular horse for his disaster:

"Dear Sir: I have just noticed your article in reference to my recent attempt at escape and also your editorial in regard to my past career entitled 'It Don't Pay.' After thanking you for your kindly notices, I have to say that both are in the main correct, and I most heartily concur in what you have to say in the last named. I would add only the same may be said of any unlawful calling. My unfortunate experience has thrown me into the society of thousands of lawbreakers in all walks of life, and in every instance the result is the same sad story, 'It Don't Pay,' in any sense. I learn that the boat will leave here in a few minutes, and I bid you and the people of Santa Barbara good-bye.

DICK FELLOWS"

Less than a year later, Dick Fellows was teaching at Folsom. His subject: "Moral Instruction."

Next semester: "Horsemanship."

SITES TO SEE

WELLS FARGO BANK HISTORY ROOM, downtown San Francisco. *(Now the bank thinks Black Bart was a humorous fellow.)*

RANCHO MISSION SAN DIEGO DE ALCALA. Home rancho of the San Diego mission, originally it was the second largest in the county, embracing 58,875 acres. In 1845 the rancho was sold to Santiago Arguello. Now it is the site of the city of San Diego.

Chapter Six *

Land Transportation
THE HARUM-SCARUM WHIRLIGIG

It was the singing wire, that earlier marvel of the age, which would tell the story to a breathless nation at the instant of its happening.

The Omaha, Nebraska, office of the Western Union Telegraph Company was the starting point of the special circuit. In early afternoon of May 10, 1869, keys began to click urgently in Western Union offices around the country; inquiries began to flood into Omaha.

Finally Omaha tapped out testily:

TO EVERYBODY: KEEP QUIET. WHEN THE LAST SPIKE IS DRIVEN AT PROMONTORY POINT WE WILL SAY 'DONE.' DON'T BREAK THE CIRCUIT BUT WATCH FOR THE SIGNALS OF THE BLOWS OF THE HAMMER.

Then, at 12:27 p.m., a message came in from Promontory Point, Utah, 2400 miles west of the nation's capital:

ALMOST READY. HATS OFF: PRAYER IS BEING OFFERED.

A silence followed, then Promontory signalled:

WE HAVE GOT DONE PRAYING. THE SPIKE IS ABOUT TO BE PRESENTED.

Chicago quickly came on the line:

WE UNDERSTAND. ALL ARE READY IN THE EAST.

From Promontory Point:

ALL READY NOW, THE SPIKE WILL SOON BE DRIVEN. THE SIGNAL WILL BE THREE DOTS FOR THE COMMENCEMENT OF THE BLOWS.

This remarkable monument in Old Sacramento suits its towering subject, Theodore Judah, who promoted and surveyed the first transcontinental railroad out of California.

After an aching moment of silence, three dots vibrated from a barren place in Utah to Washington, D.C.

At 12:47 p.m., Promontory Point signalled DONE!

The twin ribbons of iron were connected; the United States of America had itself a nation-spanning railroad.

One man above all others should have stood proudly under the bright Promontory sun on that day in early May, shaking hands and quaffing champagne and perhaps even laughing a little, although he was not much given to laughing.

But the young man couldn't make it for the best of reasons. Crazy Judah was dead.

* * *

In an era when a jet plane can thrust from coast to coast in a few hours, the place of the slow-going railroad in the transportation picture may seem a bit fuzzy.

But go back a century (plus a decade or two) and try this on for perspective:

A wagon train moving west did well to average 12 miles a day. (Oxen were favored as draft animals and oxen don't walk; they plod.)

A modern airplane flashes over more ground in an hour than a wagon train covered in *two months*. It's true that the wagon train passengers could pick wildflowers along the way, which is frowned upon if you travel by jet (ask the stewardess) but some of those wagon train folks near the end of the trail would gladly have traded a few irises for 600 miles an hour.

In an ordinary car on a modern freeway, one can cover comfortably as much ground in an hour as a wagon train jounced over in a week.

In terms of time expended in travel, the locomotive puffing along at 20 miles an hour, day and night, was as breathtaking in the 1870s as jet travel is in the 1970s.

Not everybody was an immediate convert, of course, just as today there are a few hardcases among us who can't be forced aboard a jet plane with a pitchfork.

> *Travel by stagecoach had little in common with lolling in luxury and some companies were honest about it, as in these helpful hints to tourists offered by a Nebraska newspaper.*

Tips for Stagecoach Travelers

"The best seat inside a stage is the one next to the driver. Even if you have a tendency to seasickness when riding backwards—you'll get over it and will get less jolts and jostling. Don't let any 'sly elph' trade you his mid-seat.

In cold weather don't ride with tight-fitting boots, shoes, or gloves. When the driver asks you to get off and walk do so without grumbling, he won't request it unless absolutely necessary. If the team runs away—sit still and take your chances. If you jump, nine out of ten times you will get hurt.

In very cold weather abstain entirely from liquer when on the road; because you will freeze twice as quickly when under its influence. Don't growl at the food received at the station; stage companies generally provide the best they can get.

Don't keep the stage waiting. Don't smoke a strong pipe inside the coach—spit on the leeward side. If you have anything to drink in a bottle pass it around. Procure your stimulants before starting as "ranch" (Stage Depot) whiskey is not "nectar."

Don't swear or lop over neighbors when sleeping. Take small change to pay expenses. Never shoot on the road as the noise might frighten the horses. Don't discuss politics or religion. Don't point out where murders have been committed especially if there are women passengers.

Don't lag at the wash basin. Don't grease your hair, because travel is dusty. Don't imagine for a moment that you are going on a picnic. Expect annoyances, discomfort, and some hardship."

Reprinted from the Omaha Herald, October 3, 1877

In 1830, an Indiana editor wrote about railroads:

"I see what will be the effect of it: that it will set the whole world a gadding. Twenty miles an hour, sir!—Why you will not be able to keep an apprentice boy at his work! Every Saturday evening he must have a trip to Ohio to spend a Sunday with his sweetheart . . . There will be barrels of pork, cargoes of flour, chaldrons of coal, and even lead and whiskey, and such like sober things that have always been used to slow traveling—whisking away like a skyrocket . . . Upon the whole, sir, it is a pestilential, topsy-turvy, harum-scarum whirligig. Give me the old, solemn, straightforward regular Dutch canal—three miles an hour for expresses . . . with a yoke of oxen for heavy loads. I go for beasts of burden. It is more formative and scriptural, and suits a moral and religious people better. None of your hop, skip and jump whimsies for me."

* * *

What about the stagecoach, you say? The "comfortable Concord," sprung with leather thoroughbraces, staple of every Western movie and television show? What about those mandatory scenes where the passengers from Abilene, male and female, young and old, step down energetically, ready for fight or frolic?

In reality, some of the less rubbery individuals had to be lifted off emitting little yelps.

Here's the truth, as delivered by a certain Therese Yelverton, an early Californian:

"To ride behind four well-conditioned horses would seem, in the abstract, the most pleasurable way of travelling through a beautiful country. *But practically this ride is one of the worst tortures that can be inflicted upon persons guilty of no crime recognizable by law as punishable.* This coach is so constructed, that at every pebble as large as a nut, or hole to accomodate a taw, it rolls and pitches worse than a narrow screw-steamer in a chopping sea. You are jigged, and tossed, and bounced up to the ceiling, tumbled on the floor, wedged against the window, and scattered generally in all directions; churned up in a corner, or sent sprawling into your neighbors on the middle seat and scratch your nose against a watch-chain, or a lady's shawl pin . . . What canned lobsters must feel is easy to be realized by mortals travelling per stage on a hot dusty day in California."

Railroads, anybody?

MOJAVE GHOSTS

It happened at a truck stop in the little desert town of Mojave one night in 1965.

The driver, who happened to be from Oregon, jumped down, stretched and approached the attendant pumping diesel fuel into the highway monster.

"Say," asked the driver carefully, "I don't suppose there'd be such a thing as a wild camel in these parts..."

The attendant glanced up. "A *what?*"

The driver bravely repeated, "Camel."

"About 200, they say."

"Aw, come on."

"It's a fact," the attendant said. "Miners packed ore out with 'em years ago. When the mines shut down, they turned 'em loose. Been makin' out pretty good, them camels."

The driver, immensely relieved, exhaled deeply. "A crippled cow, that's what I thought it was. So I stopped and threw a light on it. Now ain't that somethin'? A *camel.*"

The incident at Mojave in 1965 is only one of many reported over the years. But if several hundred camels are still roaming the California desert, one wonders why no photographer in recent years seems to have caught one in his viewfinder. After all, a full-grown camel is a towering beast, not likely to succeed in hiding behind the nearest bush.

There remains some doubt as to whether there still are camels in the Mojave. There is no doubt whatsoever that once there were.

The names most closely connected with the Great American Camel Experiment were Lt. Edward F. Beale, Hadji Ali and Jefferson Davis. There is no evidence that Jefferson Davis, one-time president of the Confederacy, advanced his political career by advocating in Congress the use of camels in the West. But his influence and the tireless salesmanship of Beale, a young army officer, caused the episode to become a peculiar part of history.

One of the ugliest beasts that ever lived, a camel has virtues not visible to the naked eye. On the same amount of water, a camel can cover about twice as much ground four times as fast as a mule. Furthermore, a camel can perform this feat on a diet of dry, bitter forage that would cause a mule to burn his meal ticket.

In 1857, under the nervous sponsorship of the U.S. government, the first batch of camels was imported from Asia Minor and based in

Texas. (Strictly speaking, they weren't camels, but *dromedaries*. A camel by any other name smells as foul.) The government wisely took the precaution of importing a few Arabic camel drivers, too, including Hadji Ali, whose name quickly was Americanized to "Hi Jolly." (A monument honoring Hi Jolly stands today along Interstate 10 near Quartzite, Arizona.)

Lieutenant Beale successfully shepherded the first batch of camels from Texas to Los Angeles. They were used occasionally to haul mail in southern California and Beale broke a pair of them to haul a buckboard from his Fort Tejon ranch about 40 miles south of Bakersfield into Los Angeles.

Camels turned out to be much like Siamese cats; you have to love them to put up with them. As has been mentioned, camels have this noxious odor. They also have generally nasty dispositions; on occasion, they even bite. In addition, they frighten the harness off any other animal they encounter, a trait that can be embarrassing on a narrow mountain trail, of which the frontier West had a harrowing number.

And so finally the army's emigrant camels were auctioned off at Benicia Arsenal and most of them wound up in Nevada hauling supplies into Carson Valley.

It seems that the new owners of the camels tried to resell them but found few buyers, so they turned the lanky beasts loose to shift for themselves in the sandy wastes of the Southwest, thus ending the most bizarre episode in the history of California transportation.

Are there still wild camels roaming the Mojave?

Truckers who drive through the desert at night will look you straight in the eye and say there are. Would a truck driver lie?

Given more time for Americans (both human and animal) to get used to them, the camels might have made it. But time was running out; the railroads were coming on like distant thunder. Already their advocates were prowling the halls of the U.S. Congress, pleading, cajoling, threatening, mentioning great mounds of money piling up and about to slide into the pockets of those who put the first rails through to the Pacific.

A strong double ribbon of iron connecting the Atlantic Ocean of Europe and the Pacific Ocean of the Orient, with a host of landbound American middlemen in between slicing off their pounds of flesh as the riches clicked along the rails from East to West and back again ...

Once the picture had been painted in all its tantalizing details, there was no stopping the railroads.

Land Transportation

But first there had to be a dreamer.

THE MAN CALLED CRAZY

On a winter day in 1860, a young man named Theodore D. Judah pointed out the window of his Sacramento hotel suite and said to Anna, his wife:

"If you want to see the first work done on the Pacific Railroad, look out your bedroom this afternoon . . ."

True to his promise, Judah began his survey line in the street that afternoon. It was easy, that afternoon, but to the east lay the awesome ramparts of the Sierra Nevada and if there was to be a Pacific railroad, it would have to grunt over or smash through those fearsome mountains.

Which is why the citizens of Sacramento, tired of this young man's endless harangues, began to call him "Crazy Judah." The very idea . . . a railroad from East to West across mountains that even a mule couldn't traverse in winter. Ridiculous!

The Civil War general, William Tecumseh Sherman, snorted: "A railroad to the Pacific? I would hate to buy a ticket on it for my grandchildren!"

Born in Connecticut in 1826, Judah studied engineering, then, when little more than 20 years old, helped build several Eastern railroads and a portion of the Erie Canal. At 22, he helped to plan and build the Niagara Gorge Railroad. Ambitious and in demand, Judah moved his young bride 20 times during the first six years of their marriage.

Then, when Judah was 27, a group of Californians came east in search of a man to lay out a railroad from Sacramento into the gold country.

Judah was recommended, but Judah was not interested.

Apparently the young man saw the California operation as just another little railroad job and there were plenty of those in the East. But the California delegation seemed to know their man as a dreamer of no small dreams. The possibility was mentioned that their railroad needn't stop in the foothills; why couldn't it leap right over the mountains? And once the rails had crossed the mountains, what stood in the way of a line clean across the country?

What, indeed?

Judah sent his wife a wire: "Be home tonight; we sail for California April second."

* * *

In short order, the fast-moving Judah had surveyed, graded and laid rails for the first railroad in California, from Sacramento to Folsom in the foothills.

That job done, he accepted a commission to survey a wagon road across the Sierra Nevada. One suspects that Judah's full attention wasn't given to the wagon road because he returned to Sacramento bubbling over about a pass he had discovered— a *railroad* pass!

But at the time, alas, no one shared his dream.

He talked and wrote and travelled until he was groggy; his mighty effort got him nowhere.

Finally, in September of 1859, he was able to attract a sizable gathering to San Francisco's largest assembly hall for a meeting of something called the "Pacific Railroad Convention."

Judah probably put up the money for the convention. As a reward, the convention voted to send him to Washington, D.C. (also at his own expense), to talk the U.S. Congress into appropriating money for a transcontinental railroad.

John C. Burch, a newly-elected Congressman travelling on the same ship, said of Judah: "No day passed on the voyage that we did not discuss the subject. His knowledge was so thorough, his manners so gentle and insinuating, that few resisted his appeals."

Judah was just as effective in Washington but all his salesmanship couldn't cut a hole in the fog of ill feeling swirling around the slavery issue in 1860. Northerners wanted a northern route, Southerners a southern.

No compromise was possible in the angry atmosphere, with the Civil War looming. Judah returned to California with nothing to show for a year of hard work. A lesser man might have quit.

Crazy Judah went back into the mountains.

This time he intended to map out a workable railroad route and figure the cost. He stayed until the first winter blizzards almost trapped him, then came out to Dutch Flat and drew up articles of association for the Central Pacific Railroad of California.

Some capital was pledged in Dutch Flat, but not nearly enough. Judah had to go to San Francisco in search of $70,000 more.

He failed to get it.

Aflame with anger, he ushered his wife aboard the morning boat to Sacramento. For five years, Sacramento had offered him little more than scorn. Now he bowed his neck, called meetings, talked to anyone who would listen on the streets, spread out his drawings before anyone who would look, worked desperately to show the townspeople how his railroad would bring a boom to Sacramento and California.

When he thought the time was ripe, he called a meeting.

Only a few idlers attended.

He called another meeting, this time in a room over a hardware store owned by Collis P. Huntington and Mark Hopkins. Among those who attended were Leland Stanford, a wholesale grocer, and Charles Crocker, a seller of dry goods.

Mark the names—Huntington, Hopkins, Stanford, Crocker.

Now they echo down the musty halls of California history as "The Big Four."

But there was only one big man in the room over the hardware store on that pregnant night in Sacramento; the others were smalltime merchants who got lucky.

The big man was Theodore D. Judah.

THE MISSING HOUSE ON NOB HILL

Crazy Judah knew better than to try to sell the retail merchants on his grand vision. After all, they were accustomed to dealing in nickels and dimes; Judah was thinking in terms of millions of dollars.

All he asked of them now was that they back a survey of a good wagon road to the Comstock Lode in Nevada. To the Little Four, the proposition apparently promised a lot of nickels and dimes. They bought the stock and voted themselves into corporate office.

When summer ended, Judah (being Judah) came out of the mountains not with just a wagon road but with a railroad route meticulously plotted. The route was interesting but the news he brought was even juicier: A railroad over the mountains could haul out a fortune in low grade ores that had been discarded around the mine shafts!

The ears of the nickel-and-dime merchants rose and twanged.

"Yes," said the Little Four, "we will build the railroad."

Judah was sent east to do his thing: persuade Congress to put up the money. He wisely revised his pitch to make the Pacific Railroad bill a war measure; the gold and silver of California, he pointed out, were needed to finance the Union armies.

It took a year's hard work but Judah finally greased the bill's passage through both House and Senate.

It was quite a bill. It gave railroad builders free and clear title to a vast amount of land along the railroad right-of-way and also promised millions of dollars of public money for construction.

When Crazy Judah boated back to Sacramento after this particular sojourn in Washington, he wasn't considered crazy any more.

But the Little Four, suddenly the Big Four after Judah's coup in Washington, had plans which didn't quite match Judah's.

Huntington, Crocker, Hopkins and Stanford were schemers; Judah was a dreamer. One needs the other but only for a time. The dreamer served his purpose, then was cast aside by the schemers.

History is littered with the carcasses of dreamers. Now it was time to add Crazy Judah to the pile.

* * *

Judah wanted a railroad. The Big Four wanted to get rich quick.

Perhaps Judah wanted money, too, and the Big Four had no real objection to a railroad, as such, but the difference in motivation was important, as things turned out.

Since the federal government had been so generous as to offer a railroad builder $16,000 per mile in flat country and $48,000 in mountainous terrain, why shouldn't the Big Four form their very own construction company and then, as railroad builders, offer their very own construction company a contract at a delightfully high price?

It was done.

Judah squirmed but didn't actually rebel until the Big Four decided to move the foothills of the Sierra Nevada down into the valley of the Sacramento. The government offered $32,000 per mile to build in the foothills, only $16,000 in the valley, so on the maps of the Big Four, the foothills magically moved.

The Big Four then decided that they didn't need a rebellious Judah, so they paid him $100,000 for his interest, sent him packing and did their best thereafter to wipe out his name.

In October, 1863, the dreamer and his much-travelled wife again boarded a ship bound for New York. Crossing Panama, Judah picked up yellow fever.

He lived to reach New York but died there at age 37.

He did not live to drink champagne when the rails were joined at Promontory Point nor to enjoy a mansion on Nob Hill in San Francisco.

Land Transportation

There is only one monument to Theodore D. Judah in California. This single marker is in Sacramento, at Second and L streets.

Ironically, it was Sacramento which first called him "Crazy Judah."

LITTLE GIANTS

Planning a railroad was one thing; actually building it was quite another.

The man chosen from the Big Four to be general contractor for construction was Charles S. Crocker, who weighed 250 pounds and liked to throw it all around.

"Why," reminisced Crocker, "I used to go up and down that road . . . like a mad bull, stopping along wherever there was anything amiss, and raising Old Nick with the boys that were not up to time."

Crocker's construction superintendent was James H. Strobridge and he was a dandy, too. He had one flaw: He thought that to handle the heavy work of railroad building, a man had to stand at least six feet tall and weigh at least 200 pounds.

The trouble was that when the Central Pacific began construction east into the Sierra Nevada, males of that description were in short supply. Thousands had come west during the gold rush but most of these muscular men wanted to get rich quick and there was simply no way one could do that working for the railroad at a dollar a day, plus board.

Early in 1865, Strobridge advertised all over California for 5000 husky men who wanted "constant and permanent work." This may have been a mistake; gold miners tended to be anything but "constant and permanent."

As the situation grew desperate, somebody suggested that the Central Pacific hire Chinese.

Roared Strobridge: "I will not boss Chinese. I will not be responsible for work done on the road by Chinese labor. From what I've seen of them, they're not fit laborers anyway."

Is that so, Mr. Strobridge? Hang onto your hat, Mr. Strobridge.

* * *

Less than 10 per cent of the white laborers hired by the Central Pacific stayed on the job for more than a week. Workers were given free transportation along the C.P. rails into the foothills, where the gold fields were. Smelling the rich diggings, most of them said, "Excuse me, but this is where I get off."

So Charley Crocker bellowed: "Hire the Chinese."

Strobridge decided to try a few.

The first crew of 50 coolies from Canton, China, emerged in due course from freight cars into the chill of the high country spring and shuffled through the railroad's work camp.

Watching, Strobridge groaned.

Dinky, puny, undernourished little men passed before him. Their average weight was 110 pounds; there wasn't a six-footer among them. A hard week's work surely would kill them all.

Strobridge sighed; he had no stomach for murder. The Chinese were assigned to easy jobs around camp.

The jobs were completed quickly, competently, methodically. The Cantonese seemed to learn rapidly, in spite of the language barrier.

As his eyes opened, Strobridge cautiously tried out a Chinese crew on a grading job.

After a week, it was plain even to the prejudiced Strobridge that the coolies had built more smooth grade than any Caucasian crew the superintendent of construction had been able to hire.

No fool, Strobridge telegraphed company headquarters: SEND UP MORE COOLIES.

They called the railroad the "Central Pacific," but before the whole crazy scheme was realized, most of the workers were Chinese—12,000 out of 14,000! It is highly doubtful that the job could have been accomplished at that time without the fantastic labors of the Chinese.

If railroad names reflected credit where credit was due, this one should have been called the "Chinese Pacific."

ACROSS THE GRANITE WALL

Sailing ships docked by the dozens in San Francisco Bay and a citizen who watched in wonder wrote: ". . . a living stream of blue-coated men of Asia, bearing long poles across their shoulders, from which depend packages of bedding, matting, clothing, and things of which we knew neither the names nor the uses, poured down the plank . . ."

By the thousands, they disembarked and attacked the fearsome

Land Transportation

mountains for a dollar a day. There were tunnels to be bored and bridges to be built, grades to be levelled and track to be laid. And all of this had to be accomplished not with the power tools and monstrous machines of today but with historic hand tools—picks and hammers and shovels and wheelbarrows.

A New York reporter looked in and marvelled at ". . . a great army laying siege to nature in her strongest citadel. The rugged mountains looked like stupendous anthills. They swarmed with Celestials (Chinese), shovelling, wheeling, carting, drilling, and blasting rock and earth."

In places, the rocky cliffs seemed impassable, but the clever Chinese worked out a solution.

They asked for reeds to be sent up from San Francisco; baskets were woven. Then, from the top of the cliff, the baskets were lowered, bearing one or two coolies. Dangling at a heart-stopping distance above the floor of the canyon, the coolies punched holes in the rock, stuffed the holes with powder, lit the fuse, then signalled for a quick lift, hoping to reach the top before the side of the mountain exploded and tore them apart.

Sometimes they reached the top in time. Sometimes they didn't.

The railroad kept no record of workmen killed; it might have been embarrassing. A fair guess is that as many as a thousand Chinese may have died in the mountains before the tracks were finally strung out into the deserts of Nevada.

At first the white laborers swore that they wouldn't work within 100 yards of a "heathen Chinee."

Charley Crocker bulled right into the center of the grumbling. How, he asked, could the Central Pacific hire whites instead of Chinese if whites wouldn't accept jobs? If the whites couldn't learn to get along with the coolies, Crocker added, the C.P. would have no choice but to let its white workers go and hire Chinese in their place.

The open grumbling stopped.

Crocker wrote of the Chinese: "Wherever we put them, we found them good, and they worked themselves into our favor to such an extent that if we found we were in a hurry for a job of work, it

➡

Racing eastward, the Central Pacific built many wooden trestles like this one at Secrettown, 62 miles from Sacramento. This remarkable picture shows Chinese at work with dump carts and wheelbarrows filling in the trestle with earth.

was better to put Chinese on it at once."

It's not hard to see why the Chinese came to be called "Crocker's Pets."

* * *

By 1866, there were 10,000 of Crocker's Pets swarming over the mountains and many of them now were faced with the hardest work of all—the 12 tunnels which had to be bored before the tracks reached Nevada.

The toughest was Summit Tunnel, which required cutting through 1659 feet of solid granite. If there was any lingering doubt about the courage or stamina of the coolies, Summit Tunnel wiped it out.

Five hundred Chinese were put to work and three shifts bored into the rock around the clock, working from both ends. Then a shaft was sunk at the center so that workmen could be lowered to a point where they could drill out from the middle.

Even so, the work proceeded with pitiful slowness. Sometimes a crew could grind only seven or eight *inches* through the rock during a day's work. Powder tamped into drilled blasting holes sometimes just blew out; the granite remained solid. Then the rains came and mud was a new enemy, washing out the roads and clotting up the supply lines.

But the rains were only a prelude; worse trouble came with heavy early snows. Before the winter ended, an incredible 45 feet of the stubborn stuff had fallen.

Gnashing his teeth in frustration, Crocker was forced to evacuate most of his work force, taking out all but several hundred of his best coolies. It was his hope that he could keep these few alive and working on the tunnels throughout the winter.

The crude huts of the workmen soon were buried under tons of snow; it was necessary to bore shafts through the stifling mass to provide air for the dwellings. Tunnels, some several hundred feet long, had to be dug through the snow to work sites. Those carefully selected Chinese spent most of the winter of 1866-1867 buried in snow and rock, never seeing open sky or sunlight, sometimes surviving and working on a diet of cornmeal and tea!

As the snow mass grew even more monstrous, still another threat glowered down on them—*avalanche*.

Countless tons of snow thundered down from the heights in

search of helpless victims, which it usually found in the snow tunnels. Some of the bodies, still grasping shovels and picks, weren't found until late spring when the thawing snow released its long-dead prisoners.

By August of 1867, Summit Tunnel had been broken through. By the end of November, track had been laid along it. While there was still cleanup work to be done, it could be announced in a loud, clear voice that the mountains had been defeated.

Crazy Judah and the Chinese had thrown their challenge into the teeth of the Sierras and had won one of the most remarkable victories in the history of man's efforts to bend and bore and break the earth to his own ends.

* * *

The assumption was that the Union Pacific, laying track westward across the prairies and up along the gradual ascents of the Rockies, would move much faster than the Central Pacific, which was faced with the brutal assault of the Sierra Nevada. The U.P. and the C.P., it was assumed, would join rails somewhere around the California-Nevada line.

But that assumption was founded upon a fair amount of ignorance; those who made it knew nothing of Crocker's Pets and little more of Judah's surveying genius.

This was no small matter. Federal grants of both land and money to railroaders were based on miles of track laid, so several fortunes hung in the balance.

As 1867 ended, the C.P. had laid only 130 miles of track out of Sacramento, but the slowest, most difficult work was done. U.P. had been blazing across the Midwestern prairies and boasted over 500 miles of track. But the Big Four was well aware that the U.P. had just begun to tackle the Rocky Mountains; now that cocky crowd would find out about snow and cold and avalanches at high altitude.

So Collis Huntington went to Washington, D.C., and somehow arranged for a small change in the federal rules governing the building of railroads.

Suddenly neither line had to stop at a given point; it was an out-and-out race, with the rich land grants and loans going to whichever railroad covered the most miles fastest. Ahead of the C.P. were the high, flat deserts of Nevada, which caused Charley Crocker to boast that his crews just might lay down a mile of track for every working day during 1868.

Land Transportation

And why not? The Central Pacific had a labor force of 14,000. Making up the mass of this army were no less than 12,000 experienced, hardened Chinese.

Crocker's Pets were ready to go.

Daniel and Samuel Chu, writing in their excellent book about the Chinese in America, *Passage to the Golden Gate*, described it well:

"Week after week, the procession moved eastward. Far out ahead, the surveying teams marked out the route for the track. Then came the grading crew preparing the roadbed. Following them were the track crews. And keeping pace with the track layers were the telegraph crews, setting up poles and stringing wire along the rail route. At the end of each day, a daily progress report was flashed by telegraph down the line to Sacramento.

"Month after month, the miles ticked by. Along the railroad's course, new towns sprang up almost overnight: Reno, Wadsworth, Winnemucca, Golconda.

"The routine, repeated over and over again, was boring. But it produced wonders. By the end of the year 1868, the Central Pacific's tracks reached Elko, three-quarters of the way across Nevada. The CP's work crews had made good Crocker's boast. In a year's time, they had completed more than 350 miles of track!"

TROUBLE AT THE RAILHEAD

A funny thing happened on the way to Promontory Point.

One fine day in 1869, Union Pacific surveyors working west ahead of the construction crews passed right by Central Pacific surveyors headed east. Peculiar; the plan called for one transcontinental railroad, not two.

The situation stayed relatively peaceful so long as only surveyors were involved but when the construction crews worked their way into the same Utah neighborhood, sometimes laying track only 100 feet apart, the Chinese of the Central Pacific and the Irishmen of the Union Pacific got physical. First fists and pick handles came into play. Then dynamite was set off along the right-of-way, with no warning to the other side. More blood flowed.

This remarkable Central Pacific cut near Auburn, 462 feet long and 80 feet deep, was carved through glacial debris by Chinese working with chisels, hammers, picks, shovels and primitive black powder. It looks much like this today.

When it appeared that open war was about to break out, a truce was arranged. Finally Congress awakened to the problem and told the railroads to shape up, then picked out a barren spot in Utah north of Great Salt Lake and proclaimed: "Here is where the tracks shall join."

And join they did, on May 10, 1869, as the telegraph clicked three dots signalling DONE, but not before a peaceful kind of competition had been played out.

Charley Crocker believed in his Chinese. Never a modest man, he had bragged when his crew reached 14,000 that he bossed the largest civilian work force in the world. Now he wanted to prove that he bossed the *best*.

The U.P. had once laid just a hair over eight miles of track in a day and had never stopped gloating about it, which galled Crocker no end. For one thing, the U.P. crews had put in a 20-hour work day to achieve the feat, which hardly seemed fair.

Crocker was sure his Chinese could do better, so in April, 1869, he and James Strobridge (who, if you recall, once sneered at Chinese labor) put together a crew of 848 men, 41 carts and horse teams and five train loads of material.

The cocky Crocker then invited a delegation from the Union Pacific to watch the show.

At 7:15 a.m. on April 28, Crocker turned loose his eight Irish tracklayers and hundreds of Chinese support troops. At the scene, the correspondent of San Francisco's *Evening Bulletin* wrote:

"Each of the four men ran thirty feet with one hundred and twenty-five tons. Each of the other four men lifted and placed one hundred and twenty tons at their end of the rails. The distance travelled was over ten miles, besides extra walking . . . Those eight men would not consent to shift, and are proud of their work. They, like all Central Pacific men, are water-drinkers.

"Immediately in front of the eight are three pioneers, who, with shovel and by hand, set the ties thrown by the front teams in position; while this is doing, another party are distributing spikes and fresh bolts at each end of the rail, while some of the party are regulating the gauge. These tracklayers are a splendid force, and have been settled and drilled until they move like machinery . . .

A confrontation between the old and the new occurred in 1869 when Leland Stanford's special train, en route to the golden spike ceremony, met this wagon train headed west.

"Beside the tracklayers come the spike-starters, who place the spikes needed in position; then comes a reverend-looking old gentleman who packs the rails and uses the line, and, by motion of his hands, directs the track-straighteners. The next men to the spike-drivers are the bolt screwers, quite a large force. Behind them come the tampers, four hundred strong, with shovels and crowbars. They level the track by raising or lowering the ends of the ties, and shovel in enough ballast to hold them firm. When they leave it, the line is fit for trains running twenty-five miles an hour. When all the iron thrown on the track has been laid, the handcars run to the extreme front, and the locomotive and iron train come as close to the front as possible; another two miles of iron is thrown off, and the process repeated. Alongside of the moving force are teams hauling tools, and water-wagons, and Chinamen, with pails strung over shoulders, moving among the men with water and tea . . .

"The scene is a most animated one. From the first pioneer to the last tamper, perhaps two miles, there is a thin line of 1000 men advancing a mile an hour; the iron cars, with their . . . freight, running up and down; mounted men galloping backward and forward. Far in the rear are trains of material, with four or five locomotives, and their water-tanks and cars . . . Keeping pace with the track-layers was the telegraph construction party, hauling out, and hanging, and insulating the wire, and when the train of offices and houses stood still, connection was made with the operator's office, and the business of the road transacted . . ."

With contempt for the U.P. in his heart, Crocker, at 1:30 p.m., stopped the work for lunch!

An hour later the crews went back to work; by 7 p.m., they had finished more than 10 miles of track. To prove that the work was well done, a locomotive chuffed over the new line in 40 minutes and U.P. executives had to inhale the smoke. Crocker and his Asiatic pets had made their point emphatically.

A month later, the Chinese Pacific Railroad was connected with the Irish Pacific Railroad at Promontory Point. Finally California and the East were joined by an iron artery. At the moment of the connection, transportation to the west took a great leap forward at 20 miles an hour. Wagon trains and slow boats faded out of the competition.

The rich American West was no longer far away from everywhere, reachable only by the strong, the brave and the reckless. Suddenly

Land Transportation

California was available to almost anyone at no great cost, with no great hardship. All one had to do to go a-westering was sit on a seat in an enclosed coach while clicking along behind a chuffing locomotive and the only problem was in adjusting mentally and physically to the mind-bending speed of 20 miles an hour maintained night and day.

Yessir! California, here we come!

THE FADING OF THE GLORY

Suddenly the Big Four were national heroes but . . .

Incredibly difficult as was the building of the transcontinental railroad, it wasn't half as hard as operating it at a profit.

The Big Four quickly discovered this cruel fact. Less than a year after the linking of the C.P. and the U.P., the western line was in bad trouble.

One of the dreams of the railroad builders was that a line across the U.S. would provide a land bridge for the rich trade between Europe and the Orient. It might have worked out that way except for one crushing development—only a few weeks after the ceremony at Promontory Point, the new Suez Canal was opened.

The Big Four's dreams of heavy traffic at high rates promptly went a-glimmering.

Personally, the Big Four had little to moan about. The quartet had grown rich from construction profits; additional loot could only be icing on the cake.

Before the line was finished, one of the Big Four had muscled himself into a position as Biggest of the Big Four: Collis P. Huntington.

"Ruthless as a crocodile . . ."

"Scrupulously dishonest . . ."

"A hard and cheery old man, with no more soul than a shark . . ."

And these were the appraisals of his friends!

The crafty Huntington, unable to sell his railroad or operate it at a profit, set out to create a transportation monopoly in California,

➡

Nose-to-nose at Promontory Point, Central Pacific and Union Pacific locomotives form a backdrop for a celebration of the tying together of the United States with rails.

calling it the Southern Pacific. He bought up competing railroads and steamship lines, then raised rates just as high as the traffic would bear—and sometimes a little higher. When newspapers complained about his high-handed tactics, he bought—or bought off—the newspapers. When injured, angry citizens took their case to the state legislature, they found that Huntington had gotten there first.

It was S.P. policy to insist upon the right to examine the books of shippers along its lines, then to set rates which soaked up the profits, if any. If companies went bankrupt, the rates went down, only to rise again just as soon as business improved.

When Shasta miners protested the climbing rate for shipping quartz to San Francisco, the Southern Pacific asked them to produce their accounts; then the S.P., in all its majesty, would tell them how much profit they could earn after paying the freight.

The S.P. had bought the branch line from San Pedro to Los Angeles, a one-hour trip. It cost half as much to haul a load along that short line as it had cost to ship it across the Pacific Ocean!

* * *

Plunder has its season but the moon of greed waxes and wanes. Time passes; anger mounts and pressures build; change then comes like a force of nature.

The Sante Fe Railroad built west across the deserts of New Mexico and Arizona, aiming its competitive arrow at southern California. Then it ran smack-dab into the east-building S.P. at the Needles crossing of the Colorado River. To continue, the Santa Fe needed trackage rights from the S.P.

If it didn't get the rights, said the Santa Fe, it had no choice but to build south from New Mexico across the Mexican state of Sonora to Guaymas on the Gulf of California, from which point ships could connect the rails with the Orient.

The Southern Pacific had met its match. In 1885, the Santa Fe located another roadbed through narrow Cajon Pass, which surprised the S.P. no end, then built to San Diego and north to Los Angeles.

The S.P. monopoly was dead. Competition, that great tiger-tamer, had reached into the jungle of California transportation and the big S.P. cat soon put its tail between its legs.

Huntington, Crocker, Hopkins and Stanford—the Big Four left a big mark. Their names became California by-words. Stanford University, one of the most prestigious in the U.S., rests on land which was once the farm of Leland Stanford; Huntington Library in San Marino, nationally acclaimed, is the legacy of a nephew of Collis P. Huntington; the Mark Hopkins Hotel has long been a San Francisco landmark.

* * *

The author, Rudyard Kipling, visited San Francisco in 1889 and enjoyed as a matter of course the city's most famous transportation device, then commented: "I gave up asking questions about their mechanism . . . if it pleases Providence to make a car run up and down a slit in the ground for many miles, and if for two-pence-hapenny I can ride that car, why should I seek reasons for that miracle?"

He was referring, of course, to the cable car.

The method of locomotion was promoted by Andrew S. Hallidie, who had an ax to grind—he manufactured steel cables. Having sold his cables for use in the mines, with ore buckets attached, Hallidie saw a place for his product in urban transportation, particularly on the steep streets of San Francisco, where the use of horse cars killed more animals every year than any humane person cared to think about.

Hallidie was encouraged to go ahead with his experiment. The main concern was safety. Would the endless cable stand the strain? Or would it break and allow the cars laden with screaming passengers to go plummeting down the hills to a gruesome end?

In 1873, Hallidie himself drove the first cable car down Clay Street, let go the cable and braked the car, then turned it around on a turntable, snagged the cable again and ascended the hill. By 1887, eight American cities in addition to San Francisco used cable cars, including Los Angeles and Oakland.

Now all but San Francisco's are gone.

The Hallidie Building at Sutter Street near Montgomery in San Francisco reminds the modern world of the visionary Scotsman.

But the best monuments to Andrew Hallidie are the cable cars themselves as they glide sedately up and down the fabled hills of the city by the Golden Gate, their warning bells adding a nostalgic grace note to the angry clamor of a modern city.

There have been many attempts to eliminate the cable cars; efficiency experts consider them too slow, too expensive to operate and too dangerous. So far, every effort to junk them has been beaten

down by sentimental San Franciscans.

The cable cars have become a San Francisco institution, a seedbed of folklore. An old anecdote tells of a Chinese houseboy walking to work who came upon a stalled Hyde Street cable car. He inquired gravely of the gripman: "Whattsa maller—stling bloke?"

The question became a standard San Francisco wisecrack. Stall your car on a street in modern San Francisco and chances are that sooner or later a passerby will chirp: "Whatsa maller—stling bloke?"

* * *

It is still possible to spend one's vacation riding behind steam locomotives in California. The Roaring Camp & Big Trees Narrow-Gauge Railroad operates passenger service out of Felton, Santa Cruz County, 70 miles south of San Francisco. Much of the equipment used dates back to the 1880s and 1890s.

The Arcata & Mad River Railroad (known locally as the "Annie and Mary" because two women bearing those names worked in the line's office a long time ago) runs east out of Arcata to Blue Lake.

The most famous of California's old railroads, though, bears the aromatic name of "Skunk." The California Western operates the diesel-powered Skunks between Fort Bragg and Willits in Mendocino County, through some of the state's most spectacular redwood country. During summers, an ancient steam-powered "Super Skunk" also chuffs through the trees, to the delight of thousands of oldtime rail fans who flock to Fort Bragg every year.

The passing of the steam locomotive might have been easier to bear if the evocative cry of its whistle could have been saved. Somebody once scribbled this ode to the locomotive whistle on the wall of a little depot in the West:

"Listen, my grandson, just around the hill, hear how it lifts its lonely voice and calls once more, a sound with a heartbreak in it, tired, shrill, a sound a million boys have heard before. And in the night they raised their heads, just as you are doing now, and felt a strange wonder catch hold of them in their safe beds until the sound sped far off and out of range.

"It was a sound to part the buffalo grass, long years ago; a sound with history in it heard over plain and village, mountain and pass. So listen, my grandson, and then remember it always if you can. This

San Francisco has long been the most eye-pleasing city in the United States. This nostalgic view of Sutter and Powell streets in 1896 demonstrates why.

sound will be gone forever when you're a man."

CARS, CARS, CARS

Railroads were all right in their time but highways and automobiles carried the day in California.

In the early 1970s, there were more motor vehicles registered in the state of California than in most *countries* of the world. Twenty million Californians owned thirteen million automobiles.

California's love affair with the automobile began in 1896, when a German-born machinist, John A. Meyer, finished in his San Francisco shop what is believed to be the first automobile built in California.

Meyer called the stark vehicle "The Pioneer" and bravely drove it on the first round trip of a horseless carriage from San Francisco to San Jose, with return via Oakland.

A nervous attendant on the ferry across the bay insisted that the throbbing machine be placed near the rear chain on the ferry's deck, hoping that if it exploded it could be pushed into the water and then perhaps it wouldn't take the ferry down with it, which is about all one could wish for from the autos of the day.

The Pioneer didn't explode. In fact, it putted about San Francisco for years thereafter and came into its own during the great earthquake and fire in 1906, when Meyer used it to haul machinery to safety.

The Pioneer, in immaculate condition, now rests in a proper setting, the dramatic splendor of the California exhibit in the Oakland Museum.

* * *

In modern California, the automobile rules . . . and possibly ruins.

Private cars and jet planes carry most of the passenger traffic which once nourished the railroads, while trucks snore day and night along the freeways laden with a lion's share of the freight.

But the smog-belching, freeway-clotting cars and trucks may have had their day. San Francisco is turning to rapid rail transit under the bay and is bringing back the stately ferryboats, once scorned as

In the early 1900s, a plank road may have provided a jouncy ride across the desert between San Diego and Yuma, but it was an improvement over the camel caravan. In case you were wondering about the road's narrowness, occasional turnouts allowed for two-way traffic.

impossibly slow. Los Angeles is wishing it hadn't starved out its interurban railroad system, the historic "Red Cars" which once hummed along the tracks from suburbs to central city.

History is generally viewed as a long, straight line. Perhaps history is a circle.

Anybody for a harum-scarum whirligig?

SITES TO SEE

BRIGGS CUNNINGHAM AUTOMOTIVE MUSEUM, Costa Mesa. (Big, beautiful collection of old and not-so-old sports and racing cars, both American and European; has something for everybody, from Rolls Royces to gypsy wagons; best in the state.)

JUDAH MONUMENT, Old Sacramento. (This impressive object composed mostly of piled rocks rises above the ordinary, like the man it honors, Crazy Judah.)

TRAVEL TOWN, Griffith Park, Los Angeles. (Here, quite possibly, is the finest collection of old railroad rolling stock in the U.S., certainly the best in California.)

LAWS RAILROAD MUSEUM, near Bishop. (This is the final resting place of "Slim Princess," a colorful little train which ran until 1960 over the last narrow gauge railroad to operate commercially west of the Rockies; old depot and expanding museum make this a special place for railroad buffs.)

FORT TEJON, Kern County. (A few buildings have been restored and furnished at this important old army post, which once was called home by camels.)

ORANGE EMPIRE TROLLEY MUSEUM, near Perris. (From streetcars to locomotives, gathered from as far as Ireland, many of the old trolley electrics are displayed here, just for the historical fun of it. Visit on Sunday if you want a ride between Sentiment and Nostalgia.)

Early Hell's Angels? This dashing San Diego group, caught in a rare moment of rest in 1913, demurely called itself "Pepper Tree Motorcycle Club." Oh, well...

Chapter Seven *

The Women
"WHAT'S A LADY LIKE YOU DOING IN A PLACE LIKE THIS?"

Once upon a time in California, there was a stage driver who was generally considered the roughest, toughest, one-eyed, lantern-jawed, tobacco-chewing character who ever whipped six horses along a dark mountain trail. His name was Charley Parkhurst.

He drove like a madman, they said, but he could run both front and rear wheels of his speeding coach over a half-dollar placed in the road and with a whip at 15 paces could pop a cigar out of a man's quivering mouth.

He was held up just once, but the foolish bandit didn't live long to gloat about it. It happened on Charley's second trip over the Oakland-San Jose run and he vowed to be ready next time.

He was. A month later, Charley drilled the bandit dead with one shot. Charley had lost his left eye in an argument with a horse but apparently the injury hadn't affected his marksmanship.

Charley started driving in California during the early 1850s and soon became famous. When passengers asked how, with only one eye, he could see the road through the dust raised by running horses, he replied tartly, "Don't have to. I smell it and hear it. When the wheels rattle, I know I'm on hard ground. When they don't rattle, I look down to see if the road's still there."

As the years rolled along and Charley clattered into the stage drivers' Hall of Fame, he took to wearing a patch over his missing eye, which added to his hell-for-leather look.

There was an odd thing about Charley, though. Ready to start a run, he would yell: "Mormon's Bar, Bidwell's, Jimtown and Sonora . . . all aboard!" and now and then a passenger would notice that his voice was a mite high-pitched. Only a fool or a total stranger would mention it, though, because Charley was sensitive and like as not

would knock you down not long after you opened your mouth.

Charley started his own stage line in 1860, but railroads made it unprofitable by 1873. He farmed for awhile, then went to live with friends near Watsonville, where he died in 1879.

At which point there came an interesting development — the undertaker discovered that Charley Parkhurst was a *woman!*

What's more, a physician's certificate revealed that she had once given birth to a child. It also occurred to someone that she might well have been the first woman to vote in the U.S., since she had done so in 1868, with no one the wiser.

She was buried in the Odd Fellows Cemetery of Watsonville and her grave marker can be seen there today. And why not? She was as Odd a Fellow as ever drove six snorting horses down the pike in California or anywhere else.

FIREBELLE LILLIE

There was another woman in California history who played poker far into the night, drove horses like mad and even smoked cigars on occasion . . . but she never pretended to be anything but a woman, which is exactly why she became the scandal of San Francisco along about 1865.

The dominant feature of the San Francisco skyline from almost any angle is a concrete tower thrusting up from Telegraph Hill— Coit Tower. Local lore insists that it resembles the nozzle on a fire hose. So be it.

Coit Tower is a memorial to one of San Francisco's most spectacular citizens, Lillie Hitchcock Coit, and some insist that it was she, in her free-wheeling way, who set the robust, romantic tone that today is so much a part of the fascinating aura surrounding the city by the Golden Gate as it glows and sparkles through its fabled fogs.

* * *

The major threat to the safety of early California towns was fire. Most of the buildings were made of wood and built close together (and, after each fire, rebuilt close together) for reasons which are still unclear. For the same reasons, perhaps, that Californians and

Lillie Coit, fire buff, proudly wears her Easter hat.

Alaskans continue to build smack on top of earth faults which regularly shake and shiver and slide apart.

Lillie Hitchcock, born in North Carolina, arrived in San Francisco as a child in 1851. When she first saw the city, it was licking terrible wounds after its sixth great fire; half the city lay in blackened ruins. Not long after, she was rescued from the burning Fitzmaurice hotel by a certain John Boynton, of a volunteer fire company called Knickerbocker Number Five.

And Lillie became a fire buff. She remained a chaser of fire engines almost to the end of her days.

The volunteer fire companies of those times were something very, very special in most communities. They paraded down the main stem in uniformed glory at the slightest excuse and were mainstays of every holiday celebration with their shiny trappings, prancing horses, brassy trumpets and grunting tugs-of-war. They fought fires, too, but the odds were against them. Water supplies were undependable, chemicals weren't available and flames devoured dry wood in cheek-by-jowl buildings at fearful speed.

Few of those old fire companies ever saved more than a foundation, but they were glamorous centers of community interest in an era when towns didn't have football teams, television and rapid transit. Lillie Coit was by no means alone in her hobby.

It has been established that the first fire engine little Lillie chased answered an alarm from Telegraph Hill. It was not long before she earned the position of cheerleader-mascot for Knickerbocker Number Five. Her mother did not approve of her tomboyish behavior, but apparently couldn't alter it.

When the fire alarm rang in the night, Lillie would leap out of bed, don her red blouse and black skirt, then dash toward the blaze in a hack. Waiting up for her return night after night, Lillie's father practiced on the piano while her mother wrote newspaper articles.

In time Lillie married Howard Coit, a handsome, successful San Francisco businessman, but refused to let marriage inhibit her behavior. She still drove horses as recklessly as any man, chased fires, played cards until all hours of the night and smoked cigars. By the

◄

By 1913, when this picture was taken in San Diego, fire horses like these two magnificent animals were being replaced by trucks. This splendid scene almost bridges the transportation gap—a wagon, a buggy, bicycles, cars and even a popcorn wagon.

time her husband died at age 47, Lillie had earned solid standing as a major San Francisco character and tourist attraction.

In 1923, author Gertrude Atherton visited Lillie at the Fairmont Hotel.

"You are part of our history," said Mrs. Atherton.

"Ancient history," sniffed Lillie. "A good time I had in this town, but it's no longer a wild place. Like me, it has quieted down."

She died at 88, leaving a bequest of $100,000 for beautification of her city. On October 8, 1933, a procession led by old Engine Number Five climbed Telegraph Hill for dedication of Coit Tower, a proud city's landmark for a historic lady.

WOMAN OF INDIGNATION

If readers have gained the impression that most of California's historic women were flaming eccentrics useful mostly for public entertainment, forget it.

Consider the case of one who came to Los Angeles in 1881 and immediately threw herself into a great crusade—exposure of the plight of California mission Indians drowned in the riptide of American conquest.

In 1883, Helen Hunt Jackson was appointed a special commissioner by the President. Her assignment was to study the mission Indians of California. She had attracted the government's attention with her book, *A Century of Dishonor: A Sketch of the United States Government's Dealing with some of the Indian Tribes*. Helen Hunt Jackson wrote about Indians in an angry, outspoken style; readers throughout the country got her message and reacted strongly.

She wrote: ". . . The tale of the wrongs, the oppressions, the murders of the Pacific slope Indians in the last thirty years would be a volume by itself, and is too monstrous to be believed . . .

"No one can visit their settlements . . . without having a sentiment of respect and profound sympathy for men who, friendless, poor, without protection from the law, have still continued to work, planting, fencing, irrigating, building houses on lands from which long experience has taught them that the white man can drive them off any day he chooses. That drunkenness, gambling, and other immoralities are sadly prevalent among them, cannot be denied; but the only wonder is that so many remain honest and virtuous under conditions which make practically null and void for most of them most of the

Delilah Beasley, a newspaperwoman, studied black history in California for 20 years. Her work resulted in a book, "The Negro Trail Blazers of California," published in 1919 and reprinted in 1968 by the California Historical Society and the San Francisco Negro Historical and Cultural Society. She helped mightily in pushing civil rights legislation through the state legislature in 1933.

motives which keep white men honest and virtuous..."

Helen Hunt Jackson wasn't quite finished. She said: "I am going to write a novel, in which will be set forth some Indian experiences in a way to move people's hearts..."

The novel was *Ramona*. It became an American classic.

One of the best friends California Indians ever had died in 1885. Although she had spent only a few years in the state, Helen Hunt Jackson had become a woman of California; she had earned her keep.

ANOTHER WOMAN OF WORDS

San Francisco's Gertrude Atherton gathered material for her novels by talking to the pioneers, by visiting the historic places.

The books which resulted—*The Doomswoman* in 1892, *The Californians* in 1898, *The Splendid Idle Forties* in 1902, *Rezanov* in 1906—established her national reputation.

Another nationally popular novelist who lived in California was Kathleen Norris. Then there was Gertrude Stein, who wrote up a storm of unconventional prose and poetry and who tutored Ernest Hemingway during his Paris period; she spent her girlhood in the Bay area. "A rose is a rose is a rose," wrote Stein; the rose bloomed in California and soon intrigued the world.

WOMAN OF THE SAND WALKING COMPANY

She was small and naturally nervous, anything but the robust type usually associated with pioneering. Yet it was little Juliette Brier who stood in early winter of 1849 on the summit and stared fearfully west over the awesome, desolate expanse to which her party would give a name—Death Valley.

They had left Utah in October as part of a larger party bearing the apt name of "Sand Walking Company." The plan was to avoid the snows which had trapped the Donners by veering far south into the desert before turning west into California. A good idea; too bad the entire company didn't stick with it.

Inevitably there appeared a man with a siren song, in this case a "guide" named Captain Smith, and he sang this lyric: There was a cutoff over Walker's Pass into the Tulare Valley; by taking it, the party could save 400 tiresome miles.

The Rev. John W. Brier, Juliette's husband, was a man who "always liked to give his opinion on every subject."

One hundred wagons opted for the cutoff; the Brier family was among them. Only seven wagons continued along the tried-and-true Old Spanish Trail.

For two days the going was easy along the cutoff but then the maps ran out and the canyon closed up; an old story along the trail. Owners of 72 wagons decided to turn back to the Old Spanish Trail. Even Captain Smith chose to reverse his course and didn't bother to tell the emigrants bottled up in the canyon.

Now the party without a guide huddled around a campfire at the aptly-named Misery Mountain, grumbling and worrying, and had just about decided to turn back when scouts galloped in to announce joyfully that they had discovered a pass!

Incredibly, those gathered around Misery Mountain decided to push on, not as a single group, but in three sections. A party of young, single men calling themselves Jayhawkers struck out first, followed by the Brier party. Bringing up the rear was the Bennett-Arcane section; their guide was William Manly, 21; he had never been west before.

And in this harum-scarum manner did Vermonter Juliette Brier, small and nervous, fetch up on the fearsome verge of Death Valley, along with her husband and three sons, ages eight, seven and four.

The valley is 14 miles wide and 130 miles long. Even in midwinter, it is warm and very, very dry. The barren expanse consists mostly of windblown sand, alkali flats and endless emptiness.

But they went down into the Valley of Death.

* * *

Reverend Brier went forward, looking for water.

Mrs. Brier said: "I was left with our three little boys to help bring up the cattle. Poor little Kirke gave out and I carried him on my back, barely seeing where I was going."

One morning she reached camp at 3 a.m., after crawling on her knees in the faint light of stars to seek out tracks of stumbling oxen. At a spring called Furnace Creek on Christmas morning, a man suggested to the beaten-down Juliette Brier that it might be better if she stayed there with her children.

Flaring, she replied, "I have never kept the company waiting. Neither have my children. Every step I take will be towards California."

They caught up with the Jayhawkers, who were abandoning their wagons in order to make better time. Reverend Brier asked to join the Jayhawkers, who might have refused if they hadn't been melted by the sight of skinny Juliette Brier.

Reverend Brier, never strong, had nothing left to contribute. William Manly's account said of Juliette: "She was the one who put the packs on the oxen in the morning. She it was who took them off at night, built the fires, cooked the food, helped the children, and did all sorts of work when the father of the family was too tired, which was almost all of the time."

Licking cracked lips with swollen tongues, they slogged through wind-whipped sand. At night men climbed up to snow-line and brought back snow in their shirts. Inevitably someone suggested that they return to Furnace Creek, where there was water, at least.

Mrs. Brier resisted, saying again, "Every step we take will be toward California."

By January 1, they were encamped at the head of Panamint Valley, although they didn't know it; they were completely lost and waiting for extinction. The Jayhawkers had a little strength left and pushed on, leaving Mrs. Brier in charge of the weaker ones.

What followed was unremitting horror, a diet of hawk and crow and melted ice for drinking water. Many died.

Reverend Brier tried to die, lay down, said goodbye to his wife and closed his eyes but didn't make it; he survived to father three daughters.

Finally, with Juliette wasted away to 70 pounds of true grit, the Briers stumbled into California out of the San Gabriel Mountains. On their bodies they wore rags; on their feet they wore tattered moccasins that Mrs. Brier had made from the hides of the last oxen.

But they survived; they reached California. Juliette Brier—small and naturally nervous, anything but the robust type usually associated with pioneering—made it possible. She was tougher than she looked; she finally died at Lodi at age 99 years and eight months.

THE LADY BEHIND THE EXPLORER

Some women have been largely obliterated from history because of their husband's towering images. There was a woman of California who was lost in two shadows, not only that of her husband but also that of her father.

Her father was U.S. Sen. Thomas Hart Benton of Missouri, a powerful politician who believed with his whole soul in westward expansion. Her husband was John Charles Fremont, explorer, soldier, geographer and politician.

When young Fremont first came courting his handsome daughter, Senator Benton discouraged him. He was not easily discouraged, nor was the daughter. Jessie Benton became Jessie Benton Fremont. As it turned out, John C. Fremont served not only Jessie's purposes, but her father's, too, and served them remarkably well.

The Women

With Senator Benton's hearty support, Fremont left on his first epic of western exploration only months after his marriage. After the explorer's return in 1842, his wife served as his secretary in recording and mapping the historic journey.

In March, 1843, Jessie accompanied her husband to St. Louis, from which frontier settlement a second expedition would be launched. The official line was that these treks were strictly scientific. A likely story. In truth, there was a strong element in the national government which was waiting only for the declaration of war with Mexico to latch onto these rich western lands for the U.S. War, of course, would make such a land grab legal by the international standards of then . . . and now.

John C. went forward to Kaw Landing (now Kansas City) to shape up the men and animals of his expedition. Jessie stayed behind to forward the mail.

On one fateful day there came a letter from the colonel in charge of the topographical bureau . . . John Fremont's boss. Apparently word had reached the colonel that Fremont's group had equipped itself with a howitzer, a stubby cannon not ordinarily used in geographic work. The colonel's letter said, in effect: "Come back here, boy, and explain that howitzer."

Jessie Fremont thought it over, decided that her husband couldn't be expected to obey an order he had never received and wrote to Kaw Landing that he "must not ask why, but must start at once, ready or not ready . . . only GO."

Fremont went.

When war with Mexico was declared and the fate of California hung in the balance, Fremont's presence on the embattled ground may have tipped the scales. If his wife had not made a bold decision in St. Louis months earlier, John C. Fremont might have been cooling his heels in Washington, D.C., not making tempestuous history in California.

And California of today might be Alta California, province of Mexico.

A PHILANTHROPIST NAMED PHOEBE

There was another Missouri woman who made her mark in California; her name was Phoebe Apperson Hearst. She was the wife of

This is Jessie Fremont in 1867.

The Women   199

George Hearst, mining magnate, and the mother of William Randolph Hearst, a giant figure of American journalism whose fantastic home at San Simeon is now a state park and one of modern California's most whimsical and magnificent explosions of architecture.

After a period of travel, Phoebe returned to San Francisco in 1880 and threw herself into welfare activities—hospitals, orphan asylums, kindergartens and libraries. In 1886, when she and her husband moved to Washington, D.C., Phoebe demonstrated her great interest in the education of girls by founding the National Cathedral School for Girls. Widowed in 1891, she devoted the last years of her life to the state university at Berkeley, helping to lift it to its present position as one of the outstanding schools in the U.S.

Phoebe Hearst became a university regent in 1897. In 1901, she financed Hearst Hall for women and made other large contributions to science and anthropology. Her husband had mucked the money out of the ground; Phoebe plowed it back into the intellectual air.

Physically she was an insignificant mite of a woman but mentally she sparkled. She was loaded for bear—California bear—and she will be remembered.

A SINGING SENATOR?

In 1937, she had a contract to sing with the Vienna (Austria) State Opera; she was that good. Then, in a Vienna coffeehouse, she was asked if she was pure Aryan.

Helen Gahagan Douglas tore up her contract and came home to fight racism. Affected strongly by the Depression, she teamed with her actor husband, Melvyn Douglas, to organize relief for Okies in California. She sang the national anthem at the Democratic National Convention of 1940, was chosen national committeewoman for California and then was elected to the U.S. Congress from California in 1944. Two years later, President Truman appointed her an alternate delegate to the United Nations Assembly.

In 1950, the liberal Helen Gahagan Douglas ran for the U.S. Senate in California and was defeated by Richard Milhous Nixon, of whom you may have heard; he was to become the 37th President of the

This magic kingdom is San Simeon of California, probably the most grandiose estate in the country, donated to California in honor of Phoebe Hearst, mother of the man who built it.

United States. The campaign established Nixon's reputation as a roughhouse campaigner and enthroned Helen Gahagan Douglas in the pantheon of California heroines.

L.A.'S LADY OF CULTURE

A modern woman of California was primarily responsible for giving Los Angeles its Music Center complex, a spectacular highlight of the city's downtown area. She is Dorothy Buffum Chandler, who sparked the fund drive which financed the magnificent cultural centerpiece of California's largest city.

Since 1948, Dorothy Buffum Chandler has been administrative assistant to her husband, Norman Chandler, publisher of the *Los Angeles Times,* long one of the West's most influential newspapers. Since 1955, Mrs. Chandler has been a director of the Times-Mirror Co., and a prime mover in the city's civic and cultural affairs. In 1956, she served as a member of a U.S. Commission on Education Beyond the High School.

* * *

Two of the nation's First Ladies have claimed California residence. The wife of President Herbert Hoover, Lou Henry, was born in Iowa but moved to California at age 10 and later studied geology at Stanford University, Palo Alto. The Hoovers considered Palo Alto their home both before and after his single term as President. Lou Hoover was buried at Palo Alto, then, after her husband's death, was re-buried at West Branch, Iowa, beside her husband.

Thelma Ryan Nixon—better known as Pat—was born in Nevada, but became a California resident at age 2. She majored in merchandising at the University of Southern California in Los Angeles, then taught school in Whittier, where she met the young man who was later to become President.

LITTLE LADY FROM OUT WEST

Said Alice Paul, ardent young president of the militant women's suffrage group, Congressional Union:

"We had already gone into many places campaigning with an auto. It was the easiest and least expensive way to have a campaign: drive into a town, speak *on* the car at street corners. We were there in San

Francisco, and we had to get the petition to Washington. The weather was still good. Sara was out there, free to go, willing, and lovely. A very good speaker. She was just sent to us from heaven."

It was autumn, 1915. Some states, including California, had granted women the right to vote in state and county elections but the women's suffrage groups wanted nothing less than full federal voting privileges. In 1915, the U.S. Congress was the target and Alice Paul had decided that petite Sara Bard Field of California was to be the arrow directed at the political heart of the country.

In that year, twenty million women in America could not vote. Western states had been the first to grant women local voting rights. (California, in 1911, was the sixth state to grant suffrage to women.) It was felt that Western votes would be needed to force a Constitutional amendment through the U.S. Congress which would allow women to vote throughout the country.

Two Swedish ladies, Misses Kindborg and Kindstedt, offered their new Oakland touring car, plus their own questionable services as driver and mechanic. With misgiving, but armed with a buffalo robe supplied by her fiance, Sara Bard Field set out from California on her unsentimental journey. The car was equipped with everything but a map.

This was a time, remember, when transcontinental highways existed mostly in the feverish minds of chamber of commerce members. Over long stretches of the still-wild West, a dusty road which made a bold display during the warm, dry season might bashfully bury itself under a swamp or a snowdrift when winter waxed.

But Sara Bard Field felt that the effort had to be made; the petition had to be delivered. And what a petition! It bore half a million signatures on a roll of paper *18,333 feet long* and many more would sign along the long road.

As it turned out, Sara's misgivings about the journey were well founded. They lost their way on the Nevada desert on a freezing night, then almost lost the car in a water-filled hole in Kansas and finally Miss Kindstedt, who had only recently been released from a mental hospital, announced to Sara: "At the end of this trip I'm going to kill you!"

But the trip was successful, in its own way. Sara and her co-workers succeeded in meeting President Woodrow Wilson and presenting their petition. Four miles, literally, of signatures unrolled and slapped against the far wall as a wide-eyed President watched.

Three years passed before the suffrage amendment was approved by Congress with Wilson's support. Without question, the remarkable cross-country journey of California's Sara Bard Field had provided a mighty push.

What politician could resist a pretty little lady out of California? And four miles of signatures?

BEAUTIFUL STAR

At age 108, she cut a ribbon opening a new freeway, had her appendix taken out at 110 and a year later, rode in a helicopter for the first time. In 1970, when she died in Los Angeles at age 120, she was believed to be the oldest woman in the United States receiving Social Security.

Her name, Tatzumbie DuPea, meant "beautiful star." Born in the Alabama Hills of Inyo County in 1849, she was a Paiute Indian.

She was alive during part of the lifetime of every woman mentioned in this chapter.

SITES TO SEE

SAN SIMEON, San Luis Obispo County. (This incredible estate, a wonder of the world, was donated to California in the name of Phoebe Apperson Hearst, mother of William Randolph Hearst, who built it.)

CAMPO CAHUENGA, North Hollywood, Los Angeles. (Here was signed the treaty which ended a war and nailed down the U.S. claim to California; a small museum has some interesting mementos of Jessie Benton Fremont.)

Fun and games with aeroplanes—this smirking pilot is a certain Miss Roberts, who probably never got off the ground in this Curtiss. It may be just as well. Is that tape holding the front tire to the rim?

Chapter Eight *

Agriculture
WATER, WATER EVERYWHERE

A wry Californian once remarked that the state has always had plenty of water . . . but mostly in the wrong places.

Sometimes the wrong place was a cloud drifting smugly over a parched landscape and failing to spit as much as a drop on desperate citizens squinting up. So crops died, wells went dry and the souls of men shrivelled.

It was a recurring calamity and naturally someone saw it as a business opportunity. In southern California soon after the century's turn, George M. Hatfield was his name and rainmaking was his game.

No one was quite sure what it was that Hatfield did but whatever it was, it seemed to suck moisture out of passing clouds often enough to make his name known throughout the San Joaquin Valley and as far south as San Diego. His successes, of course, were more readily remembered than his failures.

Particularly *one* of his successes . . .

The scene is San Diego; the year is 1915.

Unbroken months of dry weather had left the city's reservoir gasping for water. In desperation the city council entered into a contract with George Hatfield under which the rainmaker promised "to fill Morena Reservoir to overflow between now and next December 20, 1916."

Even though he had cagily given nature plenty of time to lend a hand, Hatfield quickly set up his mysterious tanks. Whenever pregnant clouds wafted into the neighborhood, he caused noxious chemical vapors to be released. (If he did nothing else, he may have invented

Hatfield the Rainmaker brewing his chemical magic.

industrial smog. Unlike modern smog-makers, though, he also could produce the rain to wash it away . . . he said.)

What do you know? It began to rain almost immediately, almost as if George Hatfield had turned on a faucet.

Then another faucet. And another. Then still another and by this time San Diego was experiencing a historic flood. What's more, Hatfield's deadline was almost a year away. Morena Reservoir soon overflowed, a dam was wiped out downstream and San Diego's outskirts no longer had a dust problem. The flood waters seemed to be holding the dust down nicely. Mud helped, too.

The city council was left high, dry and thoroughly confused. They blamed George Hatfield for the disaster, thereby giving him grudging credit for rainmaking, but since Los Angeles had also been inundated and the Colorado River several hundred miles to the east had run wild at about the same time, there remained some doubt as to the real identity of the hydromaniac.

Was it George M. Hatfield or was it That Great Rainmaker in the Sky?

Of the two, Hatfield was more likely to submit a bill for services rendered, so the council sternly refused to pay the contracted figure of $10,000.

"We told you merely to fill the reservoir," grumbled the council, "not flood the community."

Hatfield sued, but lost. So it goes in the rainmaking business.

Fast-growing California was going to need a veritable ocean of fresh water. Rainmaking was a fascinating art but a burgeoning state didn't dare depend on the likes of George M. Hatfield, who seemed able to turn the water on but apparently couldn't turn it off.

There had to be a better way.

THE VIOLENT DITCH OF BILL MULHOLLAND

Ever since its founding, the city of Los Angeles has had to scramble for enough water to survive . . . and fight and spend and bleed for enough water to grow.

The problem can be stated in staggering simplicity: The native water supply of southern California is less than two per cent of that available throughout the state, yet southern California is home to over 60 per cent of the state's population and Los Angeles, its metropolis, has shown the wildest sustained growth of any city in the world.

Agriculture

In southern California, drought is not so much a tragedy as a way of life. And when it does finally rain, it often pours . . . even without the help of a Hatfield. Floodwaters running out of control on their rampages to the sea do much more harm than good; that kind of precipitation California can do without.

The man with the answer debarked at San Pedro in January, 1877, with ten dollars in his pocket and in his soul, a glowing ambition to become an engineer. The Irish immigrant named William Mulholland snatched a job with the Los Angeles City Water Company and lived in a small shack near what is now Los Feliz and Riverside Drive. The shack is gone, replaced by Mulholland Memorial Fountain.

If the fountain ever goes dry, it can expect to be haunted by a leprechaun.

* * *

Say it again: History hangs on happenstance.

Riding along in his buggy one day, the president of the Los Angeles City Water Company noticed a shovel furiously working in a ditch.

The president stopped and looked; there was a husky man at the end of the shovel.

"What is your name, young man?" asked the president. "And just what are you doing?"

The sweaty face of an Irishman appeared over the lip of the ditch to snap, "None of your damn business!" Whereupon he went back to work.

Not long after, a colleague in the ditch informed the young Irishman that he had just insulted the president of the company. William Mulholland sighed, sadly laid down his shovel, picked up his coat and slogged off, expecting to collect his final pay.

Soon after, the Irishman was named foreman of the ditch gang. Apparently the company president knew a good man when he saw him at the end of a shovel.

For the next few years, the Irishman worked by day and studied geometry and engineering by night, often until 3 a.m. In 1886, he was appointed superintendent of the system.

Southern California had found its water witch.

* * *

In 1886, when Mulholland was appointed water superintendent, a young fellow named Fred Eaton was elected city engineer. A Los

Angeles native, Eaton soon threw himself wholeheartedly into water problems, much to Mulholland's satisfaction. Eaton, too, was a self-educated engineer; the men soon became cronies.

Eaton knew southern California's climate better than Mulholland; Eaton had become a water worrier. Mulholland pooh-poohed Eaton's fears, insisting that the Los Angeles River could supply the city's needs for at least half a century.

"Wait and see," muttered Eaton.

The year was 1892. Neither could have known it then but 1892 was the first year of a decade of drought that would almost destroy southern California's economy. It was also the year during which Eaton discovered a water bonanza.

Far to the north of Los Angeles, the Owens River of Inyo County drained most of the Sierra's eastern slope. It was high ground, far above the coastal plain of Los Angeles, and water flows downhill. Eaton's private dream took shape: *If somehow that Owens River water could be bought for Los Angeles and transported over 200 miles through a gravity aqueduct...*

Mulholland was still thinking about the Los Angeles River, not the Owens. As the drought stretched out, he moved to grab the last drop of the river's flow, underground as well as above. After a six-year battle, the city in 1899 won its case before the state supreme court.

From that moment forward, Los Angeles owned all rights to water in the river basin and even had power to prevent farmers upstream from pumping out of wells. The city was beginning to flex its muscle.

At the time, the San Fernando Valley was just beginning to develop irrigated agriculture. The court decision wiped out its water source and seemed to sentence the valley to a future as dry as its past.

Now the San Fernando Valley is a thoroughly urban part of Los Angeles. First the city swallowed up the valley's water, then it swallowed up the valley. So it goes in the building of a modern metropolis.

DRY AS DUST, THEN DRIER

The terrible drought continued. During the summer of 1903, Mulholland was forced to order the pumping of drinking water from the *zanja madre*, the main irrigation ditch. (This, remember, was long before pesticides and other noxious substances had polluted the

William Mulholland was the prime mover of water to southern California.

ditches; a watermaster who issued such an order today would have to be out of his mind.)

By July of 1904, with no substantial rainfall in sight, Bill Mulholland was ready to go to Fred Eaton and say: "Show me this Owens Valley. Show me this water."

Eaton did so. They studied the ground and concluded that Owens River water could be propelled to Los Angeles by the cheapest power available—gravity.

This was the last point of agreement between the two men for a long time. Eaton had bought land in the Owens Valley; he insisted on keeping a reservoir site in Long Valley that wouldn't be needed in the initial development.

The rift between the old friends grew wider and threatened the entire project. Finally Mulholland argued Eaton into allowing a low dam in Long Valley which would impound just a small part of the valley's capacity.

What the compromise really meant was that neither Owens Valley nor Los Angeles would have enough water in the event of future drought. In southern California, drought was as inevitable as sunrise, so conflict was as inevitable as sunset. Seeds of the Owens Valley War had been planted.

They would sprout soon enough.

* * *

The owner of the first automobile in the Owens Valley, Wilfred W. Watterson, was also president of the Inyo County Bank of Bishop. His brother, Mark, was treasurer.

Of a Sunday, it was Wilfred's pleasant habit to drive his 15-horsepower White Steamer over the dusty roads of the upper valley, offering rides to one and all, as a community leader should.

When the city clerk of Los Angeles arrived to complete the deals for valley land that had been initiated by Fred Eaton, Watterson dragged his feet, at one point even laid a gun on his desk in a suggestive way.

But Los Angeles bought land . . . and more land.

Finally, during the summer of 1905, Bill Mulholland was able to tell the Los Angeles council: "The last spike is driven. The options are all secured."

The Los Angeles *Times* trumpeted: "Titanic Project to Give City a River." The front page told the Owens River story; the secret was out.

Agriculture

A day too soon, for Fred Eaton's comfort. He was caught in Bishop closing out final details and only sheer bravado allowed his escape.

He left the valley by night train on July 31. Eaton was alive and breathing... but it had been a close thing.

Owens Valley citizens weren't yet ready for outright violence. The time would come.

EVERYTHING BUT THE WATER

Up to this point, argument had been confined to California. But in order to build an aqueduct across public lands, Los Angeles had to slide a bill through the U.S. Congress. It was done, but not without fanning the flames of bitterness. The controversy finally fell into the lap of President Theodore Roosevelt, who openly sided with Los Angeles.

Mulholland and his water project had carried the day. The Owens Valley was left to lick its deep wounds.

"Los Angeles has been given all that she asked for," editorialized the Inyo *Independent*, "except the water."

Mulholland and his eager beavers in the city, by now completely caught up in their heady adventure, didn't get the message.

* * *

Somebody always has to pay and in this case, it was the citizens of Los Angeles. Mulholland estimated that the great project would cost $23,000,000; bonds in that amount would have to be voted. On June 12, after a wild campaign, the votes came in—a 10-1 landslide for the Los Angeles Aqueduct!

What had been a paper project suddenly became a matter of dirt and rock and concrete and steel. It was one thing to plan the largest aqueduct in the western hemisphere; it was something else to build it.

There had never been any doubt about the choice for superintendent of construction.

"I wanted one big job before I died," the man had remarked.

William Mulholland, of course.

WATER RUNS DOWNHILL... WITH HELP

First an open ditch would carry the precious liquid south along the eastern foothills of the Sierra to the first reservoir at Haiwee. Then

a closed conduit of tunnels and siphons would be used for the next leg of the long journey along the west edge of the Mojave Desert. A covered concrete trough then would ease the flow across a corner of the desert to a point in the mountains north of Los Angeles.

Here the five-mile Elizabeth Tunnel would be employed to coax the water through the rock and after more tunnels and siphons, the Owens River would splash with well-deserved fatigue into San Fernando Valley reservoirs 223 miles below the intake.

At first men working at the tunnel faces had to drill powder holes by hand but early in 1908, electric motors were introduced to drive compressed-air drills.

In April, 1910, crews working in from the south portal set a new American hard-rock tunnel record—604 feet in a single month.

Spectacular work was being done elsewhere, too. In the so-called "Jawbone" Division north of Mojave, workmen set a world's record for soft-rock tunneling by advancing 1061 feet during a single month.

The work was hard and dangerous but it had its lighter moments, too.

Bill Mulholland much admired the Jawbone superintendent, A. C. Hansen. The tall Scandinavian was a topflight engineer, but had never developed a sense of humor. Mulholland, who liked to laugh, occasionally took advantage of the lack.

One day Mulholland turned up on the Jawbone to find that a miner had been trapped by a landslide.

Hansen said, "We have been talking to him through a two-inch pipe driven through the muck."

It struck Mulholland that if he were that miner, he would appreciate a little more than talk. "How long has he been in there?" Mulholland asked.

"Three days."

Mulholland gasped. "Then he must be nearly starved!"

"Oh, no," said Hansen. "We've been rolling hard-boiled eggs to him through the pipe."

Concealing his admiration for the trick, Mulholland asked sternly, "Have you been charging him board?"

"No..." The big Scandinavian scratched his head. "Do you think I ought to?"

The enormity of the Los Angeles Aqueduct is symbolized by this dramatic view of a siphon in Jawbone Canyon about 1913.

The entombed miner was rescued the next day; his boss chose not to bill him for hard-boiled eggs.

By the middle of 1912, 90 per cent of the aqueduct had been finished and Mulholland wearily said, "The end of our task seems fairly in sight. We are giving the city a magnificent heritage. If it were not for looking ahead to the time of reward... five or six years from now, I could not go on with the work, for I am worn out."

When it became obvious that the gigantic task was going to be finished on schedule and that it would cost no more than the $23,000,000 estimated by the superintendent, honors descended on Mulholland. His aqueduct gained recognition as America's greatest, second only to the Panama Canal as a triumph of engineering. Engineering societies showered awards on Mulholland; the University of California conferred an honorary doctorate.

Important citizens saw him as a potential mayor but Mulholland typically squelched that talk by sniffing: "Gentlemen, I would rather give birth to a porcupine backwards than be mayor of Los Angeles."

* * *

On November 4, 1913, Mulholland joined the thousands who gathered at the San Fernando Cascade.

From the platform, Mulholland watched with the crowd as the gates above them slowly lifted. First a trickle, then a rivulet and finally a flood sparkling in the sun washed down the Cascade and raced toward San Fernando Reservoir.

The program called for speeches and the like; Mulholland was to formally turn over the aqueduct to the city. But the crowd had fled to the side of the Cascade, so Mulholland simply turned to the mayor and said in a voice choked with emotion:

"There it is. Take it."

Then Mulholland joyfully joined the crowd for a drink of Owens River water.

But far to the north, in the empty reaches of proud Inyo County, there was no laughter.

A dream became reality when the first water carried by the Los Angeles Aqueduct arrived at the San Fernando Cascade. Pictured is the dedication ceremony in 1913.

THE UNNECESSARY WAR

An important man was missing from the aqueduct dedication—Fred Eaton.

Eaton, remember, had agreed to give up his private interest in the original project, but he had insisted on keeping his Long Valley ranch.

Bill Mulholland knew that Los Angeles would eventually need the ranch as a reservoir site. As the big ditch neared completion, the water superintendent talked to his old friend about Long Valley and was shocked to discover that Eaton now wanted a cool million dollars for it.

A bitter Mulholland is supposed to have snapped then, "I'll buy Long Valley three years after Eaton is dead."

Without full use of Long Valley as a reservoir, there was no way Los Angeles could guarantee Owens Valley farmers enough irrigation water for survival. If the farmers starved out, the towns died, too. Sturdy frontier settlements like Bishop and Lone Pine and Independence would no longer rest comfortably in the cool evening shadows of the Sierras; those long shadows would become a shroud.

Thus the failure of two old friends to reach agreement set the stage for violence. Drums began to beat for the Owens Valley War.

By summer, 1921, it was plain that drought had again clamped down on California and there wasn't going to be enough water for everybody.

Owens Valley farmers and ranchers weren't about to lie down and die of thirst, so they turned Los Angeles-owned water from the river into their irrigation ditches. Employees of the city ventured out to turn the water back.

Fred Eaton stationed armed guards on his creeks and kept an eye on anyone who travelled through Long Valley.

Eaton snorted: "They say I am no longer a friend of the city. I deny that. But if they try to take something of mine away from me I'll fight."

Far to the south, farmers in the San Fernando Valley sang a different song. Owens River water had turned the San Fernando desert into a green garden—green as a thousand-dollar bill. In the San Fernando Valley, there had been 3000 acres of cultivated land in 1914.

Only three years later, there were 75,000!

Water from the north had developed an agricultural paradise, with the hungry, exploding market of Los Angeles just over the hill.

But the Owens Valley began to go dry. More and more houses

stood empty, staring starkly over an encroaching wasteland. In Bishop and Big Pine, businessmen looked out at ominously quiet streets.

The bankers, Wilfred and Mark Watterson, were turned to for leadership. Other leaders emerged, among them Harry Glasscock, outspoken editor of the Owens Valley *Herald*, and Will Chalfant, editor of the Inyo *Register*.

* * *

At 1 a.m. on May 21, 1924, an eleven-car caravan rolled quietly north through Lone Pine, then turned off the highway.

Moments later the earth quaked and the town shuddered as huge chunks of concrete sailed skyward, tearing out telephone and power lines as they blasted through the echoing thunder before gouging out landing sites a quarter of a mile away.

The arrogant aqueduct had sprung a leak, a *big* leak. Dynamiters had done their work.

The damage was repaired, but on November 16, Owens Valley citizens took possession of the Alabama Gates, a main flood diversion point along the aqueduct.

The gates were opened. Immediately the entire flow of the Los Angeles Aqueduct poured across the highway and into the old bed of the Owens River.

Los Angeles quickly sent carloads of detectives and investigators north. They were met below Lone Pine by Sheriff Charles Collins of Inyo County.

"If you go up there and start any trouble," the sheriff warned, "not one of you'll get back to tell about it."

The city folks turned around.

Almost every store in Bishop closed. A sign in the center of town proclaimed: "If I am not on the job, you can find me at the aqueduct."

On November 18, more than 700 persons clustered around Alabama Gates. The scene was visited by a Western movie star of the day, Tom Mix, who was on location in the Alabama Hills; he brought an orchestra. On the following day, there was a barbecue.

But it wasn't just a picnic. There were still guns on hand and newspapers around the country began to speak of "California's little civil war."

Finally Wilfred Watterson brought assurance from Los Angeles that banking interests in the city had decided to use their influence to bring about a settlement.

Water was turned back into the aqueduct but trouble still bubbled in Owens Valley.

Southern California was booming during the early 1920s, even if continued drought threatened the water supply. A great oil field had been discovered at Long Beach; in rural spaces called Hollywood, cows had to move over as actors and actresses moved in. The land of the lotus found an even more exotic plant sprouting in its far-out garden—the movies!

As trains from the east spewed their human loads into the fabled sunshine, the need for Owens Valley water became more urgent.

Los Angeles water commissioners realized that they would have to find the money somewhere to buy what was left of the Owens Valley. It was as simple as that.

In the Owens Valley, neighbor turned against neighbor. Those who sold land to the city were considered traitors by those who had vowed not to sell. When it became clear that Los Angeles intended to suck the Owens Valley dry, merchants in Bishop demanded reparations because, if the farmers left, their businesses would collapse.

Shipments to the valley of guns and dynamite steadily increased. The guns were mostly for bluster but blasting of the aqueduct during the summer of 1927 became a ritual, like the weekly band concert. And almost as noisy . . .

THE FINAL BLOW

On August 3, 1927, an investigator from the state banking office dropped off a train in the Owens Valley and sidled up to the Inyo County Bank, the bank owned by the Wattersons, leaders in the fight against the city.

At noon of the next day, all five Watterson banks in Inyo County were closed. The investigator had discovered huge shortages. Something like $2,300,000 was missing and could not be accounted for by the Wattersons.

And so the Owens Valley War ended, not with the uproar of the last case of dynamite as it blasted concrete to bits, but with the quiet scratch of pens held in the soft, white hands of bank examiners.

With local morale shattered, it seemed that Owens Valley had no choice but to let its water stream south.

And southern California, during the next year, would have to cope with that water.

A CRACK IN THE DAM

St. Francis Dam, which almost doubled the water storage capacity in the San Fernando Valley, was finished and filled just in time to save the valley's crops in 1927, yet another dry year.

The concrete structure in San Francisquito Canyon had been built hurriedly, pushed to early completion by an aging but still hard-driving Bill Mulholland.

But during its first year of use, the dam developed a disturbing habit—it leaked. Understandable, of course; the site of the dam was along California's ancient hernia, the San Andreas Fault, and the mica schist and conglomerate upon which the structure squatted had split and split again as the earth's crust groaned and heaved along the fault line. Two cracks developed in the dam's face; they were caulked up.

Early in March, 1928, the water below the dam turned muddy, a bad sign; abutment ground might be weakening. On March 12, Mulholland checked the massive structure, decided that the muddy water was only the result of road construction and heaved a sigh of relief.

But it happened that very night, late, when most of the men, women and children downstream were asleep.

A few minutes before midnight, a large section of ground broke off, scraped across the face of the dam and fell onto the canyon floor.

Catastrophe quickly followed. The east abutment collapsed under the monstrous pressure of the millions of gallons of water in the reservoir. Then both wings of the dam burst with a mighty roar and the flood exploded around both sides of the still-standing central section.

A 100-foot wall of water stormed toward the sea, carrying great chunks of concrete bobbing like corks.

Because telephone lines had been torn away, it was impossible to pass the terrible word downstream. But at 1:15 a.m., the warning was phoned to coastal Ventura from Los Angeles. A sheriff's car roared out of Ventura with its siren wailing, warned Santa Paula, then charged on toward Fillmore. The deputy stopped at the firehouse and

➡

This pitiful column was all that was left standing when St. Francis dam collapsed in 1928. This aerial view looking downstream shows great chunks of concrete, upper right, carried well below the dam by the onrushing wall of water.

rang the bell; soon the fearsome cry echoed through the town:
"Flood! Run for the hills!"

Where telephone lines remained, operators did heroic work of warning. Fillmore suffered in its turn, then at 3:30 a.m., the monster that had escaped from St. Francis Dam hit Santa Paula with a 25-foot tide, carried houses and cars and trees and poles along like so many toys as it raged past Saticoy and Montalvo.

Soon after 5 a.m., the exhausted beast flung its burden into the Pacific Ocean and died.

Tired, old William Mulholland, builder of the dam, reacted to one of the nation's worst disasters like a man kicked in the stomach.

He said: "I envy the dead."

* * *

The toll of dead was finally fixed at 385 persons. Also lost were 1240 houses and 7900 acres of the best farmland in the nation.

The city of Los Angeles, without a quibble, accepted full blame for the disaster. The city paid claims totalling $15,000,000; not a single claim had to be taken to court.

When someone suggested to Mulholland that he needn't take all the blame, that his assistants had handled the details of the dam, the weary old man muttered:

"Fasten it on me if there was any error of judgment — human judgment. *I am that human.*"

At age 72, Bill Mulholland's flaming spirit was quenched, written off as just another casualty of that ugly night when the captive water smashed free, laughed at man's puny obstacles and plunged wildly toward its destined confrontation with the sea.

San Francisquito Canyon could not be considered a battleground of the Owens Valley War but collapse of St. Francis Dam seemed to signal the end of the long, angry fray.

Morale in the valley had collapsed with the sinking of the Watterson banks. The will to fight in Los Angeles seemed to die when the dam broke up and ground down the spirit of Bill Mulholland.

In 1930, Los Angeles voted the bonds to buy up most of what remained of Owens Valley, even paid peak 1923 prices for town lots— "reparations," if one wanted to look at it that way.

But the fact remains that Owens Valley is mostly dry today and the aqueduct still carries the water south and there are those who lived there when it all happened (and some who didn't) who feel that somehow those city dudes stole the water.

Not really; those city dudes bought and paid for it. In money, in blood, in labor, in suffering.

The Owens Valley War rings out in California history not only because of its violence but because it painted in bold, bright colors the continuing pageant of California's water wars.

Those who have the water want desperately to keep it, or sell it dearly; those who don't have it want desperately to snatch it, or buy it cheaply.

Because, in the drought-plagued land called California, water is life.

OTHER WATERS, OTHER WARS

There is another stream flowing into the sight of Californians and this one makes Owens River look like a long, thin puddle.

The Colorado, it is called. This monster, nurtured by the deep snows in the Rocky Mountains, is one of the three largest water systems in the United States. It drains part of seven states and empties into Mexico.

California cocked an eye at the Colorado for one very good reason: The great river passed tantalizingly close to what was surely (next to Death Valley) the hottest, driest, bleakest, emptiest, godforsakenest expanse of the state—the Salton Sink and the Colorado Desert.

Arizona was already irrigating from the river in the Yuma Valley. They say on the desert, "Where mesquite grows, fence posts will bloom if watered."

Someone quickly pointed out that the market was very limited for blooming fence posts. There was no way to make the Colorado Desert bloom, grumbled the cynics; alkali was too close to the surface.

A dreamer named George Chaffey thought it could be done. The founder of Ontario and other California towns, Chaffey had established a worldwide reputation as a reclamationist.

Chaffey went to work and by spring, 1902, distribution canals fed water to 100,000 acres of desert which suddenly grew fantastic crops of wheat and barley. The Colorado Desert became the Imperial Valley of California, farmland beyond compare.

It was a good beginning, but it was only a beginning.

There had to be a dam—a very big dam.

Bill Mulholland got involved, of course; he could see no end to the thirst of his employer, the city of Los Angeles. And Phil Swing, an Imperial Valley lawyer, was learning the ropes in Washington, D.C., learning them so well that he was to become California's most effective water lobbyist at the federal level.

The California interests had two major objectives: the Colorado Aqueduct to Los Angeles, which would insure the big city a supply of water for a long time to come; and the All-American Canal, which would free the Imperial Valley from Mexico's claims on the water and guarantee that this ancient wasteland would become the world's biggest oasis.

But rivers, remember, have minds of their own; they flood or they trickle, as nature calls. Dams were needed to impound the flood water and insure a steady supply in dry years. To be truly useful to man, water must be stored.

Only after a nine-year fight was Boulder Dam (now Hoover Dam) approved. It was dedicated in 1935 by President Franklin D. Roosevelt. Behind it grew Lake Mead, largest man-made lake in the U.S. (But it shrinks each year as river-borne silt fills it. Engineers said silt wouldn't choke it for 300 years; now 100 years sounds more reasonable as erosion and other pollution run wild. Rivers resent being used as sewers.)

* * *

William Mulholland died on July 22, 1935. Los Angeles mourned and work was stopped on the Colorado Aqueduct for a minute of sorrowing silence. The water witch was dead, but the water still flowed.

The aqueduct was finished in 1941. Among the California cities which began to enjoy its water were Pasadena, Santa Monica and Long Beach. During the same year, the All-American Canal began to deliver water.

It wasn't enough, of course. There will never be enough if California continues its record-shattering rate of growth. Southern California, in particular, has always generated feast or famine, dust or mud.

But the water made a miracle, a California phenomenon admired

Oroville Dam, new keystone of California's water system, is the tallest man-made pile of dirt in the world. Spillway is at left.

around the world — the food factory, the automatic farm. The formula is simple: earth plus water plus fertilizer plus year-around sunshine.

California, with about four billion dollars worth of crops annually, has led the United States in agricultural production for more than 20 years. Two billions more are piled on each year by processing those crops.

Yet California is nowhere near America's so-called "Farm Belt." The state, by itself, has become a Farm Belt, complete with buckle.

California irrigates about 8,000,000 acres of land, not counting suburban lawns. That resounding figure represents about one-quarter of all the irrigated land in the United States!

Until World War II, water development had been mostly a local affair. By 1960, when the state's voters committed themselves to the California State Water Project, water planning had become a statewide concern. Federal agencies also became involved, both in planning and financing, particularly the Army Engineers and Bureau of Reclamation.

The state water project took giant strides during the 1960s, highlighted by the completion of the tallest pile of dirt in the world, Oroville Dam. How much earth is needed to build a dam like this monster?

Eighty million cubic yards, most of which consisted of tailings left from gold mining operations which conveniently covered thousands of acres south of Oroville. The first dam contract was let in July, 1962. All facilities were in operation in mid-1969.

Oroville Dam on the Feather River and the great lake behind it have become one of the most remarkable sights in California. To a first time viewer approaching from below, the dam is disconcerting; rabbit brush grows out of its face. He relaxes only when he learns that under all that earth rests a concrete core which locks the rabbit brush to bedrock.

* * *

By 1970, California's mountains were pretty well peppered with

Winemaking has long been a California specialty. This scene shows champagne being corked at Buena Vista Vineyard, Sonoma, in the early 1870s. Chinese workers made the wicker baskets in the foreground, in which bottles were packed for market.

dams, while the lowlands were ribbed and criss-crossed with canals.

It had to be this way. About 75 per cent of the native water supply is in northern California but 75 per cent of the need and use are in southern California. So nothing would do but to move the precious fluid from one place to another. In the process, the state has developed one of the world's most elaborate water transportation systems.

* * *

Cattle and the American West are part and parcel, like potatoes and gravy. The origins of the industry are Mexican, without a doubt. Working cattle from the back of a horse, branding, trail driving, roundups—these were tricks brought up from south of the border. The legendary Longhorn steer came from Mexico, too. The thick book of laws governing ranching and mining in the West of today was based on the *regulamientos* of Spain. Water rights by which California agriculture lives or dies in the modern era are based on prior usage, not on the English system of "riparian rights," under which the person who owned land along a stream also owned use of the water. The Mexican way, again.

* * *

The Californios provided the model for the original American cowboy. It was said that a Californio wasn't much interested in anything that couldn't be done from the back of a horse, whether it was grabbing a chicken buried in the sand, a favorite sport, or lassoing a bear. It was a simple time, with simple pleasures. The Oakland Museum displays a few lines from a song of that earthy time:

"A ranchero if he's lucky
  has a pair of pants and wooden stirrups
  and some good leather reins."

This, believe it or not, is the south end of a tractor going north. Benjamin Holt of California built this amazing machine for farming the marshy Sacramento delta. There had to be a better answer and Holt soon found it in the track-laying tractor, or "caterpillar," which he first built in 1904. The British placed large orders with Holt Manufacturing Co. during World War I for monstrous track-laying war machines. In an attempt to confuse the enemy, the British let it be known that the vehicles would be used to haul water to troops in the desert, hence the name "tank." Tanks they are called to this day.

* * *

Name any crop or livestock-poultry product and it's probably produced in ridiculous quantity somewhere in California. (The two major exceptions are tobacco and soybeans.) The state's climate and water supplies encourage what may well be the most diversified agriculture in the world. California farmers lead the country in production of 46 different crops, from alfalfa seed to walnuts, skipping lightly over garlic and rabbits. Cattle and calves lead the way with about 19 per cent of the state's total production, followed by dairy products with 11 per cent. Also consistently in the top twenty are eggs, grapes, hay, tomatoes, cotton, lettuce, nursery products, oranges, rice, peaches, cut flowers, sugar beets, almonds, potatoes, turkeys, barley, walnuts and strawberries.

* * *

An important goad and guide for California's leap to the forefront of agriculture in the U.S. has been experimentation carried on by the University of California, Division of Agricultural Sciences, with busy campuses at Davis, Berkeley and Riverside. The factory farm works only because science and technology make it work. The concept is based solidly on two pillars—machines and chemicals. Over the years, California's agriculture researchers have helped to develop many of both. Since farming on such a vast scale has drastically altered the state's ecology, the Davis campus is now called the "College of Agricultural and Environmental Sciences." If field burning pollutes the air and pesticides foul streams and lakes, it is agriculture's responsibility to do what it can to correct the situation. The scientists at Davis will have to meet the problem head-on.

THE SAGE OF SANTA ROSA

"I firmly believe, from all I have seen," he wrote in a letter to his old home in New England, "that this is the chosen spot of all the earth, as far as nature is concerned. The climate is perfect . . . everything is like a beautiful spring day all the time."

The writer was referring to the Santa Rosa Valley about 50 miles north of San Francisco. He had come west as a young man carrying 10 potatoes in his luggage—"Burbank" potatoes, fittingly enough,

Luther Burbank of Santa Rosa earned world renown with his plant magic.

for the young man's name was Luther Burbank and he had developed the variety in Massachusetts.

Luther Burbank was destined to live a long, productive life in the Utopian valley he had discovered and when he died in 1926 at age 77, the world knew his name. His grave under a Cedar of Lebanon in the yard of his old home draws reverent visitors from about 60 foreign countries every year. The world knows him well.

Luther Burbank simply wanted to make plants better, more useful to man and more beautiful to look upon. His accomplishments ran the gamut from the little white Shasta Daisy to the spineless cactus which he developed for use as cattle feed in the Southwest.

Both the daisy and the cactus can be seen in Burbank Memorial Gardens, which are maintained by the city of Santa Rosa as a monument to the man who talked to plants. His home and greenhouse are on adjoining property along busy Santa Rosa Avenue.

Burbank's birthday, March 7, is commemorated as California's Arbor Day; at schools throughout the state, trees are planted in his name.

One wonders what this Californian known-around-the-world would say if he were resurrected long enough to tour a modern San Joaquin Valley factory farm . . .

SITES TO SEE

LOS ANGELES COUNTY MUSEUM OF SCIENCE & INDUSTRY, Exposition Park, Los Angeles. (Among many other fine exhibits, there is a giant relief model of the Metropolitan Water District, including the Colorado Aqueduct.)

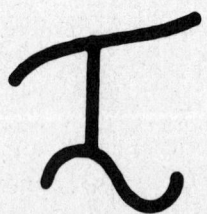

RANCHO SAN PASQUAL. A brand registered by Manuel Garfias on September 5, 1843, was used at the rancho, which now encompasses Pasadena, South Pasadena and San Marino.

Chapter Nine *

The Hyphenated Californians
AMERICANS WITH JAPANESE FACES

A teenager named John Aiso won an oratorical contest at Hollywood High School in 1926, and earned a much-desired trip to Washington, D.C., where he would compete in the national finals.

But John Aiso didn't go to the nation's capital. His debating partner went instead, and won the national contest.

John Aiso was cheated of the trip because, through no fault of his own, he sprang from the wrong race. He was Nisei—second generation Japanese-American—and Californians of that day would not have felt properly represented in Washington by John Aiso, American citizen by birth . . . but a Nisei.

The subject of the debating contest was "The American Constitution."

On June 7, 1969, officials of the state of California placed a plaque on the grounds of a school in El Dorado County, where Japanese 100 years earlier had established a visionary project called "Wakamatsu Tea and Silk Farm Colony." The colony didn't last long, but by 1910 there were 72,157 Japanese living in the U.S.

An immigrant Japanese showed California how to grow rice, which constituted a great leap forward for the state's agriculture. Japanese-Americans were first to demonstrate that potatoes could be a commercial crop in California.

A report to the governor in 1921 from Col. John P. Irish, president of the California Delta Association, stated:

". . . They had seen the Japanese convert the barren land like that at Florin and Livingston into productive and profitable fields, orchards and vineyards, by the persistence and intelligence of their industry. They had seen the hardpan and goose lands in the Sacramento Valley, gray and black with our two destructive alkalis, cursed with barrenness ... and not worth paying taxes on, until Ikuta, the Japanese, decided that those lands would raise rice. After years of persistent toil, enduring heartbreaking losses and disappointments, he conquered that rebellious soil and raised the first commercial crop of rice in California. Due to the work of this great Japanese pioneer, this State now has a rice crop worth 60 million dollars (in 1921) ... they had seen that 70 per cent of the total 74,000 acres owned by Japanese were these lands that disfigured the State until they had been reclaimed by Japanese genius and industry ..."

* * *

The scene: Honolulu, Hawaii. The date: Sunday, December 7, 1941.

A 17-year-old, Daniel Ken Inouye, woke up early, turned on his bedside radio and stiffened in horror as he heard:

"Pearl Harbor is being bombed by the Japanese! I repeat: This is not a test or a maneuver! Japanese war planes are attacking Oahu!"

By December 11, 1941, 1370 persons of Japanese descent had been "detained" on the mainland and in Hawaii.

Panic swept the country. Rumors snapped and crackled through the fear-fogged atmosphere. Frantic reports threatened invasion of the West Coast by Japanese air and naval forces. After all, hadn't the mighty U.S. fleet been destroyed at Pearl Harbor? After a disaster of that magnitude, anything seemed possible.

Late in December, 1941, two San Francisco Japanese talked together.

"Sab," said one, "I hear they're going to put all the Japanese in concentration camps. Do you know anything about that?"

"Who says so?"

"The chief of police in Oakland. He told me everybody, Issei, Nisei, even the little kids, will be interned."

Sab snorted. "He's crazy. They can't do that. We're American citizens. We've got our rights."

* * *

Nisei (pronounced nee-say) are Japanese-Americans born in the United States. Issei (ee-say) are Japanese-Americans born in Japan. Nisei have American citizenship as a right of birth. In 1941, Issei couldn't become naturalized citizens even if they wanted to, under the 1924 Exclusion Act.

A syndicated columnist, Henry McLemore, wrote: "Herd 'em up, pack 'em off and give 'em the inside room in the badlands. Let 'em be pinched, hurt, hungry and dead up against it . . . Let us have no patience with the enemy or with anyone else whose veins carry his blood . . . Personally, I hate the Japanese. And that goes for all of them."

Another columnist, Westbrook Pegler, bellowed: "The Japanese in California should be under guard to the last man and woman right now and to hell with habeas corpus until danger is over."

On December 19, the Western Defense commander, Lt. Gen. John L. DeWitt, wrote a memo to his Washington superiors, asking "that action be initiated at the earliest practical date to collect all alien subjects fourteen years of age and over, of enemy nations and remove them to the Zone of the Interior."

Note that there is no mention of "Japanese" or "Japanese-Americans."

The 1940 census had turned up 126,947 persons of Japanese descent in the U.S. The majority lived in California. Of the total in the West, 71,484 were citizens by birth; 40,869 were aliens who were barred from citizenship by law.

It is interesting and ironic to consider that in 1941, there were 51,923 aliens of Italian ancestry in California and 19,422 Germans, most of whom could have become citizens if they had cared to. And the U.S. at the time was at war with both Germany and Italy . . .

But finally it was only the Japanese, aliens and citizens alike, young and old, who were uprooted, removed and locked up under armed guard—*every last one of them in California and in the western halves of Oregon and Washington!*

It happened in the United States of America; it happened in the sovereign state of California.

And not so long ago . . .

* * *

Thus the clamor rose, spreading like wind-driven fire in the dry grass of California, fueled by hysteria which trailed the grim smoke of Pearl Harbor.

Mayor Fletcher Bowron of Los Angeles spoke on the radio to urge the removal of the Japanese. He was joined by such groups as the

American Legion, the Military Order of the Purple Heart, the Farm Bureau Federation and the Native Sons of the Golden West.

On February 19, 1942, President Franklin D. Roosevelt signed Executive Order 9066, which gave the Secretary of War the power to designate certain "military areas" and to exclude "any or all" persons from such areas.

At a hearing in San Francisco several days later, Attorney General Earl Warren of California testified: "I want to say that the consensus . . . among the law-enforcement officers of this state is that there is more potential danger among the group of Japanese who were born in this country than from the alien Japanese who were born in Japan . . . We believe that when we are dealing with the Caucasian race we have methods that will test the loyalty of them, and we believe that we can, in dealing with the Germans and the Italians, arrive at some fairly sound conclusions because of our knowledge of the way they live in the community . . . But when we deal with the Japanese we are in an entirely different field and we cannot form any opinion that we believe to be sound . . ."

So racism reared its ugly head again in America.

The inscrutable Oriental, the Yellow Peril.

Italians and Germans, even though aliens, were safe because they were white. But those slant-eyed Japs, you had to watch them, right? *Right* . . .

(Yes, this Earl Warren is the same honored citizen of California who became Chief Justice of the U.S. Supreme Court, the same Earl Warren who was tarred and feathered on all those billboards which appeared in the 1960s after the so-called "Warren Court" had laid the legal foundation, at long last, for the civil rights of minorities in America. Fear fades and with it fades hysteria; times change; people change; only the irony of history is constant and constantly startling.)

* * *

Sabotage.
Fifth Column.
Dark Rumors.
Shadows in the Night.
Odd Noises.

Days dawned in fear, and dusk set the fear afire. In the glorious golden sunsets oozing out of the ocean which surged against the California shore, there suddenly blossomed colors more yellow than orange and red.

The cries of the hysterical rent the air:

A Jap's a Jap, right? Hadn't those lousy Japs in Hawaii marked the targets for the bombers at Pearl? Hadn't they cut the phone lines and stolen fuses from the ack-ack shells? Hadn't they blocked the streets with their junk cars so the sailors and soldiers and marines were delayed in getting to their stations?

As it turned out, they hadn't.

But this cool knowledge came later, much too late to help the Nisei and the Issei.

When all was said and done and the terrible war was over and men of different races could look at each other without mortal fear in their eyes, it was concluded that Japanese-Americans, alien or otherwise, *had not committed a single, solitary, documented act of sabotage or espionage in Hawaii or on the mainland.* On the contrary, they had only worked hard and fought fiercely and suffered brutally for their adopted country, the land of the free and the home of the brave.

As it turned out, the internal enemy was not the Japanese-American.

The internal enemy was fear and its sick handmaiden—racism.

* * *

Most of the Nisei and Issei in California lived in the urban and suburban areas of San Francisco and Los Angeles.

There is a horse racing facility near San Francisco called Tanforan. There is another near Los Angeles called Santa Anita. Both had hundreds of stalls for horses. At the time, the stalls seemed like logical dwelling places for "Japs." The tracks needed only barbed wire and gun towers to make them really cozy; it was done.

On Terminal Island, Los Angeles, the human vultures flocked to "buy" the household effects of the dispossessed Japanese-Americans—$5 for an almost new washing machine, $10 for a refrigerator, $25 for a piano. The Nisei and Issei sold at those blood-sucking prices; they had no choice.

In the rural areas, the situation was much worse. Farmers of Japanese descent, faced with imprisonment for an indefinite period, were forced to sell carefully-tended farm land for a fraction of its real worth. The fruit of decades of labor was torn away by vultures and lost forever to the rightful owners.

* * *

There were 12 assembly centers in California: Marysville, Sacramento, Stockton, Tanforan Racetrack near San Francisco, Turlock, Salinas, Merced, Pinedale, Fresno, Tulare, Santa Anita Racetrack in Los Angeles and Pomona.

The only relocation centers—or semi-permanent camps— in California were Manzanar near Independence and Tule Lake in the northeast. At the latter camp were segregated what the War Relocation Authority considered "disloyal" Japanese-Americans.

Said a Sansei (third generation) child after her first day in an assembly center, "I don't like Japan, Mommy. I want to go home to America."

By the end of 1942, 110,000 persons had been evacuated.

On January 2, 1945—three years after the evacuation had begun —the Supreme Court of the United States ruled that confinement of the Japanese-Americans had been a violation of their constitutional rights. Anticipating the decision, the army had opened the gates of the concentration camps one day earlier. The long exile was over.

Only half of those who had been evacuated still remained in the camps when the bars were dropped. Many had been scattered over the country by the War Relocation Authority, spread from Maine to Mississippi, where they tried to make new lives in areas which did not consider them a threat to the war effort. (Nisei sent to the south had startling experiences. Southern whites thought of them as white, Negroes thought of them as black. Whites insisted that they act like whites, sit at the front of busses and use white rest rooms and drinking fountains. Blacks murmured to the Nisei: "Down here, we colored folks have got to stick together." Surely no other experience could have demonstrated so well the infuriating stupidity of American racism.)

Still others, mostly young men, had gone into the armed forces. Apparently the Nisei who made this choice tried to prove something.

They did.

The 442nd Regimental Combat Team, mostly Nisei, was formed in early 1943 and trained at Camp Shelby, Mississippi. The 442nd's motto was "Go For Broke." It was derived from a Hawaiian gambler's phrase meaning, "Shoot the works."

Forced out of their homes, Nisei lived in quarters like these at Tanforan racetrack near San Francisco.

The 442nd shot the works in Italy and France. When the blood stopped flowing, the unit had taken part in seven major campaigns and had suffered 9486 casualties—300 per cent of its original infantry strength—and had earned more than 18,000 individual decorations for valor!

* * *

In 1942, the army realized that its intelligence and propaganda efforts in the Pacific were in trouble; Japanese linguists were needed badly.

Whereupon somebody thought: *What about all those Japanese-Americans?*

The call went out for Nisei to enroll in the language and intelligence program. Thirty-seven hundred men were interviewed, but only *three per cent* spoke fluent Japanese! Apparently Americanization had been too successful.

A school was established at Camp Savage, Minnesota, and the first Nisei linguists were trained and sent to the Pacific, where they translated captured battle plans, messages and diaries; they interrogated prisoners and broadcast propaganda.

Soon the order came back to the States: "Send us more Nisei linguists."

In Europe, the 442nd fought the noisy, bloody war and won its part of it. In the Pacific, Nisei linguists fought the quiet, secret war and perhaps contributed as much to the final victory.

The last of seven Presidential Distinguished Unit Citations earned by the 442nd Regimental Combat Team was presented by President Harry S Truman in a ceremony on the White House lawn. The President said: "You fought not only the enemy, but you fought prejudice—and you won. Keep up that fight and we will continue to win—to make this great republic stand for what the Constitution says it stands for: 'The welfare of all the people all the time.'"

* * *

As one of his last acts as governor of California in 1953, Earl

Smiling teenagers en route to school . . . a classic scene. Except that these young persons are Japanese-Americans and the buildings in the background of this Ansel Adams photo are part of California's Manzanar Relocation Center and the happy people are prisoners in their own country during World War II.

Warren named John F. Aiso a municipal court judge in Los Angeles, making Aiso the first mainland Nisei to be named to a judicial post. This is the same John Aiso, the debater, who in 1926 was cheated of a trip to Washington, D.C. because of his race. This is the same Earl Warren who in 1942 saw great danger in the presence of Nisei along the California coast, the same Earl Warren who helped to strike mighty blows for civil liberties as chief justice of the U.S. Supreme Court. Irony and history march arm-in-arm down the years.

* * *

In 1971, San Jose elected a new mayor. Nothing unusual about that. But this particular mayor was unusual. He happened to be Norman Y. Mineta, 39, first Japanese-American ever chosen to head the government of a major American city. Mineta's political experience included two years as a prisoner in a relocation camp during World War II. Said Mineta about his imprisonment: "This is the kind of history from which we must learn, so nothing like it can happen again."

* * *

Capt. Dan Inouye of the 442nd (elected U.S. Senator from Hawaii in 1962) lost an arm in combat. On his way home in 1945, he passed through San Francisco. Wearing his combat decorations and with his sleeve empty, he entered a barber shop.

The barber said, "We don't serve Japs here."

It happened in the United States of America, in California, during the not-so-distant past.

AMERICANS WITH MEXICAN FACES

At sunrise on May 3, 1965, a brown worker got up from his knees in a field of roses near the Kern County town of McFarland, yelled, *"Huelga!"* and walked out to the dusty road.

The man, Epifiana Camacho, was one of 80 on that fateful morning who took those long, long steps away from his work.

In Spanish, *"huelga"* means "strike."

A few miles north of McFarland 22 years earlier, a 17-year-old Mexican-American refused to sit in the segregated section of a movie theater in the town of Delano and was thrown into the street.

Although both events took place in the San Joaquin Valley of

California, they are connected in time only by a thin thread.

The teenager kicked out of the Delano theater was Cesar Chavez.

The "Strike of the Roses" was the first work stoppage organized by the first truly successful farm workers' union in California . . . or in the United States.

Its leader was Cesar Chavez, Mexican-American. Or, if you prefer, "Chicano."

The headquarters of his union is in Delano.

WHERE DID ALL THE SPANIARDS GO?

Old Spanish families settled California, right? You've seen the pictures in the history books of the dashing caballeros, charros, senoritas, casas grandes and all the rest.

Well, there were some true-blue Spanish, all right. A few. Among the 23 individuals listed in the Bancroft Library at Berkeley as the founding fathers of Los Angeles are "Two Espanoles."

Also included were "Eight Mulattos, Two Blacks, Nine Mexican Indians, One Mestizo."

So scratch that myth. In fact, most of California's early settlers before the American conquest considered themselves not Spanish, but Mexican residents of Sonora, northern province of Mexico.

For a long time, even Mexican-Americans in California helped to perpetuate the Spanish myth. Too many Mexican Americans like to point to their golden skins and murmur, "Spanish," trying to kick under the carpet the ancient and remarkably sophisticated cultures of the Mexican Indians . . . if they were aware of them.

The lumps under the carpet were too obvious to be ignored.

Language, as is so often the case, helped to create the confusion. A tongue called Spanish — or more exactly *Espanol* — is the national language of Mexico. Naturally; it was introduced by Spaniards as a fringe benefit when those aggressive, greedy Europeans conquered the sun-swept land of the Aztecs. To compound the confusion, the first California Constitution in 1849 recognized both Spanish and English as official state languages.

A logical, sensible language, Spanish is, with every syllable pronounced, but it still manages to slide softly into the ear; it is a language which avoids the gutturals of German while escaping the too-fluid slurring of French; a language made for the singing of romantic songs, for carrying on quiet conversations under moon-washed jacaranda by the plaza.

There are other languages spoken in Mexico to this day, ancient Indian languages, but these are heard mostly in the south.

A Mexican visiting Spain might have a little difficulty in being understood here and there, but it is the same language. Spaniards brought it to Mexico; Mexicans adopted it and it has thrived and spread because it is a very fine language.

In California, Mexican-Americans are sometimes referred to as "Spanish-speaking." Or they have "Spanish" surnames.

They are no more Spanish because they speak a language called that than other U.S. citizens are English because their language is called that.

* * *

The late 1960s saw the growth of an awareness among Mexican-Americans of their Indian heritage, an awakening that promised to grow into pride.

So how important is all this to California?

Consider the fact that Mexican-Americans in California constitute 7.5 per cent of the total population. It was estimated in 1970 that there were 200,000 legal Mexican aliens living in the state and 70,000 more who had entered the country illegally. Mexicans in the northwestern states of Mexico have traditionally treated the California-Mexico border as a mere line on a map, not as a Berlin Wall.

Eight hundred thousand Mexican-Americans live in the Los Angeles metropolitan area. In all the world, only Mexico City and Guadalajara boast more citizens of Mexican ancestry than does Los Angeles. The Mexican-American community of Los Angeles is big enough to rank as one of the 10 largest cities in the U.S.

More than half of California's 285,000 farm workers are of Mexican descent. Their leader: Cesar Chavez. The most prominent Mexican-American in the United States in 1970 was the same man, the last, best hope of the nation's migrant workers, those hard-pressed residents of the affluent society's mobile ghetto.

How did it begin? By what route did California's farm workers and Cesar Chavez arrive at the tense time, the 1970s, and the crucial place, the farm factories of California?

FOREIGNERS IN THE FIELDS

Native California Indians were California's first farm workers.

Some clear-eyed observers have said that they were California's first farm slaves.

If they were slaves, they escaped slavery by a simple method: They died. By 1850, there weren't enough Indians left alive to till the fertile fields of California.

Enter the Chinese, who built the Central Pacific Railroad, then looked around for other work to do. Many found it on the land. But they worked too well (and too cheaply) to suit the whites who wanted their jobs. The Federal Exclusion Act of 1882 solved the problem by barring Chinese.

So along came the Japanese. They not only worked cheaply and well, but bought and developed land of their own, much of it ground that other farmers had given up on.

Europeans, Hindus and Armenians were the next source of cheap farm labor. Racists, having disposed of the Yellow Peril, simmered down. The Europeans, mostly white, stayed and thrived. Many rich farmers in modern California are children of those immigrants.

Filipinos were imported by the thousands during the 1920s, just in time to serve as competition for the hordes of Mexicans who fled their homeland after the 1910 revolution. Most of the Mexicans were illegal immigrants, but local lawmen were inclined to close their eyes if the growers needed help. Thus appeared the term "wetback," applied first to Mexican immigrants who swam the Rio Grande River in the dark of night.

Growers had no objection to hiring farm workers who had entered the country illegally. At any rate, they showed little interest in turning such workers over to the U.S. Border Patrol for deportation. (Unless, of course, such workers gave them trouble, in which case out they went.)

The Great Depression of the 1930s was a boon, in a way, to California's big farmers, in that it helped to create an exodus from Oklahoma, Arkansas and Texas of thousands of farmers whose Dust Bowl land was literally blown away. (California novelist John Steinbeck told the story as well as it will ever be told in his novel, *The Grapes of Wrath*.)

"Okies," they were called. When they appeared in hordes (350,000 all told) looking for work in the fields of California, local lawmen suddenly took a new interest in enforcing the immigration laws. Mexican farm workers were deported in large numbers.

Okies were mostly of the white race, but they were usually treated like a racial minority. A California writer, Carey McWilliams, spoke of entering a motion picture theater in Bakersfield and seeing a sign: "Negroes and Okies Upstairs."

Then, on a quiet Sunday morning, the Japanese bombed Pearl Harbor.

"BIENVENIDOS, BRACEROS!"

Not long after the war began, California agriculture again developed an acute need for Mexican labor.

The Philippine Islands had gained their independence in 1934 and importation of sturdy Filipinos had fallen off. Most of the Chinese who had once worked in the fields had long since settled in the cities. The Japanese were in concentration camps—or plainly headed that way. The Okies had drifted into the shipyards and airplane factories, where the pay was better. The Europeans had graduated from working on farms to running them.

California farmers, faced with an emergency, thought up the bracero program. Agreements were hammered out with the Mexican government under which Mexican nationals in large numbers would be trucked into southwestern U.S. for harvest time and trucked out when the crops were in. Braceros were the salvation of California's wartime agriculture; they worked hard and they worked cheap. Their wages didn't loom large by U.S. standards but they let the braceros cut wide swaths when they returned to Mexico, if such was their inclination.

The war ended. California growers argued the U.S. Congress into extending the bracero program.

Thus setting the stage for Cesar Chavez and his United Farm Workers Organizing Committee.

* * *

The San Jose barrio from which he came was called *Sal Si Puedes*. Translation: "Escape if you can."

His father and his uncle had been active unionists in the dried-fruit industry since 1939. Workers often met at the Chavez house. Said Cesar much later: "It made a deep impression on me . . ."

At age 19, he joined the National Agricultural Workers Union.

If one learns from defeat, membership in that union was highly educational. The N.A.W.U. worked no better than farm unions which had preceded it. But young Chavez learned from it how *not* to organize.

He came to Delano in the summer of 1962, to the great valley where he had labored as a boy in the vineyards. He did manual labor to survive and if there was enough money for gasoline, he went in the evening from town to town and talked with *campesinos,* the farm workers.

He organized for a year and signed up a grand total of 10 dues-paying members at $3.50 a month.

Chavez said, "Talk about being scared, I had to get dues in order to eat. I suspect that some of the members were paying dues because they felt sorry for me." The time came when he had to beg for food; he and his children were just plain hungry. "It turned out to be the best thing I could have done, although at first it's hard on your pride. If people give you their food, they'll give you their hearts."

The first meetings were in private houses; often only two or three persons attended.

During this time, Cesar's wife, Helen, worked in the cotton fields. He said, "If you haven't got your wife behind you, you can't do many things. We were together then and still are. I think I'm more of a pacifist than she is. Her father, Fabela, was a colonel with Pancho Villa in the Mexican Revolution."

In the beginning, there were two women and four men. The women were Helen Chavez and Dolores Huerta; the latter was to become chief negotiator for the union.

Pretty, intelligent and very female, Mrs. Huerta said of her work: "When we are deadlocked, I cry. The bosses are men, and they can't stand a woman's tears."

The men were Chavez, Gilbert Padilla, Antonio Orendain and Larry Itliong, the latter of Filipino descent.

In 1965, the U.S. Congress closed out the bracero program.

In the grape-growing areas of California, the cry "Huelga!" rose stridently along the dusty roads as union pickets marched, carrying signs in Spanish and English, plus Tagalog for the Filipinos, beseeching the workers to leave the fields.

It was anything but a fair fight. According to the California Chamber of Commerce, "agri-business" contributes more than nine billion dollars each year to the state's economy.

Chavez said wryly, "We had $85 in the treasury at the beginning of the strike."

THE LONG STRUGGLE

The followers of Chavez had grievances aplenty, many of them arising from the fact that farm workers were not covered by the National Labor Relations Act.

Pay was low and fringe benefits virtually nonexistent; housing provided for workers was sometimes unfit for livestock; hiring was usually handled through labor contractors who often profiteered at the workers' expense; field toilets for the workers, required by law, were seldom provided in sufficient quantity, if at all.

The growers argued that meeting union demands would force them out of business. It would be impossible, they said, to farm successfully if unionized workers could strike at harvest time. Agriculture in California, they insisted, was completely dependent on a plentiful supply of cheap labor. If Chavez and his U.F.W.O.C. were victorious, the growers warned, they would have to mechanize to survive and many fewer workers would be hired.

U.F.W.O.C. leaders chose the state's table grape industry as the first target. Chavez had no illusions about the task confronting his union; he predicted that it might take as long as 10 years to achieve the first contract with a grower.

The first weapon employed was the traditional one—the strike.

The growers showed no signs of caving in.

Firmly committed to non-violence, Chavez watched worriedly as angry incidents occurred. Speeding trucks brushed against picketing workers at the roadsides; bloody beatings took place in the tense towns; threats were made with abandon; shots rang out in the night. Chavez saw that another weapon was needed to ease the pressure on the pickets, to increase pressure on the growers.

He found his weapon in the boycott.

U.F.W.O.C. members fanned out over the country to picket wholesalers and retailers who sold California table grapes. The boycott was surprisingly effective and helped to gain much national support for Chavez and his people.

The growers, badly pained in the pocketbook, protested that boycotts were specifically forbidden by the National Labor Relations Act.

A high point in the farm workers' struggle is captured on film. Ending a climactic fast in 1968, Cesar Chavez, second from right, converses with the late Sen. Robert F. Kennedy at a mass meeting in Delano. At left is Helen Chavez, Cesar's wife; at right is his mother.

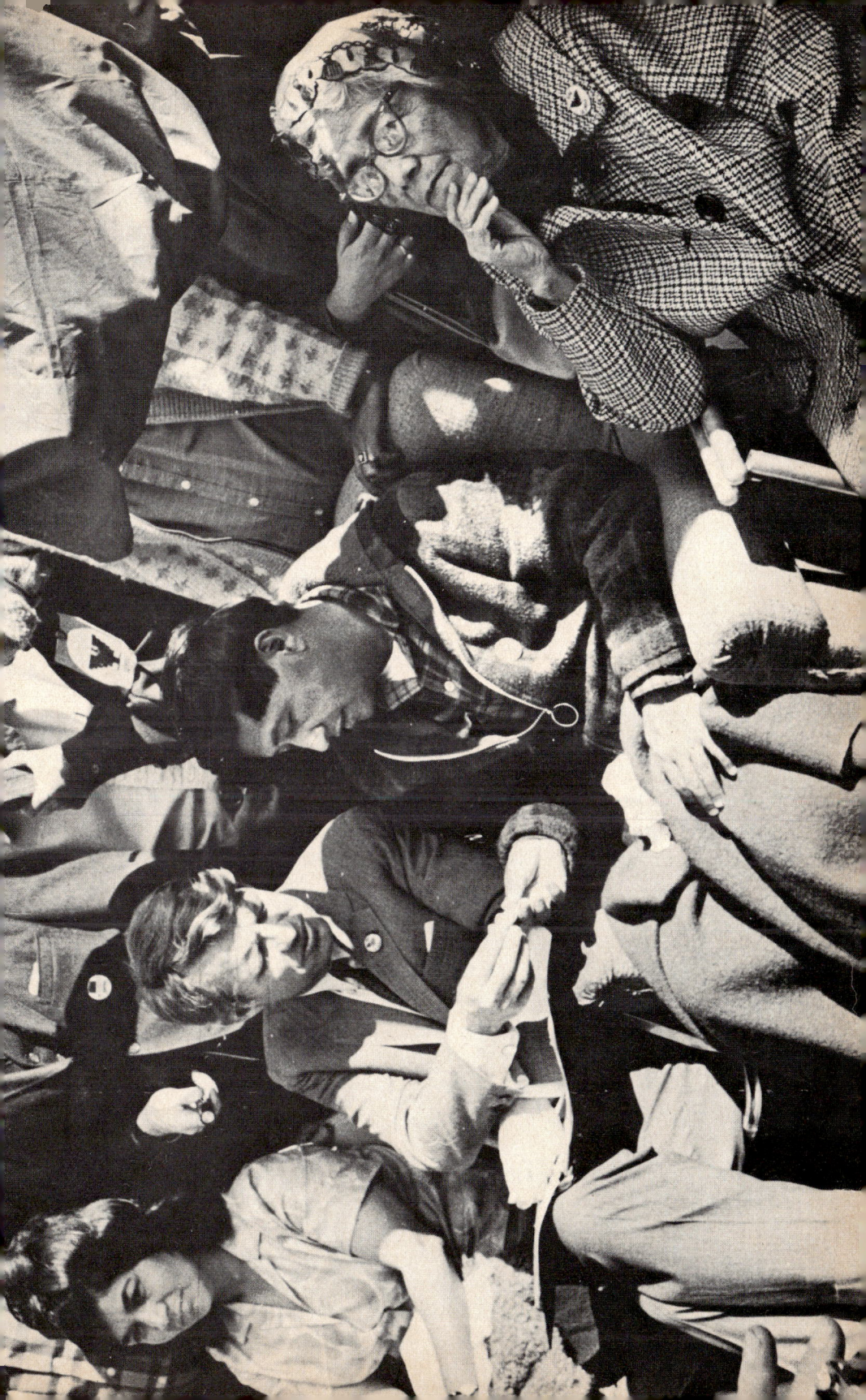

Farm workers, Chavez reminded with a small smile, were not covered by th act, had always been excluded from its protection.

The breakthrough came in springtime, 1970, when a few small Coachella Valley growers signed contracts with U.F.W.O.C. By July of the same year, it was estimated that 30 per cent of California's table grapes were being grown under union contract.

Flexing its new muscle, U.F.W.O.C. took another long step during the same year when strikes were launched against vegetable growers in the Salinas Valley. There was talk, too, of extending the effort to adjoining states, particularly Arizona and Oregon.

In 1970, it seemed safe to say that a farm workers' union had been successful in the U.S. for the first time.

While Cesar Chavez was always quick to express pride in his Mexican blood, he angrily fought attempts to turn U.F.W.O.C. into a purely Mexican-American organization, branding such efforts as nothing more nor less than racism. He reminded the proponents of *La Raza* ("The Race," referring to militants of Mexican Indian blood) of the great efforts put forth by the U.F.W.O.C. Filipinos, in particular. He threatened to resign over the issue; he even went on a widely-publicized fast to make his point. He made it.

*   *   *

And so it happened that California's Mexican-Americans, struggling along with other minorities during the late 1960s to gain a full share of citizens' rights and opportunities, found themselves with a hero respected across the nation as a towering figure in the labor movement and admired by liberals of all races and political parties.

But perhaps history finally will spotlight his name not because he led a farm union in California but because he made it clear that a policy of non-violence, doggedly adhered to, can produce startling results.

Such as, in early 1971, the announcement by a spokesman for the President that unionization of farm workers had suddenly become a major goal of the administration.

AMERICANS WITH CHINESE FACES

Some of them, mostly the old ones, still refer to America as *gum san*—Land of the Golden Mountains. The first individual to arrive in California was said to have been the cabin boy of the good ship *Bolivar* in 1838 but if all the facts were known, the cabin boy might well have been a Johnny-come-lately.

The mysterious record shows that 75 Oriental junks had washed up on the American side of the Pacific Ocean by the year 1875. Surely some of those sailors came ashore on what they formally called *Mei Kwok*—Beautiful Land—and formed the vanguard of the Chinese in America.

The Chinese were different from most California immigrants in that they did not intend to stay. They were *gum san hoch,* or sojourners. Even death couldn't hold them in *gum san;* it was an article of faith that their bodies must be returned to China.

But the old attitudes flaked away. More and more sojourners became residents. Many thousands of their quiet, industrious kind are now valued citizens of California. The Chinese-Americans, exotic migrants from the Celestial Empire, are here to stay.

The gold had its attractions for them, of course. The historic image of the Chinese in the gold fields is that of the coolie patiently plodding along the stream beds well behind the whites, content to sift out the meager leavings.

But in the Yuba River district, a pair of Chinese picked up a dandy little nugget that white miners had overlooked. It weighed 240 pounds and was worth $30,000!

On the middle fork of the Feather River, other Chinese stumbled onto a 40-pound nugget. Fearing trouble, they whacked it up into little pieces and sold it with their dust.

What mainly annoyed Americans about the Chinese was that they didn't contribute much to the cutthroat economy of the gold fields. Instead of squandering their gold in the roaring saloons and gambling dens, they shipped much of it back to China. This sneaky trick was obviously un-American and could only lead to trouble.

Which it did.

* * *

The Celestials called Sacramento "Second Port of the Golden Hills." San Francisco was "First Port of the Golden Hills," and "Third Port of the Golden Hills" was Marysville.

The largest Chinese settlements in the gold country were at Auburn, Coloma, Angels Camp, Hornitos, Nevada City, Coulterville, Chinese Camp and Placerville. In these places today, one can still see colorful reminders of the Celestial presence.

Poetic they may have been but welcome competitors they were not, most emphatically. When 18,400 Chinese debarked in 1852, white miners panicked. A mass meeting in the Columbia district on May 28 of that year led to a raging complaint that certain shipowners and merchants were swamping the mines with "long-tailed, horned and cloven-hoofed inhabitants of the infernal regions."

They were referring to the Chinese, in case you wondered. Suddenly the Yellow Peril had reared its ugly head—and tail and horns and hooves.

In the Agua Fria district around Mariposa in 1856, this message was posted:

"Notice is hereby given to all Chinese on the Agua Fria and its tributaries, to leave within 10 days from this date, and any failing to comply shall be subjected to 39 lashes and moved by the force of arms."

Other, more subtle methods were used as well. Landlords were reminded that Chinese tenants were a fire hazard, what with their cooking in pans over open fires, shooting off firecrackers on holidays and burning punk in religious ceremonies. A tax was levied on foreign miners and was used mostly to oppress the Chinese. Even Chinese who weren't miners had to pay it. No small potatoes were involved; the levy produced the thumping total of five million dollars between 1850 and 1870.

So why didn't the Chinese take their case to a court of law?

Simply because Chinese couldn't testify in the courts of California until 1873, when the California Revised Code took hold.

The legal switch may have been a product of guilt. Two years earlier in Los Angeles, in October of 1871, 22 Chinese residents of an area ironically called "Nigger Alley" died at the wrong end of taut ropes—lynched by a white mob.

It was one of the worst massacres of Chinese in America.

THE BARS GO UP

American have always had difficulty in relating comfortably to Orientals in their midst and to the Chinese in particular.

Californians fell easily into the national habit of creating a stereotype, then shoehorning all Chinese into it. "John Chinaman," in the

Scene: Los Angeles, at Temple and New High Streets. Time: the early 1870s. Subject: lynching of a Chinese.

minds of most whites, grew into a sinister figure, a slant-eyed, shuffling, un-Christian opium-smoker.

As a matter of plain historical fact, the Chinese who entered California probably produced more economic good and created less deliberate trouble than any other immigrant nationality. An earlier chapter points up the immense contribution of Chinese to the first transcontinental railroad. Down through the years, the juvenile delinquency rate among California Chinese has been almost unbelievably low. The Chinatowns of California cities, despite the sinister stereotype, are usually the safest urban places in which to stroll after dark.

But the stereotype was drawn in indelible ink.

Gold fever dropped and railroad building passed its raucous peak. Suddenly the indefatigible Chinese became dangerous competitors for scarce jobs.

By an act of the U.S. Congress in 1882, Chinese were excluded. That act was not repealed until 1943.

One wonders how Chinese would have been received in California if they had been willing from the beginning to consider themselves Californians and not merely sojourners.

When a Communist revolution swept over China during the 1940s and the Nationalist government fled to Formosa, many Chinese in America no longer felt the pull of their ancient homeland. America became their homeland, and California their home.

The largest settlement of persons of Chinese ancestry outside of the Orient is in San Francisco.

Originally "Little China" in the city by the bay covered 12 blocks, with the lines drawn at Kearny, California, Stockton and Pacific streets. It wasn't exactly a ghetto. Partly by their own choice, Chinese immigrants re-created a bit of their homeland in this favored place. In Chinatown, San Francisco, they could conduct business as usual, almost as if they had never left Canton. Chinatown was their security blanket in a new land that often showed a hostile face.

In 1906, an epic earthquake and fire wiped out the old Chinatown, but a new and better one bloomed in the ashes. Now Grant Avenue is the Main Street of Chinatown, San Francisco, one of the state's major tourist attractions.

As one might expect, Los Angeles did it differently.

Modern Chinatown in Los Angeles is an Oriental shopping center, a reproduction of Peking City. (A few cynics call it "Disneyland,

Far East.") Old Chinatown in Los Angeles didn't burn; it was replaced in 1938 during one of the first fits of urban renewal. It is a commercial center, not a place of residence.

At the west gate of Chinatown in Los Angeles, a camphor wood arch proclaims: *The best things Chinese are gathered here.*

The feel and odor and sound of the Orient are in it. It adds richness to the cosmopolitan mix that makes California the intriguing place that it was ... that it is.

AMERICANS WITH BLACK FACES

Wednesday, August 11, 1965 ...

It had been hot—95 degrees—and muggy in Los Angeles during the afternoon. Until that fateful day, summer had been unusually cool and comfortable, making August 11 that much more difficult to bear. Adding irritation on August 11, a gray-yellow pall of smog clutched the throat of the city.

It was a good day for trouble. During that day and that night and during the incredible week which followed, Los Angeles was to experience a great human eruption, the like of which it had never seen before.

America's festering racial problem was coming to a head ... in California.

* * *

Marquette Frye, 21, lived in Watts, the black ghetto of Los Angeles.

During the early evening of August 11, 1965, with several shots of vodka under his belt, he drove his mother's 1955 Buick along Avalon Boulevard in Watts. He drove the car a little too hard—50 miles an hour in a 35-mile zone—and somewhat erratically, according to Lee Minikus, the California highway patrolman who stopped the Buick near 116th Place just a block from Frye's home.

On that hot, sticky day, the arrest took too long. Idlers along Avalon Boulevard began to gather at the scene. Somebody recognized Marquette Frye and informed his mother, who soon came running.

More policemen arrived. The crowd grew to 150 persons, then to 1000, mostly black.

A few rocks were thrown as the sun sank in a smog-smeared sky. The Fryes were taken away in the squad car. The 1955 Buick followed, dangling like a dead whale on the hook of a tow truck. It could have ended then and there, but it didn't.

An officer drew a wet hand away from his neck and realized he had been spit on by a black woman. He plunged into the crowd after her; Vesuvius erupted.

The Watts Riot promptly scorched its way into California history.

* * *

Citizens who were able to do so stayed at home, behind locked doors. If there were guns in the houses, they were at hand. Those who ventured onto the freeways by night saw a city burning and in its agony casting a ghastly glow against the sky. The peak of the erupting volcano was 103rd Street in Watts, where business buildings were being looted and burned. By the end of the frightful week, 103rd Street would have richly earned its new name: Charcoal Alley.

Thirty-three persons died; ninety million dollars worth of property was destroyed.

In the aftermath, a stunned Los Angeles mumbled: *Why?*

Wasn't it common knowledge that Negroes were treated better in Los Angeles than anywhere else in the country?

In the East, ghettos were little more than high-rise rabbit warrens but not in Los Angeles. In Watts, blacks lived mostly in individual houses, surrounded by lawns, garlanded by palm trees, insulted by very few of those sullen signs: "White Trade Only." The bus stations and the railroad stations didn't separate their waiting rooms by race, nor their rest rooms, nor their drinking fountains. In Los Angeles, there was no "back of the bus" treatment for blacks; in fact, the driver of the bus, sitting as far up front as one can get, often was a Negro.

So why did the landmark black revolt of modern times happen in Los Angeles, California?

Perhaps because in California, blacks saw a glimmer of light at the end of the tunnel. There was racism in California, but it was not a native sickness, ingrained over the centuries; it had been imported. At the end of the tunnel in California there was a glimmer of hope.

Perhaps there was hope because once California had been an open society.

* * *

Minorities

If anyone should ask, "Will California ever have a black governor?" some knowing soul is likely to reply, "So what else is new?"

Pio Pico, last Mexican governor of California before the U.S. takeover, was a distinguished member of a mixed-blood family. His paternal grandparents were a Spanish-Indian, Santiago de la Cruz Pico, and a mulatto, Maria de la Bastida.

* * *

Another remarkable Afro-American who had made his mark in early California was Jim Beckwourth. He was a mountain man, a guide and scout, spinner of yarns beyond compare and probably the most successful horse thief in California history.

He was positively versatile, Jim Beckwourth was, and he proved it in 1846 by swiping the ridiculous number of 1800 horses (eighteen hundred!) and driving them to Colorado for sale.

In 1847 and 1848, this same jack-of-all-trades, legal and illegal, served as a U.S. army scout between Missouri and California, and moonlighted as a horseback mail carrier from Monterey south. Apparently the U.S. government did not hold a little horse stealing against a man. (Not if he confined his activity to Mexican horses, at any rate.)

Earlier Beckwourth had been an important man among the Crow Indians. It is on the record that he was married to a Mexican woman in 1840, in New Mexico. Also, he was one of the original settlers of Plumas County, California. When he died, he was again living with the Crow Indians.

The pattern is plain. Before California was taken over by the United States, not many Californians were concerned about a person's racial derivation. One's neighbor might be part Indian, part Mexican, part Spanish, part black, part white. And perhaps, slightly Asiatic...

* * *

An outstanding summation of black influence on the development of early California is presented concisely in *Afro-Americans in the Far West* by Jack D. Forbes.

Forbes points out that the blood of the Spanish explorers who ventured to the West Indies after the voyages of Columbus was thoroughly mixed. Trade routes had introduced many Africans into Spain for centuries prior to 1492 and the Moorish conquest of Spain accelerated the flow.

Long before the historic landing at Plymouth Rock, Africans

Jim Beckwourth was a mountain man, explorer and teller of tall tales. In his spare time, he stole horses on a grand scale.

had landed in the West Indies. Most of those early arrivals were slaves but many became free after arriving in the New World. Forbes suggests that blacks may have been the first non-Indian residents of what is now the United States.

It happened like this: The Spanish expedition of de Ayllon attempted to establish a colony along the Carolina coast during 1525-1527 and brought Negro slaves. Defeated by illness and Indian enmity, the Spaniards departed, leaving behind a number of slaves who had revolted. These intermarried with Indians and became permanent residents.

And all this occurred 80 years before Jamestown was settled!

When the Spanish moved north to strengthen their grip on Mexico, many persons of African ancestry took part. It was difficult to recruit Europeans for the dangerous, life-sapping expeditions through the harsh wastes of the immense Sonora Desert. Negroes, Indians and mixed-bloods of all varieties filled the gaps in the struggling columns.

Especially useful to the Spanish were Christian Negroes who spoke Spanish. Many of these were put in charge of Indians at the missions; they also developed many new mining towns.

When the Spanish decided to take Baja California under their enormous wing, mulattoes crossed the gulf from Mexico's mainland to work as miners and soldiers. In 1790, Forbes states, mulattoes constituted about 21 per cent of the Spanish-speaking population of Baja. (Approximately 50 per cent bore the interesting designation of *casta*, or too-mixed-to-identify.)

Sonora, Sinaloa and Baja were the bases from which the Spanish colonized Alta California. The Africans, Indians and mixed-bloods moved north, doing much of the hard work along the trail. The adventure which hung so often by a slender thread could not have succeeded without them.

* * *

The Portola expedition which founded San Diego and Monterey included among its *soldados de cuera*—leather jacket soldiers—a certain Juan Antonio Coronel, a mulatto. Also with Portola were several mulatto mule drivers.

The de Anza party of 1775 included 29 soldiers; one-fourth were mulattoes.

In those critical years late in the 18th century, about 20 per cent of the Spanish-speaking residents of California could claim African blood.

Of the 46 *pobladores* who first settled Los Angeles, more than half had African blood. The rest were Indian and a Chinese from Manila and a couple of Spaniards. (This last pair, no doubt, is primarily responsible for the mostly mythical old Spanish heritage of Los Angeles.)

The Watts district of Los Angeles may be a California-style ghetto but the city did not start out in such a narrow-minded way. The first city lots were passed out to the immigrants in a color-blind manner, with complete integration of races.

Had this not been true, the first pure whites in Los Angeles—miniscule, defenseless minority that they were—might have been forced into a very tiny ghetto.

THE "CENSUS WHITES"

The Los Angeles pattern was carried out elsewhere.

Forbes writes in *Afro-Americans in the Far West*:

". . . Santa Barbara possessed a Spanish-speaking population which was more than half non-white or mixed blood. Afro-Americans constituted at least 19.3 per cent of Santa Barbarenos in 1785. San Jose, now one of California's major cities, possessed a population in 1790 which was at least 24.3 per cent part-African and 59.5 per cent non-Espanol. In the same year Afro-Americans constituted 18.5 per cent of the settlers at Monterey . . . at San Francisco, eight years earlier, the military garrison was at least 18.1 per cent Afro-American and more than half non-Espanol, but by 1790 persons *designated* as part-African comprised only 14.7 per cent of the total population . . .

"The percentages which have been given above must now be qualified somewhat. In California, as elsewhere in the Spanish empire, it was quite easy for a person to experience a 'change of race.' Individuals could often purchase the status of 'Espanol' but in California it was easy to 'lighten one's color' by simply living in a community, acquiring local status, and perhaps, being on good terms with the census-taker. For example, between 1781 and 1790 eight of the original settlers of Los Angeles were reclassified from mulatto to Indian-Spanish, from Indian-Spanish to Spanish, and from Indian to Indian-Spanish. Thus all became officially lighter."

* * *

Whaling captain William T. Shorey and family. Mrs. Shorey said of the baby: "Victoria is a remarkable sailor. She knows all the ropes, and has perfect command of her father."

Francisco Reyes was the first rancher in the San Fernando Valley; he was mayor of Los Angeles from 1793 to 1795. He was a mulatto.

* * *

Grafton T. Brown was one of the first San Francisco lithographers. His paintings were widely exhibited. He was a Negro.

* * *

Capt. William T. Shorey, well-known in California maritime circles, was one of few blacks who held a master's license for sailing ships of more than 700 tons.

* * *

One of San Francisco's early leaders was William A. Leidesdorff, a Negro born in the Virgin Islands. He was a prominent businessman, member of the council and city treasurer. Appropriately, he lived in one of the biggest houses in town. He built a hotel at Clay and Kearny streets and was responsible for the first steamship to cruise San Francisco Bay. (In July, 1970, the San Francisco Negro Historical and Cultural Society sponsored a walk to city landmarks in honor of Captain Leidesdorff.) The captain died as a relatively young man in 1848. Perhaps it was just as well; California's first era of racial justice was about to end. The Constitution framed in 1849 took voting rights away from "Indians, Africans, and the descendants of Africans."

Blacks were forced to segregate themselves for protection and progress, mostly in San Francisco and Sacramento. They established many churches, a newspaper called *The Mirror of the Times* and an educational-cultural institution, the San Francisco Athenaeum, which had its own library. They had to organize private schools, too, since blacks were barred from public education.

Blacks could be tried in the courts of California but couldn't testify in those courts, making a joke of equal justice under the law. In 1855, 49 delegates from 10 counties travelled to Sacramento for a "Convention of the Colored Citizens of the State of California." They presented a petition to the legislature, got nowhere, so tried another convention the following year, this time with 61 delegates from 17 counties. It didn't work, either. It took the Civil War and the resultant smashing of "Chivalry" Democrat power to turn the tide. Blacks gained the right in 1863 to testify in California court

Wilson Riles, California Superintendent of Public Instruction, was elected in 1970, the first black to be voted into such a post since Reconstruction days in the South a century ago, the first black elected to statewide office in California.

cases in which whites were defendants; a decade later, all the bars to Negro testimony were torn down.

Ratification of the Fifteenth Amendment to the U.S. Constitution gave Negroes voting rights in 1870. California refused to ratify, but enough other states did to put the amendment into effect.

* * *

Watsonville had a real problem in early days. The town had a grand total of *two* colored families and the resident whites had no intention of integrating the public schools. So a white teacher was hired for the sole purpose of instructing those few black children. Separate but unequal; if that white teacher was any good, blacks probably got a better education than whites in Watsonville. Irony strikes again.

And again. In 1970, Wilson Riles was elected superintendent of public instruction in California. He was the first black to be elected a state school superintendent since the days of Reconstruction in the South, the first black to be elected to statewide office in California. Riles rolled up more than three million votes; it is believed that this is the largest tally for a black candidate in a free election in the history of the world!

Also in 1970, Marcus A. Foster was chosen as superintendent of Oakland schools. He is a Negro.

During the same landmark year, John L. Miller was chosen as leader of the Democrats in the California Assembly. He was the first black ever to be elected to the leadership of either party in the legislature.

* * *

According to Forbes in *Afro-Americans in the Far West,* Negroes in California made up approximately 1.8 per cent of the state's population in 1940. By 1960, this figure had increased to 5.6 per cent. Many blacks immigrated during World War II, when their labor was needed desperately in the weapons factories. Since these factories were concentrated in southern California, it is hardly surprising that more than half of the state's black population lived there in 1970.

But blacks didn't have the numbers, not nearly enough, to elect Wilson Riles. There had to be a lot of white votes, too, and experts were reasonably sure that the winning margin was pulled to the polls when Riles received the endorsement of a Japanese-American,

Minorities

Dr. S. I. Hayakawa, the politically potent president of San Francisco State College.

It could only have happened in California.

SITES TO SEE

WATTS TOWERS, Watts district, Los Angeles. (Strange structures built by Simon Rodia out of bits and pieces are worth a second look.)

CHINESE HISTORICAL MUSEUM, Adler Place, downtown San Francisco. (Small but intriguing museum operated by Chinese Historical Society of America.)

CHINATOWN WAX MUSEUM, San Francisco. (Excellent re-creation of Chinese scenes in China and the U.S., including a fortune cookie factory!)

OLVERA STREET, Puebla de Los Angeles. (Highly commercial, but Mexican shops and trade center are of interest to the tourist-shopper.)

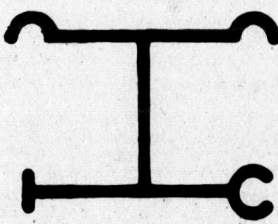

RANCHO SANTIAGO DE SANTA ANA. This brand was first recorded in 1826 by Don Bernardo Yorba. Descendants of Don Bernardo still occupy some of the land on both sides of the Santa Ana River Canyon. Originally, the rancho covered the width of the county and included the towns of Santa Ana, Tustin and Orange.

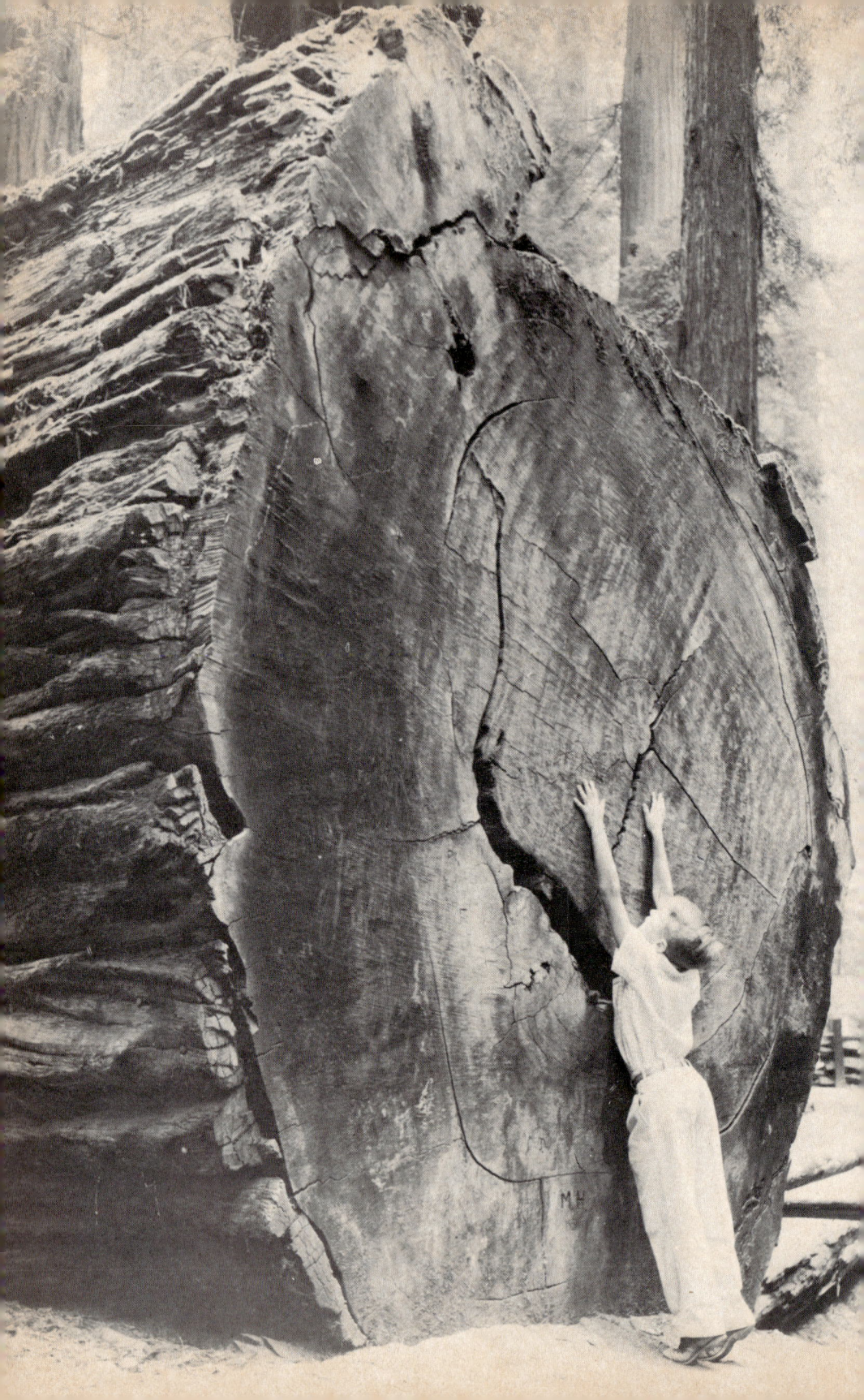

Chapter Ten ✶

Commerce
ALL THE GOLD AIN'T IN THEM HILLS

"Californians are people who were born somewhere else and then came to their senses."

So quoted William Graves in a *National Geographic* article. He reports on a meeting of "Old Settlers of California" attended by the humorist, Will Rogers, whose ranch is now a Santa Monica park. After the meeting, Rogers wrote: "No one was allowed to attend unless he had been in the State two and one-half years."

An adopted Californian went through stages, according to an adage: "First a knocker, then a booster, and finally a liar."

Remi Nadeau, who has written some of the best books about the state, commented: "Few statements about California are completely true, or are even approximately true for very long."

You have been warned.

✶   ✶   ✶

They say a Texan can out-brag an Alaskan without clambering down from his horse but an Alaskan holds his own pretty well once he gets warmed up, which is seldom. The only reason either one creates a stir is that the Californian hasn't yet found time for a lot of bragging; he's been too busy getting rich. If he ever does have a free moment, the Texan might as well ride off into the sunset and the Alaskan surely will burrow into the nearest snowbank. Let's pick over some of the shot in the Californian's locker:

The state of California has a gross economic product (dollar volume of everything produced) higher than all but six *countries*

Hey, kid, you broke it! A fallen redwood like this one in Richardson Grove 80 miles south of Eureka, gives little boys something to reach for.

of the world! (If it matters, the countries which lead California are U.S.A., Soviet Union, Japan, West Germany, France and the United Kingdom.)

Twenty million Californians own (and endlessly drive) 13 million automobiles, a remarkable 10 per cent of the U.S. total. By contrast, 236 million Russians drive about a million cars. (To Californians caught in a clot on a freeway, this may seem like an empty boast and a mixed blessing.)

California has over 12 million telephones. Only U.S.A. and Japan have more. (The state is also third highest in wrong numbers.)

There is as much electrical power generated and used by 20 million Californians as by 700 million Chinese.

After the 1970 census, California was officially certified as the most populous state in the U.S.A. For some years before 1970, Los Angeles County has claimed the honor (and borne the burden) of being the most populous county in the entire country.

California is the major aerospace center of the world, top farm state of the U.S.A. and recognized birthplace of photochemical smog.

So eat your hearts out, you Texans and Alaskans.

WEALTH ABOVE, WEALTH BELOW

California, during its career as a political subdivision, may have had more luck than sense. (In time, it may choke on its luck, but we'll save acid comments about that for the next chapter.)

First, in our time span, there were the California Indians, who had developed a satisfying, rather psychedelic way of life on what must have been in those old days one of the most lovely lands on earth.

Along came the Mexicans, led by a few European Spanish and Portuguese who had been charged by their distant nabobs with conquering the world for long enough to pick the gold out of its teeth. Seasick on the same ships and trudging in the same dusty columns up the long, hot land were the Franciscans, Catholics from the old country who burned to turn heathens, whatever their color, into Christians. God, after all, did not discriminate; a heathen was a heathen.

The rancheros built a satisfying life under the soothing sun of California and enjoyed it so much that they failed to guard their flanks. When the cry of "Gold!" echoed through the Sierras, white Americans were listening and soon came running.

This fantastic mansion, built in Eureka by lumber baron William Carson in the 1880s, still stands in all its splendor. It is now used as a private clubhouse.

There was more material wealth in California than the Indians or the Spanish or the Mexicans or the Franciscans or the Americans had ever dreamed of.

* * *

The Indians (most sensibly, as it may yet turn out) adjusted to nature, accepted it as good, just as it was, and built their lives around its bounty, which, in California, was considerable. The Mexicans based a comfortable economy on a livestock industry. The Americans prospered with gold grubbed out of the California mountains, then, when the gold petered out, grew fat on Nevada silver.

About the time that gold and silver played out for lucky California, oil gushed from cracks and crevices in the countryside. At first, nobody knew quite what to do with it except swear in its direction. They learned, though, as years went by and a petroleum-hungry world fought for a place in line with a big, big bucket. The gold rush was a thing for pikers; California's total take from gold over all the years is approximately equal to the modern income from petroleum products for just *one year*.

As if gold, silver and oil weren't enough, it turned out that sun-bleached California, given frequent dousings of imported water, would produce more farm products than any other state. As if gold, silver, oil and factory agriculture weren't enough, it also turned out that California was a fine place in which to design and build and fly airplanes and finally to design and build and fly remarkably sophisticated objects which in 1969 would waft men to the moon and packages of instruments far beyond the moon.

There seemed to be no end to the bounty. In the highlands of the north and soaring over the eastern mountains were trees of monstrous size, just one of them big enough to furnish the inside and outside of three or four houses in everlasting redwood.

Such an incredible land was certain to become a magnet for a series of incredible races of people—ambitious people, competitive people, stimulating and stimulated people, scientists, writers, artists, teachers, mountain climbers, super salesmen, con men, skin divers, motorcycle riders, religious cranks, irreligious cranks, nature nuts, hippies, super squares, Upton Sinclair, Aimee Semple McPherson and Lawrence Welk; not to mention Dr. Francis E. Townsend, who

The Pioneer, first car manufactured in California, is displayed in the Oakland Museum.

caused a colossal commotion in the country by demanding that senior citizens be given $200 every month by the federal government.

Then along came World War II, a worldwide disaster which caused California's economy to boom as never before. It is an ill wind, indeed, which fails to blow a few dollars into California.

ICKY, STICKY GOO

To the Forty-Niners, that black gunk which oozed out of the ground here and there was mostly a slippery nuisance. Some historians suggest that Andres Pico distilled California crude oil for use in lamps at San Fernando Mission as far back as 1854 but others insist that it never happened. There is no question, though, that asphalt was mined about the same time and applied to streets and roofs. The Spanish word for the stuff was *brea*. The American word was "tar" and who needed it? Well, practically everybody, as it turned out.

The first well, some say, was drilled at Petrolia, Humboldt County, in 1861, although Contra Costa and Ventura counties also claim the distinction. That early boom didn't amount to much because California's thick, asphalt-based crude oil resisted refining. In fact, some of it was so lumpy it had to be picked up with a shovel. (One early driller feared a gusher, he said, because most of the petroleum would get hung up in trees.)

California's first commercial refinery was built by Star Oil Works at Newhall in 1876. Restored, it can be seen there today. (Star Oil Works mated with Standard Oil Co. and the offspring was Standard Oil of California, a major modern company.) In 1919, oil production took over as the state's top industry and between 1920 and 1926, California pumped out more oil than it had been able to produce in all the years preceding. Heavy producers were such new fields as Huntington Beach, Santa Fe Springs and Signal Hill in Long Beach. Union Oil Company, still one of the bigger companies, was formed in Ventura County way back in 1890 when three small outfits threw in together.

After "whipstock" drilling was invented, a pump no longer had to be positioned directly over an oil pool. Some of those wells visible today along the southern California coast are actually sucking oil from under the ocean. The next step was drilling from platforms

This gusher at Signal Hill, Long Beach, blew out about 1925.

offshore. This type of well caused a huge ecological flap in 1969 when a leak caused spillage of hundreds of thousands of gallons of crude oil into the ocean off Santa Barbara. Oil companies spent many months and much money cleaning up the mess. (There was a peculiar aspect of that controversy; few persons thought to mention that oil in Santa Barbara Channel was anything but a recent development. Capt. George Vancouver spotted a huge oil slick in the channel in 1792-93 and other early explorers had learned to recognize this stretch of coastal water by its oily iridescence.)

THE FLYING PROFESSOR

California comes honestly by its dominance of aerospace.

Young John Montgomery, a graduate scientist, put a glider into the air way back in 1883 over the sun-browned hills of Otay Mesa south of San Diego.

To put things into perspective, one must realize that Americans in that year were trying to get used to railroads and wondered if the human body could stand sustained speeds of 40 miles an hour. Horses and buggies were still considered the only sensible transportation devices and the Model T wasn't even a glimmer in the eye of Henry Ford.

After the Otay Mesa flight, Montgomery hired on as a professor of applied sciences at St. Joseph's College in Humboldt County, then took a similar job at Santa Clara College. In 1905, as a large crowd watched at Santa Clara, a Montgomery glider dropped from a balloon and descended safely to the ground in controlled flight from a height of more than 4000 feet.

Montgomery's last flight in 1911 was recounted by Martin Cole in an article published in the *American Aviation Historical Society Journal* in 1967.

It had been a great day at Evergreen, near Santa Clara. On this October day, the 53-year-old Montgomery had soared on strong thermals, then turned gracefully and landed near his starting point. Cole writes:

"Cornelius Reinhardt rushed forward with a camera to record

A young test pilot, Daniel Maloney, rides a Montgomery glider being lifted by a hot-air balloon at a San Jose racetrack. Maloney would ascend as high as 4000 feet, then cut loose and glide to a landing. Just such a flight finally killed him when ropes dangling from the balloon damaged the glider's wings.

the... smile on Montgomery's face, but the Professor waved him off.

"'Wait until I make one more flight,' he said. 'I want to try something special.'"

Cole reported Reinhardt's recollections:

"As the glider rolled swiftly down the runway, Montgomery pulled his elevator controls apparently too sharply. The glider suddenly rose up... at a sixty degree angle... He pulled himself up in the framework, trying to change the controls, but the glider slipped sideways and threw the back of his head against the projecting end of one of the stovebolts...

"... I was with him in a moment and he said to me, 'What is happening... how is the machine?' And I answered, 'How are you?'...

"I knelt beside him and saw the small hole just above and back a little from the ear..."

Montgomery lived only two hours longer.

A state historical monument on Otay Mesa south of San Diego marks the site of Montgomery's trail-blazing 1883 flight.

History has unfairly hidden John Montgomery's light under a bushel. While others were gaining glory, Montgomery was working his way to an understanding of aircraft control which far surpassed that of other flight pioneers. According to Arthur D. Spearman, S.J., University of Santa Clara, even the fins of early space rockets demonstrate the influence of Montgomery's designs.

THE EARLY BIRDS

While John Montgomery first put California on the aviation map, many worthy pilots and constructors followed in his slipstream.

Outstanding was Glenn L. Martin, who ran a bicycle shop in Santa Ana, then took over an abandoned Methodist church and started to build airplanes. In 1908, he put together what may have been the first powered aircraft built in the West, a pusher biplane which he flew in 1909. He established a training school for pilots in Griffith Park, Los Angeles, and had managed by 1915 to set up an airplane factory at the present site of L.A. International Airport.

In 1910, a brave flyer named Ely flew his biplane off the U.S.S. Pennsylvania in San Francisco Bay and survived, thus proving something. In 1911, he landed on the same ship.

Meanwhile another major personality of early aviation, Glenn H. Curtiss, was making in 1911 the first successful hydroplane flight, taking off and landing on San Diego Bay.

Other great names were just getting off the ground. Lockheed Aircraft was formed in Santa Barbara in 1916, then moved to Burbank. In 1920, an engineer for Martin, Donald Douglas, started his own aircraft company in the back room of a Santa Monica barbershop! Here he built three torpedo planes for the U.S. Navy and was making a plane per week by the end of 1922.

In March, 1924, two huge Douglas biplanes—single-engined, with a top speed of 110 miles per hour—roared off from Santa Monica's Clover Field. When they returned 190 days later to be greeted by a crowd of 50,000, they had startled the world by doing nothing less than flying completely around it!

It was Douglas Aircraft of California which built the first truly modern all-metal, low-wing airliner, the DC-1, and in the process transformed the world's commercial aviation. Now called "McDonnell Douglas," the firm continued to play a prominent role when aviation became aerospace and sent the first men to the moon. Douglas was the contractor for the top stage of the Saturn V rocket which started U.S. astronauts on their incredible journey.

Another major California aerospace firm, North American Rockwell, built the command module which carried the spidery landing craft to the vicinity of the moon as the Apollo program captured the imagination of the world in the late 1960s.

During World War II, southern California became the major assembly line for Allied aircraft, turning out hundreds of thousands of war birds at plants bearing proud names like Consolidated Vultee, Northrop, Hughes, Ryan Aeronautical, Lockheed, North American and Douglas. (It was especially good to hear again from Ryan, whose San Diego factory built the plane which Charles Lindbergh flew across the Atlantic in 1927. A replica of this plane is a main attraction of the San Diego Aerospace Museum.)

From John Montgomery in 1883 through Curtiss and Martin and Douglas and Hughes . . . down the years, the buoyant air of

⬅

A 1910 air show at Dominguez Field, Los Angeles, must have been a hair-raising event but one would never guess it from the bored attitudes of the men in the foreground. Perhaps this sort of flying frenzy was safer than it looks; those old planes paddled along very slowly.

California supported and nurtured the flying machine. It was only natural that the state should become the world's paramount aerospace center.

AN ATTITUDE CALLED HOLLYWOOD

California's money-makers seem to succeed at almost anything they attempt, no matter how fantastic.

You want to make a movie? Hollywood, California is the place. Or at least it *was*. Now Hollywood's big thing is television. (In truth, though, Hollywood was more a state of mind than an actual geographical location, when it came to moviemaking. A great many movies were produced in places like Burbank and Culver City. "Hollywood" caught on because it sounded like a place where one would make movies.)

You don't want to make a movie? You want to ship a ton of them to Singapore? California can do that for you, too, with major ports at Los Angeles-Long Beach (these pump a lot of oil into tankers), San Francisco-Oakland, San Diego, and if lumber is your game, you might try Eureka in Humboldt County.

You would like to take your ship inland? That *big* ship? Seems like a strange request, sir, but California can accommodate you at Sacramento and Stockton, if you don't mind a little river ramble and a jaunt along a canal. In the old days, the Sacramento River carried some of the biggest, fanciest boats that ever dipped a paddle into water; an ocean-going merchantman isn't likely to cause it to burst its levees.

Oil, agriculture, aerospace, lumbering, film-making, water commerce, tourism, real estate development, banking (California's Bank of America happens to be the world's largest)—you name it and somebody in California has gotten rich from it and is getting rich from it and will get rich from it. Even, praise be, the working man . . .

➡

Once the British ruler of the seas, the great ship Queen Mary was pushed in 1971 to its permanent home off downtown Long Beach. This aerial photo offers an excellent view of another pride of the Port of Long Beach, Pier J, one of the world's largest man-made peninsulas. Between Pier J and the city can be seen still another distinctive feature of the Long Beach shoreline, an oil island, dressed up to look like a resort hotel. Oil revenues help mightily to make this port one of the fastest-growing in the world.

Wage earners in California constitute an aristocracy; their per capita income in 1970 of more than $4000 was the highest in the world.

It wasn't always that easy. California history in this century recorded two of the major landmarks of the labor struggle in the U.S.—the Mooney case in San Francisco, the McNamara affair in Los Angeles.

At 1 a.m. on October 1, 1910, an explosion destroyed the plant of the Los Angeles *Times,* owned by Gen. Harrison Gray Otis, leader of the city's anti-union forces. Twenty-one persons died in the building; many more were injured.

In April, 1911, James B. McNamara and a man with the unlikely name of Ortie McManigal were arrested in Detroit and charged with the crime. McManigal confessed and implicated John J. McNamara, brother of James. The McNamaras were taken to Los Angeles for trial; their attorney was the renowned Clarence Darrow.

It was Darrow who rose in court on December 1, 1911, to announce that the defendants wanted to change their pleas to "guilty as charged." James McNamara went to prison for life, while John got off with 15 years.

* * *

In 1916, a tense nation that had grown weary of labor strife was bracing for more serious warfare in Europe against the massive forces of the Kaiser. In San Francisco on July 22, a Preparedness Day parade was torn apart by a thrown bomb; 19 persons died.

Arrested were Thomas Mooney, a labor organizer; his wife, Rena; and Warren K. Billings. Mooney was sentenced to be hanged. Billings was slapped with life imprisonment. When protests exploded around the world, Mooney's sentence was reduced to life in 1918.

It still didn't wash, because Tom Mooney wasn't guilty. He had been railroaded as a radical, nothing more. To the power structure of those days, radicalism was a worse crime than bombing.

Snapped the Colfax, California, *Record:*

"We may as well be candid and kindergartenish with you. The reason that Mooney and Billings are in prison is because a majority of the people of the state of California want them there and the Supreme

Bombing of the Los Angeles Times building in 1910, violent landmark in labor-management warfare, left this smoking hulk. Note eagle still on its perch atop the building and classic fire engine in foreground.

Court and the Governor dare not disobey that majority. It is quite beside the point whether or not they are guilty of the particular crime of which they were charged and convicted. The question is: Are Mooney and Billings the sort of people we want to run at large? We have decided this in the negative and we have them locked up. We intend to keep them there, despite all fulminations from Greenwich Village."

Not until January, 1939, when one of California's outstanding liberal governors, Culbert Olson, took office, was Mooney pardoned.

Three years later, Tom Mooney died in a San Francisco hospital and was mourned around the world. California's Mooney case had long since become a landmark of international labor history.

SITES TO SEE

AEROSPACE MUSEUM, Balboa Park, San Diego. (This has much to offer any flying buff; outstanding collection of old aircraft engines; a very special place for aviation historians.)

BALCLUTHA, Fisherman's Wharf, San Francisco. (This great old Cape Horn sailing ship has been lovingly restored; the very complete museum aboard reeks of the sea.)

CABRILLO BEACH MARINE MUSEUM, San Pedro. (A salty spot of great charm and interest developed over many years by the city of Los Angeles; full of fascinating sea things, from ship models to seashells.)

HARBOR CRUISES, Los Angeles-Long Beach, San Francisco, San Diego. (No better way to see and feel and smell California's maritime heritage.)

LOS ANGELES COUNTY MUSEUM, Exposition Park, Los Angeles. (The historic movie exhibit is worth a long look; it may be unique.)

MARITIME MUSEUM, San Francisco. (Another ocean-oriented dandy; many good things here, including restored old vessels that you may tour.)

MONTGOMERY MEMORIAL PARK, Chula Vista, south of San Diego. (Towering wing and stone marker honor John Montgomery at site of his first flight.)

MOVIE WORLD, Buena Park. (Here are old cars and planes galore, many of which saw Hollywood service.)

STANDARD OIL MUSEUM, downtown San Francisco.

STAR OF INDIA, Embarcadero, San Diego. (Another handsome restoration said to be the oldest sailing ship afloat.)

UNION OIL MUSEUM, Santa Paula.

Finally out of prison, Tom Mooney led this triumphal parade up Market Street in San Francisco.

Chapter Eleven *

Ecology
THE BLEEDING LAND

It was always restless ground, California, with its own strange ways and its own peculiar creatures living and dying upon a section of the earth's mantle that seemed only loosely attached to the central core.

California is a land of highs and lows, with the highest mountain (Whitney) and lowest sink (Death Valley) in the mainland United States, so close together one can be seen from the other. Small wonder. A million years ago, give or take a millenium, earthquakes stirred under the land, causing it to rumble and roar and explode the tops off towering mountains, unleashing floods of steaming lava to run hissing toward the sea, twisting and buckling and wrenching and grinding and tilting the peaks, thrusting up new ranges, creating canyons and valleys, turning inland seas into deserts in a mere tick of time, tipping large chunks of land almost upside down before the warring forces of the inner earth subsided and geological peace was declared.

Not *peace,* exactly; more like an armed truce with frequent violations. The violent convulsion had left wounds in the subterranean crust under California that may never heal. Faults, they are called, weak places in the top crust where the earth builds up pressures which periodically demand that the land above slip and slide and rise and sink.

As they did at 5:13 a.m., April 18, 1906 . . .

On that fearsome morning, it was reported that an inmate in the state insane asylum at Agnews (Santa Clara) had cried out: "I'm going to heaven in a chariot of fire! Don't you hear the rumble of the chariot wheels? It's coming low to get me!"

Off Point Arena in Mendocino County moments earlier, a steamer

John Muir stands beside one of the giant trees he loved and fought for.

seemed to strike an obstacle with great force, yet its captain knew his vessel rode in water at least 70 feet deep.

The convulsion rippled southward along the ancient fault, touching land first near Point Arena. Where the fault crossed flatlands in Sonoma and Marin counties, the earth opened up, then crunched together with a twisting, grinding effect. When the horror had passed, land west of the fault line was as much as 21 feet *north* of its original location!

There was danger well away from the rupture itself. Fifty-two died in ruined buildings in Santa Rosa, the city hardest hit by the shock, although it lies 20 miles east of the fault.

The 5:15 train for San Francisco was about to depart from Point Reyes when it lurched one way, then the other, before tipping over.

In San Francisco Bay, Alcatraz Island and its prison were untouched; the monster seemed to be saving its strength for the city across the bay.

San Bruno felt it after San Francisco; then the conduit which might have fed a billion gallons of water to San Francisco in its time of desperation was ripped beyond repair.

Two died at Stanford University as buildings toppled, 21 more at San Jose, and a full hundred more when the insane asylum collapsed at Agnews.

At last, after ripping through the Pajaro Valley of Monterey County 192 miles from its first assault on the awakening land of California, the rupture went underground.

In Los Angeles, windows rattled; that was all.

But San Francisco's agony was only beginning.

* * *

When sailors jumped ship in San Francisco Bay to run toward the gold fields, hundreds of sailing vessels were left to rot at anchor. A few of the ships were used as business buildings (and one as a jail!) but in time dirt was dumped around them, or over them, and the city thereby became a little larger and the bay a little smaller. (The filling and diking process has continued into modern times. Once there were 700 square miles of San Francisco Bay; now there are only 400.)

It was the filled land near the waterfront which suffered most

Tilted, twisted buildings in San Francisco after the big quake. The little house in the middle got along just fine until its towering neighbors leaned on it.

terribly during the brief time—less than a minute—when the earth shook and rumbled and split. Houses slid down hillsides; streets sank; walls bulged and fell, trapping victims underneath; chimneys toppled all over the city (it was finally estimated that 95 per cent of the city's chimneys were damaged or destroyed); a hotel cupola fell through a firehouse, carrying the fire chief down to the first floor, killing him; walls fell away from houses and hotels, revealing startled persons in their beds.

San Franciscans were accustomed to earthquakes but nobody had thought to warn the tourists. Among them was opera star Enrico Caruso, who apparently panicked completely and puffed into Union Station wearing a towel around his neck and carrying a framed picture of Teddy Roosevelt.

Within minutes after the convulsion, ruptured gas mains, broken electrical wires, toppled lamps and shattered chimneys caused fires to spring up throughout the city. There was plenty of fuel to feed the flames and little water with which to fight them, because few mains were left intact. (Modern San Francisco has huge underground reservoirs throughout the city; in the event of another holocaust, it wouldn't be victimized by fragile pipes.) San Francisco had felt quakes before and had burned before but never such a quake, never such a fire, and now the proud city would have to cope with them simultaneously.

"Down to the south," said a fireman from the Howard Street station, "the sky was a streak of orange, with huge flames leaping up into the air."

In desperation, firemen resorted to dynamiting buildings to halt the spread of flames but the great fire would burn for three days and two nights and would destroy three-fourths of the city. When the ashes finally cooled, nearly 500 persons had died and 300,000 more were homeless.

Yet within a week, proud survivors of the disaster were referring to their "damnedest, finest ruins" and were starting to nail together new buildings.

And building again directly over the San Andreas Fault . . .

San Francisco quaked and then burned in 1906. This view shows a few of the thousands who lived in the streets for days afterward. Other heavy quakes hit Santa Barbara in 1925, Long Beach in 1933 and Los Angeles in 1971.

ORANGES AND SNOWCAPS

Ask an American who has never travelled west about California and he will probably paint a verbal picture of orange groves (foreground), a palm or two (middleground), and snowcapped mountains under a brilliant blue sky (background).

Once it actually was like that. The picture isn't a lie; it's merely outdated. Now many of the orange groves have been replaced by cookie-cutter houses and all but one of the palm trees in the picture have been cut down. The snowcaps are still there, and the blue sky, too, but you may be able to see them clearly on only a few days each year, usually right after a heavy rain, when elderly citizens sigh and murmur: "Used to be like this all the time."

In the 1920s and 1930s, before the state became so ridiculously populated, California must have been a heaven on earth, a wonderland of climatic and scenic variety. It still is, but one may have to go to the north to appreciate it.

The outsider's image is of the southland, but north of Sacramento and San Francisco lie long, tall reaches of mountainous, wooded land carved up in fascinating fashion by rocky canyons and rapid streams, tens of thousands of incredible, unknown acres which put to shame many of the national parks in less fortunate parts of the United States.

In that country there is Mt. Shasta, a romantic vision of a mountain. Sun-struck in early morning or as daylight wanes in February, Shasta is . . . well, Shasta is Shasta. A classic. One has to see it to disbelieve it.

In the north, there is also Mt. Lassen, most recently active of America's volcanoes, and the angry, dissipated earth which surrounds it in Lassen National Park. West of the great mountains, watered by fog and storms off the sea, there lives a kind of plant life which exists nowhere else. A sprig, a twig, a little horticultural oddity which grows in northern California to the unreasonable height of 367.8 feet —*Sequoia sempervirens*, better known as Coast Redwood, which grows nowhere in the world but in a narrow belt 540 miles long between Monterey and the Oregon border.

In Mendocino County, there grows another oddity unique to California called the pygmy cypress. At best, these trees reach a height of 10 feet. Most are much smaller. Anyone who has been utterly cowed

Little boys and big trees have always smiled upon each other. These monster redwoods tower in Bull Creek-Dyerville Forest south of Eureka.

by *Sequoia sempervirens* along the coast and *Sequoia gigantea* in the Sierras might soothe his ego with a glance at a pygmy cypress.

Once it was thought that redwoods were the oldest living plants in the country. Not so; the bristlecone pine of the Sierras is older. There is one in California which is said to be 4600 years old, another across the line in Nevada 4900 years old. (Sorry about that, Californians, but don't give up. A Sierra juniper in Tuolumne County may prove to be 6000 years old.)

The Feather and the Klamath and the Trinity rivers, Shasta Dam and red-banked Shasta Lake, the inland population center around Redding, the lumber-oriented coastal beehive at Eureka, the splendid isolation of lovely Susanville . . . this is northern California, with few palm trees and no orange groves. Some day, unfortunately, it may be discovered.

* * *

Crowded, polluted and noisy as it is, fully discovered and promoted until it hurts—even with all its bleeding sores, southern California remains a geological wonder of the world.

Consider the Salton Sea. Once it was a salty arm of the Gulf of California. Then silt from the Colorado River threw up a dam and the northern end of the gulf became a lake; then the lake dried up. The Colorado taketh away but the Colorado also giveth. In 1905, the flooding river overflowed Salton Sink to a depth of 83 feet and a length of 45 miles. Fed by irrigation runoff, the immense lake has no outlets. So why doesn't it flood the desert? Sunshine almost every day of the year, plus blistering summer heat, cause enough evaporation to keep things in balance.

Consider also La Brea Tar Pits, part of Hancock Park in Los Angeles. Eons ago, weird animals slithered up for a drink and slipped to an oily death in the treacherous pools. Their oil-impregnated skeletons were preserved remarkably well. The elephants' graveyard became a heaven for archaeologists, zoologists, anthropologists and paleontologists. Since 1906, when the finding of the remains of an enormous bear set off the California Bone Rush, they have been happily grubbing around in what they consider the richest source of Ice Age remains in the world.

The pygmy cypress is one of California's most modest claims to fame. The world's smallest tree, it grows only in Mendocino County. This is an adult specimen.

* * *

Let us now say a kind word for southern California's Death Valley, castigated the world around as one of the world's champion nowhere-and-nothing places. Ridiculous; under a warm January sun, Death Valley offers rainbow-hued rocks in a display of geological splendor not easy to match.

The enormous deserts of southern California have a strong appeal for those attuned to the quiet message of their immense spaces, their healing sun and their skinny, hard-nosed, indomitable flora and fauna.

The sea lapping 200 miles of the southern shore is warm eight months of the year. New southern Californians tend to become either sea people or desert people at first; then, if they are wise, they become both, in season. Wheels make it possible for a southern Californian to live in perpetual summer, if he chooses.

Wheels may also sentence him to living in eternal hell . . . if he chooses.

In peacetime, the car is the leading killer of young Californians. At age 36, cancer and heart disease take over. For every person killed by the automobile in California, three more are permanently maimed. California has more licensed drivers than registered voters, more cars than families or houses. In the Old West, a gun was considered the equalizer among men. In the New West of California, the car is the new equalizer in the world's first Automobile Society.

* * *

In 1969, Mrs. Sharon Sites Adams, a 100-pound California housewife, sailed alone from Yokohama, Japan, to San Diego aboard a 31-foot boat. She knew she was nearing home when, 90 miles off San Diego, the fog turned brown and smelled of sulphur. Then sharks stopped eating barnacles off her boat; they preferred the garbage floating out from California.

* * *

The grizzly bear is the symbol of California, right? There hasn't been a grizzly in California since 1912, when the last recorded kill was made in the Cuyama Mountains. Monarch, the last captive grizzly,

California's vast deserts, completely charming in season, display many exotic plants, including these Joshua trees.

was put out of its aged misery in the Golden Gate Park zoo in 1911. The state flower is the California poppy, which once clouded most roadsides with its warm yellow-orange glow. Now one must hunt long and hard to find a field of them.

* * *

One out of 10 Americans now lives in California. By 1985, it is estimated by criers of doom that one out of five will live in the state. In 1970, California boasted one-fifth of one inch of public beach per resident. By 1985 . . .

* * *

Once the Santa Clara Valley just below San Francisco Bay was a green and quiet land of farms. The air was clean, the pace was slow, the sky blue and the sun warm. In 1950, the county had a population of 290,000; in 1970, *more than a million*. Santa Clara County has been one of the fastest-growing areas in the United States. It is wildly prosperous. Its metropolis, San Jose, has become a major California city. The air isn't clean, the sky is rarely blue and the pace isn't slow any more in the Santa Clara Valley. What happened in this lovely place of long ago? Growth happened, that's all; "progress" happened, California boosterism at its most successful, a triumph of per capita income over per capita livability. Santa Clara Valley is not alone; some towns in southern California increased their populations by *1000 per cent* between 1960 and 1970! Problems? Sure, all kinds, quite naturally, with no easy solutions in sight. But how could any reasonable person expect anything else? By 1985 . . .

* * *

Around Benicia in the Bay area, horses are dying from lead poisoning; the air is dangerous. In southern California, pine trees are turning brown and expiring in the mountains; the air is dangerous. In many

California's shoreline has always worn two masks, fearsome and friendly. In 1923, one of the world's worst peacetime naval disasters occurred north of Point Arguello, near Lompoc, when seven U.S. Navy destroyers racing from San Francisco to San Diego crunched to sudden death on the rocks of "La Guijada del Diablo," the Devil's Jaw, during a stormy, fogbound night. Twenty-three sailors died. The picture shows all seven ships, although one or two may be hard to find. The seven destroyers were stripped, abandoned and finally ground to bits against the rocks by the surging sea.

urban school districts in California, physical exercise is sharply restricted on days of heavy smog; the air is dangerous. By 1985 . . .

* * *

During a single day Californians throw away, per person, 20 pounds of solid wastes — garbage and rubbish. Over a year, that amount of junk and goop would build a wall 100 feet wide and 30 feet tall from the Oregon border to Mexico. By 1985 . . .

A MAN NAMED MUIR

There is a man of California who is justified in crying out to Californians of today: "I told you so!" but he can't cry out, except from the grave, because he died in 1913, exhausted by his losing battle to prevent Hetch Hetchy Reservoir from despoiling one of his favorite places, Yosemite National Park. The name is John Muir and without pretending to be more than a geologist and botanist, he turned out to be California's first immigrant ecologist, one of the few whites who held the Indian view of man's place in nature.

In 1867, he *walked* 1000 miles, John Muir did, from Indiana to the Gulf of Mexico, studying plants and rocks along the way. Then he travelled west and made his headquarters in Yosemite Valley while he studied the Sierra Nevada, with exploratory side trips to Alaska and way stations. In 1880, he married and went to live near Martinez; his home there is now a National Historic Site.

In 1892, John Muir was elected first president of the Sierra Club, the California-based conservation organization which became the most influential group of its kind in the U.S.

John Muir wrote at length about his beloved land, talked at even greater length in praise of it, fought to save its wild beauty and finally died in its defense.

The Martinez house is not the best memorial to this natural man; a better monument is a preserve of growing things in Marin County just north of San Francisco: Muir Woods, a breathtaking place of redwoods reaching toward the sky and California laurels strangely hugging the ground, where sweeps a dappled green sea of ferns among

Most recently active of California's volcanoes, Mt. Lassen is shown in eruption during its last angry fit, which lasted from 1914 to 1917.

alder, tanoak and azalea, all of it enjoyed by black-tailed deer, squirrels, chipmunks, skunks and a veritable United Nations of birdlife.

There are also tourists, shuffling along the trails in all seasons, paying their respects in their various ways to nature's display and to John Muir.

Each tourist who enters Muir Woods National Monument receives a small brochure, courtesy of the U.S. Government Printing office. The brochure's last paragraph might well be the rallying cry of Californians as they enter the critical 1970s, with their state teetering on the brink of ecological disaster:

"Please observe these regulations: Portable radios must not be played, as they are an intrusion on the quietness of the forest. Park bicycles in the parking area; the trails are restricted to pedestrians only. Leave natural features undisturbed."

We can't help but feel that the dedicated pedestrian, John Muir, the man who loved natural California more than most, would approve.

SITES TO SEE

CABRILLO BEACH MARINE MUSEUM, San Pedro. (Tide pools protected by the state offer easy lessons about life in the sea.)

DESERT MUSEUM, Palm Springs. (This explains the wonders of the desert, if they can be explained; the murals are exceptional.)

LIVING DESERT RESERVE, near Palm Desert. (Part of the Desert Museum, this outdoor school offers a long, lovely, lonely walk on the desert, complete with smoke trees; a wonderful way to spend a winter afternoon.)

SEARLES LAKE, near Trona, San Bernardino County. (Glacier melt after the Ice Age deposited in this lake—usually dry—a great chemical storehouse; in fact, here can be found half of the chemicals known to man.)

John Muir, on the lead horse at left, rides in Yosemite, his special place. Riding at Muir's left is President Theodore Roosevelt, another outdoorsman.

CALIFORNIA FACTS AND FIGURES

Total area: 158,693 square miles (third largest in U.S.)
Population: 20,098,863 (first in U.S., 1970 census)
State capital: Sacramento
Counties and county seats: Alameda (Oakland); Alpine (Markleeville); Amador (Jackson); Butte (Oroville); Calaveras (San Andreas); Colusa (Colusa); Contra Costa (Martinez); Del Norte (Crescent City); El Dorado (Placerville); Fresno (Fresno); Glenn (Willows); Humboldt (Eureka); Imperial (El Centro); Inyo (Independence); Kern (Bakersfield); Kings (Hanford); Lake (Lakeport); Lassen (Susanville); Los Angeles (Los Angeles); Madera (Madera); Marin (San Rafael); Mariposa (Mariposa); Mendocino (Ukiah); Merced (Merced); Modoc (Alturas); Mono (Bridgeport); Monterey (Salinas); Napa (Napa); Nevada (Nevada City); Orange (Santa Ana); Placer (Auburn); Plumas (Quincy); Riverside (Riverside); Sacramento (Sacramento); San Benito (Hollister); San Bernardino (San Bernardino); San Diego (San Diego); San Francisco (San Francisco); San Joaquin (Stockton); San Luis Obispo (San Luis Obispo); San Mateo (Redwood City); Santa Barbara (Santa Barbara); Santa Clara (San Jose); Santa Cruz (Santa Cruz); Shasta (Redding); Sierra (Downieville); Siskiyou (Yreka); Solano (Fairfield); Sonoma (Santa Rosa); Stanislaus (Modesto); Sutter (Yuba City); Tehama (Red Bluff); Trinity (Weaverville); Tulare (Visalia); Tuolumne (Sonora); Ventura (Ventura); Yolo (Woodland); Yuba (Marysville)
Elevation: 282 feet below sea level (Death Valley) to 14,495 feet above (Mt. Whitney)
Statehood: 1850
State motto: "Eureka" ("I have found it")
State flower: Golden poppy
State bird: California valley quail
State tree: Redwood
State animal: California grizzly bear
State colors: Blue and gold
State fish: South Fork golden trout
State song: "I Love You, California"

SELECTED BIBLIOGRAPHY

Abdill, George B.; PACIFIC SLOPE RAILROADS; Bonanza; 1959.
Altroochi, Julia Cooley; THE OLD CALIFORNIA TRAIL; Caxton; 1945.
American Guide Series; CALIFORNIA: A GUIDE TO THE GOLDEN STATE; Hastings House; 1939.
THE AMERICAN HERITAGE BOOK OF GREAT HISTORIC PLACES, American Heritage; 1957.
AMERICAN WEST; January, 1969.
Barzman, Sol; THE FIRST LADIES; Cowles; 1970.
Bean, Walton; CALIFORNIA: AN INTERPRETIVE HISTORY; McGraw-Hill; 1968.
Bidwell, Gen. John; ECHOES OF THE PAST; Citadel; 1962.
Bolton, Herbert Eugene; OUTPOST OF EMPIRE; Knopf; 1931.
Chalfant, W. A.; GOLD, GUNS AND GHOST TOWNS; Stanford; 1947.
Chu, Daniel, and Samuel Chu, Ph. D.; PASSAGE TO THE GOLDEN GATE; Doubleday; 1969.
Combs, Barry B.; WESTWARD TO PROMONTORY; American West; 1969.
Conot, Robert; RIVERS OF BLOOD, YEARS OF DARKNESS; Bantam; 1967.
Craib, Roderick; PICTURE HISTORY OF U. S. TRANSPORTATION; Simmons-Boardman; 1958.
Davenport, William; THE MONTEREY PENINSULA; Lane; 1964.
Fisher, Anne B.; THE SALINAS; Farrar & Rinehart; 1945.
Forbes, Jack D.; AFRO-AMERICANS IN THE FAR WEST; U.S. Gov't Printing office; n.d.
Fowler, Harlan D.; CAMELS TO CALIFORNIA; Stanford; 1950.
Gentry, Curt; FRAME-UP; Norton; 1967.
Gleichman, Joan; "Sierra Siesta for a Slim Princess;" DESERT MAGAZINE; July, 1969.
Gudde, Erwin G.; 1000 CALIFORNIA PLACE NAMES; U. of California; 1969.
Hillinger, Charles; THE CALIFORNIA ISLANDS; Academy; 1958.
Holbrook, Stewart H.; THE STORY OF AMERICAN RAILROADS; Crown; 1959.
Holdredge, Helen; FIREBELLE LILLIE; Meredith; 1967.
Hornung, Clarence B.; WHEELS ACROSS AMERICA; Barnes; 1959.
Hosokawa, Bill; NISEI: THE QUIET AMERICANS; Morrow; 1969.
Hughes, Langston, and Milton Meltzer; A PICTORIAL HISTORY OF THE NEGRO IN AMERICA; Crown; 1968.
Hutchinson, W. H.; CALIFORNIA: TWO CENTURIES OF MAN, LAND, AND GROWTH IN THE GOLDEN STATE; American West; 1969.
Iacopi, Robert; EARTHQUAKE COUNTRY; Lane; 1964.
INDIANS OF CALIFORNIA: PAST AND PRESENT; American Friends Service Committee; 1960.
Jackson, Joseph Henry; BAD COMPANY; Harcourt, Brace; 1949.

Jensen, Oliver, Joan Paterson Kerr and Murray Belsky; AMERICAN ALBUM; American Heritage, 1968.
Kennedy, John Castillo; THE GREAT EARTHQUAKE AND FIRE; Morrow; 1963.
Kirsch, Robert and William S. Murphy; WEST OF THE WEST; Dutton; 1967.
Kitagawa, Daisuke; ISSEI AND NISEI; Seabury; 1967.
Kroeber, Theodora; ISHI IN TWO WORLDS; U. of California; 1961.
Leadabrand, Russ; EXPLORING CALIFORNIA BYWAYS II; Ward Ritchie; 1968.
Lee, Calvin; CHINATOWN, U. S. A.; Doubleday; 1965.
Lillard, Richard G.; EDEN IN JEOPARDY; Knopf; 1966.
Matthiessen, Peter; SAL SI PUEDES; Random House; 1969.
McWilliams, Carey (ed.); THE CALIFORNIA REVOLUTION; Grossman; 1968.
MONTEREY PENINSULA HERALD; June 1, 1970.
Morley, Jim; MUIR WOODS; Howell-North; 1968.
Nadeau, Remi; CALIFORNIA: THE NEW SOCIETY; McKay; 1963.
Nadeau, Remi; THE WATER SEEKERS; Doubleday; 1950.
NATIONAL GEOGRAPHIC; various issues.
Okubo, Mine; CITIZEN 13660; AMS Press; 1966.
THE PACIFIC HISTORIAN; various issues.
Payne, Doris Palmer; CAPTAIN JACK, MODOC RENEGADE; Binfords & Mort; 1938.
Riesenberg, Felix, Jr.; THE GOLDEN ROAD; McGraw-Hill; 1962.
Robinson, John and Alfred Calais; STATE PARKS OF CALIFORNIA; Lane; 1961.
Ross, Ishbel; SONS OF ADAM, DAUGHTERS OF EVE; Harper & Row; 1969.
Ryland, Lee; "The Outlaw Who Couldn't Ride a Horse;" TRUE FRONTIER; March, 1969.
SAN FRANCISCO CHRONICLE; various issues.
Spearman, Arthur Dunning, S. J.; JOHN JOSEPH MONTGOMERY, FATHER OF BASIC FLYING 1858-1911; U. of Santa Clara; 1967.
Speck, Gordon; BREEDS AND HALF-BREEDS; Clarkson N. Potter; 1969.
Sproull, Harry V.; MODOC INDIAN WAR; Lava Beds Natural History Ass'n; 1969.
Steiner, Stan; LA RAZA; Harper & Row; 1970.
Stewart, George R.; THE CALIFORNIA TRAIL; McGraw-Hill; 1962.
Stewart, George R.; ORDEAL BY HUNGER; Ace; 1960.
Stone, Irving; MEN TO MATCH MY MOUNTAINS; Doubleday; 1956.
SUNSET TRAVEL GUIDE TO NORTHERN CALIFORNIA; Lane; 1970.
Terkel, Studs; HARD TIMES; Pantheon; 1970.
TIME; various issues.
Twain, Mark; ROUGHING IT; Harper; 1871.
Utley, Robert M., and Francis A. Ketterson, Jr.; GOLDEN SPIKE; U. S. Dept. of the Interior; 1969.
Wagner, Jack R.; GOLD MINES OF CALIFORNIA; Howell-North; 1970.
WESTWAYS; July, 1968.
Wood, R. Coke and Leon Bush; CALIFORNIA HISTORY; Fearon; 1963.
Yelverton, Therese; ZANITA: A TALE OF THE YOSEMITE; Hurd & Houghton; 1872.

INDEX TO PERSONS AND PLACES

Adams, Sharon Sites 299
Aerospace Museum 280, 286
Agnews 289, 290
Aiso, John F. 233, 242
Alameda 118
Alameda County 139, 306
Alcatraz Island 56, 76-77, 290
Ali, Hadji 155-156
Alleghany 129
Alpine County 306
Altadena 37
Alturas 306
Amador County 306
Amador, Jose Maria 74
Anderson, R. A. 62-63
Angels Camp 251
Anza, Juan Bautista de 10, 18, 259
Arcata 129, 179
Ascension, Father 9
Atherton, Gertrude 191, 193
Auburn 251, 306

Bakersfield 114, 146, 156, 246, 306
Balclutha 286
Barncho 56
Bartleson, John 108
Bastida, Maria de la 257
Beale, Edward F. 155-156
Bear Valley 85, 87, 88, 92, 98, 99, 101, 102
Beckwourth, Jim 257
Belden, Josiah 108
Benicia 33, 156, 301
Bennett, Charles 117
Benton, Thomas Hart 195
Berkeley 6, 118, 199, 230, 243
Bernard, Captain 43-46
Bidwell, John 108, 116
Bidwell Mansion 114
Bigler, Governor 133
Big Pine 217
Billings, Warren K. 284-286
Bishop 129, 184, 210-211, 216-217
Black Bart 139-142
Black Jim 53, 56-58
Blue Lake 179
Bodega Bay 116
Bodie 128-129
Bogus Charley 53, 56
Boston Charley 53, 56-58
Bowron, Fletcher 235
Branciforte 16
Brannan, Sam 118-119
Breen, Patrick 83-84, 88-90, 96-98, 104
Bridgeport 128, 306
Bridger, Jim 81-82
Brier, John W. 193-195
Brier, Juliette 193-195
Briggs Cunningham Automotive Museum 184

Brown, Grafton T. 262
Brown, Willie Jr. 33
Bruff, J. Goldsborough 76
Bryant, Edwin 104
Buena Park 286
Burbank 280, 281
Burbank, Luther 230-232
Burch, John C. 158
Burger, "Dutch Charley" 96
Burns, Walter Noble 136
Butte County 60, 62, 128, 306

Cabrillo Beach Marine Museum 286, 304
Cabrillo, Juan 3, 6
Cabrillo National Monument 11
Calafia 2, 6
Calaveras County 141, 306
Caliente 143-145
Camacho, Epifiana 242
Campo Cahuenga 202
Canby, E. R. S. 51-53
Captain Jack 42-58
Carmel 9
Caruso, Enrico 292
Castro, Jose 26, 28
Catalina Island 6
Cermeno, Sebastian 8-9
Chaffey, George 224
Chalfant, Will 217
Chandler, Dorothy Buffum 200
Chandler, Norman 200
Chavez, Cesar 243, 244, 246-250
Chavez, Helen 247
Chico 108, 114
Chinatown Wax Museum 265
Chinese Camp 251
Chinese Historical Museum 265
Chula Vista 286
Coachella Valley 250
Coit, Lillie Hitchcock 187-191
Coit Tower 187, 191
Cole, Martin 33, 274-276
Colfax 284
Collins, Charles 217
Coloma 117, 128, 251
Colton Hall 30, 34
Columbia 128, 252
Colusa 306
Colusa County 306
Contra Costa County 272, 306
Copperopolis 141
Coronel, Juan Antonio 259
Cortez, Hernando 2
Costa Mesa 184
Coulterville 251
Crescent City 306
Crespi, Father 16-17
Crocker, Charles 159-162, 163-166, 167, 170-172, 176

Culver City 281
Curly Headed Doctor 45, 47, 51, 52, 54
Curtiss, Glenn H. 280

Darrow, Clarence 284
Davis 230
Death Valley 193-195, 223, 289, 299, 306
Delano 242-243, 247
Del Norte County 306
Denton, John 98-99
Desert Museum 304
De Witt, John L. 235
Dolan, Patrick 90, 92-93
Dolores, Juan 66
Donner, George 80, 81, 88, 96, 102
Donner, Jacob 88, 96
Donner Lake 86, 105
Donner, Leanna 98
Donner Memorial State Park 114
Donner, Tamsen 102-104
Douglas, Donald 280
Douglas, Helen Gahagan 199-200
Douglas, Melvyn 199
Downieville 128, 306
Drake, Francis 8, 11
Du Pea, Tatzumbie 202
Dutch Flat 158
Dyar, L. S. 52-53

Eaton, Fred 207-211, 216
Eddy, James 97, 102
Eddy, William 83-84, 90, 92-94, 97-98, 102-104
Eddy, Mrs. William 97
El Centro 306
El Dorado County 233, 306
Ellen's Man George 53
Elliott, Milt 80, 83-84, 96-98, 102
Eureka 281, 297, 306
Exposition Park 232, 286

Fair, James 120
Fairfield 306
Fallon, W. O. 104
Fellows, Dick 142-149
Felton 179
Ferrelo, Bartolome 6
Field, Sara Bard 201-202
Fillmore 219-222
Flaco, Juan 31-32
Flood, James 120
Florin 233
Folsom 148-149, 158
Fort Bragg 179
Fort Ross 23, 40, 116-117
Fort Tejon 156, 184
Fosdick, Jay 93-94
Foster, Marcus A. 264
Foster, W. M. 92-94
Fremont, Jessie Benton 195-197, 202
Fremont, John C. 26-28, 32, 87, 195-197
Fresno 37, 239, 306
Fresno County 306
Frye, Marquette 255

Galvez, Jose de 15, 17
Garcia, Three-Fingered Jack 133-136
Gardner, Erle Stanley 37
Gillem, Colonel 54-55
Gillespie, Archibald H. 31-33
Glasscock, Harry 217
Glen Ellen 36
Glenn County 306
Golden Gate 8, 10, 118, 177, 187
Golden Gate Park 301
Good, Hiram 62-63
Governor's Mansion 40
Grass Valley 126, 128
Graves, W. C. 84, 91
Graves, Mary 92
Graves, "Uncle Billy" 93
Grey, Zane 37
Griffith Park 184, 276

Haiwee 211
Halladie, Andrew S. 177
Halloran, Luke 82, 84
Hancock Park 297
Hanford 306
Hansen, A. C. 213-214
Harris, Benjamin Butler 123-126
Hastings, Lansford W. 79-80, 81-82, 85, 90, 104
Hatfield, George M. 205-206
Hayakawa, S. I. 265
Hearst, George 199
Hearst, Phoebe Apperson 197-199, 202
Hearst, William Randolph 199, 202
Herron, Walter 85, 90
Hidalgo, Father 24
Hollister 306
Hollywood 218, 281, 286
Hook, William 101
Hooker Jim 52, 53, 56
Hoover, Lou Henry 200
Hopkins, Mark 159-161, 173, 176-177
Hornitos 251
Huerta, Dolores 247
Humboldt County 272, 274, 281, 306
Hume, J. B. 139, 141, 143-144, 146, 148
Humphrey, Isaac 117
Huntington Beach 272
Huntington, Collis P. 159-161, 167, 173-177

Ide, William B. 28
Imperial County 306
Imperial Valley 223
Independence 216, 306
Inouye, Daniel Ken 234, 242
Inyo County 202, 208, 214, 217, 306
Ishi 58-70
Ishi Discovery Site 77
Itliong, Larry 247

Jackson 306
Jackson, Helen Hunt 191-192
Johnson's Ranch 87, 94, 97, 98, 102
Jones, Thomas ap Catesby 27
Juan Flaco Marker 40

Judah Monument 184
Judah, Theodore D. 152, 157-161, 167, 184

Kern County 114, 146, 184, 242, 306
Keseberg, Ada 99
Keseberg, Lewis 81, 83, 84, 88, 96, 102-105
Kings County 306
Kipling, Rudyard 177
Klamath Basin 50
Kroeber, A. L. 60, 64-70, 73

La Brea Tar Pits 297
Lake County 306
Lake Mead 224
Lakeport 306
Lassen County 109, 306
Lassen National Park 295
Lassen, Peter 109-112
Lava Beds National Monument 41
Laws Railroad Museum 184
Leidesdorff, William A. 262
Lindbergh, Charles 280
Living Desert Reserve 304
Livingston 233
Lodi 195
London, Charmian 36
London, Jack 36
Lone Pine 216, 217
Long Beach 218, 224, 272, 281, 286
Long Valley 210, 216
Los Angeles 16, 31-32, 33, 34, 40, 72, 77, 87, 143, 144, 146, 156, 176, 177, 184, 200, 202, 206-218, 219-223, 224, 232, 237, 239, 243, 244, 252, 254, 255-256, 259-260, 262, 265, 276, 281, 284, 286, 290, 297, 306
Los Angeles County 37, 268, 306
Los Angeles County Museum 286
Los Angeles County Museum of Science and Industry 232
Lopez, Father 16
Love, Harry 133-136

Mackay, John W. 120
Madera 306
Madera County 306
Manly, William 194
Marin County 11, 290, 303, 306
Mariposa 128, 133, 252, 306
Mariposa County 306
Maritime Museum 286
Markleeville 306
Marshall, James 115, 117, 120, 128
Martin, Dennis 107
Martin, Glenn L. 276-280
Martinez 303, 306
Marysville 104, 126, 239, 251, 306
Mason, R. B. 117
Mayfield 147
McCutcheon, William 84-85, 87-88, 90
McFarland 242
McKinstry, George 98
McManigal, Ortie 284
McNamara, James B. 284
McNamara, John J. 284

McPherson, Aimee Semple 270
Meacham, Alfred B. 50-51, 52-53
Mendocino County 179, 289, 295, 306
Merced 239, 306
Merced County 306
Meyer, John A. 180
Miller, John L. 264
Mineta, Norman Y. 242
Minikus, Lee 255
Mission San Carlos Borromeo de Carmelo 13, 15, 39
Mission San Diego de Alcala 14, 17, 39-40
Mission Dolores 39
Mission San Fernando 272
Mission San Francisco de Solano 14, 39
Mission San Juan Capistrano 39
Mission San Luis Obispo 39
Mission San Luis Rey 39
Mission Santa Barbara 39, 72
Moak, Sim 62-63
Modesto 306
Modoc County 306
Mojave 155, 213
Mono County 306
Montalvo 222
Montalvo, Garcia Rodriguez Ordonez de 1
Monterey 9, 13, 15, 17, 18, 30, 31, 36, 87, 259, 260
Monterey Bay 9-10, 15, 16-17, 27, 28
Monterey County 290, 306
Monterey Peninsula 34, 36
Montgomery, John Joseph 274-276, 280, 286
Montgomery Memorial Park 286
Mooney, Thomas 284-286
Morena Reservoir 205-206
Morse, Harry N. 139, 141-142
Mount Lassen 62, 109, 112, 295
Mount Shasta 46, 295
Movie World 286
Muir, John 303-304
Muir Woods National Monument 303-304
Mulholland, William 206-216, 219, 222, 223, 224
Murieta, Joaquin 132, 136-137, 143
Murphy, Lem 91, 93

Nadeau, Remi 267
Napa 306
Napa County 306
Needles 176
Nevada City 128, 251, 306
Nevada County 114, 128, 306
Newhall 272
Nixon, Richard Milhous 37, 40, 199-200
Nixon, Thelma Ryan 200
Nobles, William H. 112
Norris, Kathleen 193
North Hollywood 202

Oakes, Richard 77
Oakland 118, 139, 177, 180, 185, 234, 264, 281, 306
Oakland Museum 180, 228

Old Town (San Diego) 40
Olson, Culbert 286
Olvera Street 265
Ontario 223
Orange County 37, 306
Orange Empire Trolley Museum 184
Orendain, Antonio 247
Oroville 58-60, 64, 77, 128, 139, 226, 306
Osbourne, Fanny 36
Otay Mesa 274, 276
Otis, Harrison Gray 284
Owens Valley 208-211, 216-218, 222-223

Padilla, Gilbert 247
Pajaro Valley 290
Palm Desert 304
Palm Springs 304
Palo Alto 200
Panamint Valley 195
Parkhurst, Charley 185-187
Pasadena 224
Paul, Alice 200-201
Peralta, Luis 118
Perris 184
Petrolia 272
Pico, Andres 28, 272
Pico, Pio 28, 257
Pico, Salomon 137
Pico, Santiago de la Cruz 257
Pike, William 84, 86
Pinedale 239
Pioneer Village 114
Placer County 306
Placerville 122, 251, 306
Plumas County 257, 306
Point Arena 289-290
Point Loma 11
Point Reyes 290
Pomona 239
Pope, Saxton "Popey" 66, 70
Portola, Gaspar de 10, 15, 16, 18, 259
Promontory Point (Utah) 109, 151-152, 160, 169, 172, 173
Puebla de Los Angeles 40, 265

Quincy 139, 306

Ralston, William 120
Red Bluff 306
Redding 129, 297, 306
Redwood City 306
Reed, James Frazier 80-85, 87-88, 90, 99, 101-102, 104
Reed, Jimmy 99
Reed, Margaret 80, 83, 85, 96, 98-101
Reed, Patty 98-102
Reed, Tommy 98-102
Reed, Virginia 85, 96-97, 99
Reed-Donner Party 76, 79-105, 106, 107
Reinhardt, Cornelius 274-276
Reyes, Francisco 262
Reyes, Senora 32-33
Riddle, Frank 52, 53
Riddle, Toby 52, 53

Ridge, John Rollin "Yellow Bird" 136
Riles, Wilson 264
Rivera, Fernando de 15, 16
Riverside 230, 306
Riverside County 37, 306
Rodia, Simon 265
Rogers, Will 267

Sacramento 24, 33, 40, 77, 86, 102, 104, 109, 114, 119, 133, 157, 158-159, 161, 184, 239, 251, 262, 281, 295, 306
Sacramento County 306
Sacramento Valley 80, 94, 116, 234
Salinas 36, 239, 306
Salinas Valley 250
Salton Sea 297
Salton Sink 223
San Andreas 306
San Benito County 26, 306
San Bernardino 306
San Bernardino County 304, 306
San Bruno 290
San Diego 11, 14, 15, 16-17, 18, 40, 176, 205-206, 259, 274, 276, 280, 281, 286, 299, 306
San Diego Bay 6, 15-16, 40, 280
San Diego County 306
San Fernando Reservoir 214
San Fernando Valley 208, 213, 216, 219, 262
San Francisco 14, 31, 33, 34, 39, 64, 70, 104, 118, 120, 122, 136, 141, 149, 158, 160, 163, 170, 176, 177-179, 180, 187, 190, 199, 200-201, 230, 237, 239, 242, 251, 254, 260, 262, 265, 281, 284-286, 290-292, 294, 303, 306
San Francisco Bay 6, 22, 34, 64, 76, 79, 87, 118, 162, 290, 301
San Francisco County 306
San Francisquito Canyon 219, 222
San Joaquin County 306
San Joaquin Valley 37, 137, 208, 232, 242
San Jose 16, 33, 104, 108, 147-148, 180, 185, 242, 246, 260, 290, 301, 306
San Juan Bautista 104
San Luis Obispo 147, 306
San Luis Obispo County 202, 306
San Mateo County 306
San Miguel 6, 39
San Nicolas Island 72
San Pedro 6, 9, 176, 207, 286, 304
San Quentin 142, 143, 146, 147
San Rafael 306
San Simeon 199, 202
Santa Ana 276, 306
Santa Anita 237, 239
Santa Barbara 9, 72, 143, 148-149, 260, 274, 280, 306
Santa Barbara County 306
Santa Catalina 9
Santa Clara 147, 274, 289
Santa Clara County 301, 306
Santa Clara Valley 147, 301

Santa Cruz 16, 147, 306
Santa Cruz County 179, 306
Santa Fe Springs 272
Santa Monica 6, 224, 280
Santa Paula 222, 286
Santa Rosa 230-232, 290, 306
Saroyan, William 37
Saticoy 222
Searles Lake 304
Serra, Father 10, 13-18, 34, 39, 40, 73-74
Serra Museum 40
Scarfaced Charley 47-50, 55
Schallenberger, Moses 105-107
Schonchin, Old 50
Schonchin, John 53, 56, 58
Shacknasty Jim 53, 56
Sharon, William 120
Shasta County 306
Shasta Lake 297
Shorey, William T. 262
Sierra County 306
Signal Hill 272
Sinclair, Upton 36-37, 270
Siskiyou County 306
Sloat, John Drake 28
Slolux 56
Smith, Jedediah 26
Snyder, John 83-84
Solano County 306
Soledad 147
Sonoma 14, 18, 27, 39
Sonoma County 36, 40, 290, 306
Sonora 124, 129, 185, 306
Southwest Museum 77
Spearman, Arthur D. 276
Spitzer, Augustus 91, 97
Standard Oil Museum 286
Stanford, Leland 159-161, 173, 177
Stanislaus County 306
Stanton, Charles 84-86, 91, 92
Star of India 286
State Indian Museum 77
Steamboat Frank 56
Steele, Elisha 50
Stein, Gertrude 193
Steinbeck, John 36, 245
Stevens, Elisha 105, 107
Stevenson, Robert Louis 36
Stockton 40, 108, 136, 239, 281, 306
Stockton, Robert F. 31-32
Strobridge, James H. 161-162, 170
Summit Tunnel 166-167
Susanville 297, 306
Sutter's Fort 73, 77, 80, 85, 86, 87, 88, 92, 98, 101, 114, 115-116, 119, 123
Sutter's Fort State Historic Monument 102
Sutter's Mill 108, 115, 117, 122
Sutter, August 119
Sutter County 306
Sutter, John 24, 73, 85, 88, 90, 104, 108, 109, 115-119, 123
Sutro, Adolph 120
Swing, Phil 224

Tanforan 237, 239
Tehama County 62, 108, 306
Telegraph Hill 187, 190, 191
Thomas, Eleazar 52-53
Thomas, Evan 54-55
Thomes, Robert 108
Thompson, Snowshoe 122
Thorn, Ben 141
Townsend, Francis E. 270
Travel Town 184
Trinity County 306
Trona 304
Truckee Lake 86, 87, 88, 91, 94, 97, 101, 105
Tulare 239
Tulare County 306
Tulare Valley 193
Tule Lake 48, 54, 239
Tulelake 41
Tuolumne County 124, 128, 297, 306
Turlock 239
Twain, Mark 36, 122

Ukiah 306
Union Oil Museum 286

Vallejo 33
Vallejo, Mariano 24, 28, 117
Vasquez, Tiburcio 137, 139, 143
Ventura 6, 219, 306
Ventura County 272, 306
Visalia 306
Vizcaino, Sebastian 8-10, 17, 34

Walker's Pass 193
Warren, Earl 37, 236, 240-242
Waterman, T. T. 60, 64, 66-70
Watsonville 187, 264
Watterson, Mark 210, 217, 218
Watterson, Wilfred W. 210, 217, 218
Watts 255-256, 260, 265
Watts Towers 265
Weaverville 129, 306
Webber, J. B. 59
Weber, Charles 108
Webster, Daniel 30
Welk, Lawrence 270
Wells Fargo Bank History Room 149
Wheaton, Frank 42, 46, 51
Whittier 33, 37, 200
Williams, Bayliss 91
Williams, Eliza 80, 96
Willits 179
Willows 306
Woodland 306
Wright, Thomas 54-55

Yelverton, Therese 154
Yerba Buena 31
Yolo County 306
Yorba Linda 37
Yosemite National Park 303
Yreka 50, 306
Yuba City 306
Yuba County 306

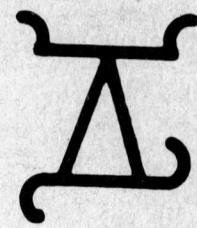

RANCHO SAN JOAQUIN. This ancient brand was brought by Don Jose Andres Sepulveda from Rancho San Vicente of Santa Monica to his newly-acquired rancho. Such well-known cities as Corona Del Mar and Irvine now occupy part of it.

RANCHO LOS PALOS VERDES. The Rancho Los Palos Verdes, now the location of Palos Verdes Estates and Marineland, consisted of 31,629 acres. The brand was issued to Jose Loreto Sepulveda on February 24, 1839.

RANCHO LA BREA. Antonio Jose Rocha registered his brand for the famous Rancho La Brea on August 2, 1845. The former rancho is now the site of the Wilshire Boulevard Miracle Mile and La Brea tar pits.

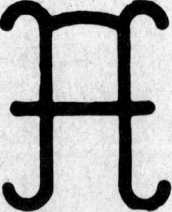

RANCHO SANTA GERTRUDES. Manuel Nieto was granted this brand for his Rancho Santa Gertrudes in 1785. The rancho covered 17,602 acres. Modern Downey is located within the boundaries of the former rancho.

RANCHO RODEO DE LAS AGUAS. The very exclusive city of Beverly Hills now lies within the original boundaries of Rancho Rodeo De Las Aguas, which used the brand of Demetrio Villa and which was registered February 7, 1844.